When Silence Screams

When Silence Screams

LIVING WITH BIPOLAR DISORDER

JOURNALS 1997 - 2011

KATHERINE L. FOGG

iUniverse books may be ordered through booksellers or by contacting:

iUniverse
1663 Liberty Drive
Bloomington, IN 47403
www.iuniverse.com
1-800-Authors (1-800-288-4677)

Because of the dynamic nature of the Internet, any web addresses or
links contained in this book may have changed since publication and
may no longer be valid. The views expressed in this work are solely those
of the author and do not necessarily reflect the views of the publisher,
and the publisher hereby disclaims any responsibility for them.

Any people depicted in stock imagery provided by Thinkstock are
models, and such images are being used for illustrative purposes only.
Certain stock imagery © Thinkstock.

ISBN: 978-1-4917-4692-9 (sc)
ISBN: 978-1-4917-4693-6 (e)

Library of Congress Control Number: 2014921376

Print information available on the last page.

iUniverse rev. date: 07/27/2015

Introduction

IN 2011, I WAS finally diagnosed as being Bipolar with severe anxiety and social phobia. Up until this time, I lived life through an internalized microscope. The feelings of sadness and despair followed me like a shadow and I couldn't control the feeling of hopelessness that encompassed my every waking hour. I turned to my journals as a refuge; as a way to release those inner demons that sat heavy on my mind and soul. From the time I was 18 until now, these journals have been my only confidante.

I turned to various means in an effort to control what was ultimately out of control. I developed an eating disorder, had bouts of alcoholism, moments of hyper-mania energy, depressive episodes that lasted months at a time, and I finally retreated in solitude to try and figure out just what was going on in my head.

It wasn't until 2011 that I got an answer as to why my mind and body fluctuated so erratically between highs and lows. I was diagnosed as Bipolar. At first I rebelled against the idea of having this disorder affixed to my name, but it is what it is.

After finally seeking treatment, the disorder has steadily come under control, something I have strived for since the first episode I recall having when I was 18 years old.

There are days when the depression overwhelms me still and there are nights I can't sleep and moments when my energy seems to override every other sense of my being.

Bipolar disorder is what afflicts me but it no longer defines me.

These are my journals. These are my thoughts, ideas, and dreams.

This is me.

Welcome to my world.

This book is lovingly dedicated to my grandmother,
Isobel Smith, who passed away October 20, 2014.
She was my biggest supporter and best friend.
Gram, I miss you and love you forever.

To my friends and family who have stood by me
through the highs and lows, the ups and downs, the
struggles, failures, and successes, I thank you all.

For my mother, Penny; my father, Jeff; my sister, Jen; and
my dear friends, Hannah and Katt: Your love, support,
and encouragement has given me the courage and
motivation to begin and finish this book. I love you all.

Love always, Kat

1997 – 1999

High School Years

AUGUST 1997

I AM BACK AGAIN, dear Journal. I've been away for a while. In fact, I destroyed you. I hope you hold no resentment for that. I felt the need to incinerate my past and that meant destroying some of the memories I had written down in you. Of course, now I wish I hadn't but I promise this time I won't treat you so badly. Well, I'll treat you as well as I treat myself, how's that? That could get ugly too. Oh! But who cares! I'm a junior in high school! Can you believe it! Where have these years gone? Suddenly I'm 16 years old and entering my next to last year in school; scary, but exciting. What's this year going to hold for us all? I just don't know. Year to year, you never know. But I've got my license now, I've got a cool car, my Firebird, which has saved my life this past summer, traveling to and fro to softball practices and friend's houses so I could relinquish the hold my parents had on me by always having to give me a ride. Of course now the problem is going to be money. For now, I get twenty dollars a week from my parents for lunches and what not so if I skip lunch I'll have plenty of gas money! Some things can so easily be worked out.

I know how much you must have missed me, J, but here I am. And now that I'm here again, I can begin to tell you about….. Me! Aren't you happy? I know you are because I am. If I'm happy, you're happy; if I'm sad, then you're sad; if I'm angry, than you're going to be angry too. We are, essentially, one in the same.

In my past journals I thought I had to write diligently and effortlessly. That effortlessness has been burned; has been lapped up in the flames of one impassioned, angry moment when I lit a match. So I really am going to try this all again. And I'm not going to fail anymore. Well, the real reason I got rid of all my other journals was because I was afraid someone was going to find out too much about me. Now I don't care. Let them know who I am. Let them like me, let them hate me, let them know me as me, not as how they want to see me. I'm not going to feel ashamed for being myself and I am certainly not going to apologize for being who I am. The question remains though, exactly who am I?

AUGUST 1998

WELL DEAR J, I haven't written in a while. I never have been good at keeping journals, or relationships of any kind. Sometimes I wish I hadn't destroyed all my other journals. It would be interesting to read them now. But they have been incinerated and the dust has blown away on the wind.

You'd think with all I've been through, I would've figured it out sooner; I can't stand being in relationships. It drives me crazy to be around the same person for so long. I will live the rest of my life out by being single and alone – most of the time, I am sure. Besides that, I seemed to have rambled on. I'm sorry, but the new school year is approaching: my senior year, 1999. Ecstatic as I am, I will confess that I'm frightened as well. Not of AHS (after high school) but of the times in high school, in this, my last year. Every year is more of the same. You never know though, something absolutely wondrous may happen to me and I'll be left staring wide eyed at the unprecedented event. Maintaining healthy relationships? Maybe. That would be a small miracle in and of itself. We'll see, we'll see, oh how we will see. A desperate cry I scream out into the night for this last year to be filled with love and hope and peace around the world. Such foolish hopes for a grown girl don't you think? I am only seventeen though. All of my hopes have not been dashed yet. The world, it seems, is just spiraling down into the void of despair and chaos. I wonder what this year will bring to us. Still, I have a part in me that will not give up hope at any cost. I'll always strive to pick up the pieces and try to fit it all back together again somehow. Like I said, Dear J, we'll see.

DECEMBER 20, 1998

HEATHER DECIDED TO HAVE a party for her birthday which just happens to fall on Brad Pitt's birthday. I have the same birthday as Danny DeVito, quite a difference. But anyway, the party was a big mistake on my part. I don't even know where to begin. First I went over to Lindsay's with Bret and Shawn and we, for some stupid reason, decided to jump on her trampoline that was covered with a foot of snow. I suppose it was fun in the beginning but after becoming soaked through with wetness and falling and nearly breaking every major bone in our bodies, it got tiring. We went inside and that's when something happened to me. Believe me, I want to know as much as you, but I don't know what it was. I had an onset of major depression in a split second and could not get out of it. I don't know what triggered it. Nothing as far as I can tell but it was sudden, and I was beyond depressed. I felt suicidal. Shawn, Lindsay, and Bret all noticed the change immediately and asked what was wrong, but I said, 'nothing' and went outside pretending I had forgotten something in my car. I tried to shake the feeling, but it was so persistent. I cast it aside though and decided to go to the party.

When we got there, my mood started to lift as I was surrounded by my friends. Kirsten was there and it was so good to see her again. I started off slowly but soon found myself being fed Jell-O shots by Lindsay. I had ten of those before enough was enough. Then Kirsten made strawberry daiquiris, those were a refreshing change of pace. Then we did tequila shots. By then, you can imagine, I was a little more than tipsy. I vaguely remember seeing Jonas and saying something to him, though I can't remember what. Next thing I know, Brad is falling down the stairs and Lindsay is telling me it's time to go. I went with her and got my car at her house and she followed me home making sure I drove safely. She was the sober one. I went inside and realized I didn't want to be there. So I left and headed back to Heather's house. It was idiotic on my part, but I did it nonetheless. I think I drove about 70 the entire way. Stupid.

I got back and picked up where I had left off. Keegan and I played our DICE game. The rules are: whoever rolls the lower di, drinks, and Kirsten always drank with the loser. Ben came into the kitchen and took my keys away from me, much to my dismay. I smoked a cigarette or three with Brad and the smoke made me sick and light headed so I ran to the bathroom and threw up red Jell-O. That's when I realized I had to leave. Since they took my keys, I had no transportation. And I knew I shouldn't be driving anyway. I said I needed fresh air and went outside. I sat down by the wheel of someone's car and I got hit with this self-loathing feeling and knew I really had to get out of there. So I started to walk the five miles back to my house. I didn't care at this point that it was five degrees outside, in the middle of winter, at three o'clock in the morning. I just had to leave, go home, somewhere, anywhere other than where I was.

I dove in the ditches and over snow banks when cars came. I did little commando rolls to avoid the headlights, which was kind of fun, more like a game than anything else. And by the grace of God, I made it home. I walked the entire five miles in my worn through combat boots and a thin spring jacket. It was so cold and my hands were blue and purple by the time I got home at five o'clock in the morning.

The next morning was even worse. I didn't have a hangover but I hated myself more than words can say. I don't know why. No one was home and I was left alone so I lost it. I cried, I screamed, I tore my room apart and punched my mirror. My hand was cut from the glass and I was bleeding all over everything, down my forearms and onto the floor. I just sat there and watched the blood come out of me. I found it sickly fascinating. Then I realized what I'd done and was like, "What is wrong with me?!" I felt like a bad after-school movie of the week.

I called Lindsay. She came over, helped me clean up my room and bandage my hand. Before we left for her house, Amanda called me and asked what happened to me last night. She said everyone was so worried about me and they couldn't find me anywhere; that she, Kirsten, and Keegan all walked down to the dam where they thought I might be and then, I think it was the liquor in them gone astray, they thought I had committed suicide because the saw footprints leading down and into the water.

My parents asked what happened to my hand. I told them

a screw had come loose on my mirror and it fell off the door and I cut my hand on a stray shard of glass while I cleaned it up. Nice little white lie. My little stunt will surely make its way through the hallways tomorrow. Hey, you have to laugh at the best and worst things about yourself, don't you? My best attribute is sometimes just 'playing along'.

APRIL 19, 1999

HAVE YOU EVER STOOD in the middle of a road during the darkest hour of the night? I did that tonight, J. I was trying to make sense of everything, looking for an answer within the stars. Everything seems to be falling apart. I don't exactly know what or why, but there seems to be a building, foreboding panic deep within me.

The moon was full and the sky was bright as I stood there. But the darkness of the world was insurmountable. I strained my eyes to see into the darkened night but I could see no further than the end: the end, where everything fades to black as your eyes close down upon the sunlight. Even with the aid of a light, the world is too dark. There is a sheer black veil that envelops everything around, and sometimes inside, of you. And you know what happens then don't you? Tragedy. A tragedy of mind, body, and heart. A tragedy at its highest expense.

And no matter what way I chose to look, it all ended in a completely isolating darkness.

It's the kind of darkness that surrounds and consumes you so you can never see the real picture. It's a violent darkness that stretches across the sky tonight, one that presents itself in a camouflaging ray of light.

AUGUST 24, 1999

I GUESS THE ONE thing I've learned so far is that life is what you make of it. There will be outside influences but in the end, ultimately, the choice is yours of what kind of life you're going to lead.

AUGUST 1999

THESE FAMILIAR FACES THAT are home to me will be no longer. Soon I will be thrust into this strange world and forced to face my own reality. I won't be able to rely on the same people I've known my whole life. Their smiles won't be there to brighten my day and their laughter will no longer fill the rooms in which we shared our thoughts, dreams, and our secrets. Their touch will no longer be felt by my hand and their eyes will be looking at someone else. They won't see me. I won't be able to hide behind them. I'll become visible to the world; to strangers. What will I fall back on? And who will be there to catch me when I do?

All these thoughts rushed through my mind last night as I shared my last meal with my friends. Some friends I've known for 13 years and they will be pulled away from my grasp. I feel as if I am slowly drowning. I can still see above the water but I can't breathe. They're here now but are drifting down the river leaving me behind to struggle and gasp for air.

Who will I have to breathe life into me when I find myself and wash upon the shore?

It is strange how suddenly one can find themselves in the midst of their own denial. The thoughts crash upon me like the angry waves of the sea. It will all be over soon. No more midnight calls of anxious excitement over the nights events. No more planning for the weekends or after school. No more summer fun, careless and free, shared together. I wonder how people can leave each other so easily. How do you let go? Are you supposed to forget or are you supposed to put the memories in the back of your mind and pretend they're not there? Memories of the days when life was easy; when your friends were always there and nobody left, nobody said goodbye. Why should goodbye be so final? Why is it that, when it's said, it feels like the end?

SEPTEMBER 7, 1999

To have the capacity to love people you don't know means you have a good soul – one that is tired of the pain and one that wants to ease the suffering of others; a soul that just wants to love and be loved. Sometimes, the kindness of strangers help people get through their times of unrelenting sorrow – because they know people care.

SEPTEMBER 20, 1999

So my journey begins. Today I take the first step towards independence as an adult (as short lived as it may be). I left my house this morning to head towards Indiana. Unknowingly and frankly quite naïve, I have somehow managed to find my way to New York. My security lies within the confines of my own vehicle; a 1990 Pontiac Firebird.

As I sit here writing at eleven at night, the rain falls down. Sometimes it seems the raindrops are my tears. At times I wish things never had to change. If you could only pick one moment in time to live, when would it have been? What was your happiest time?

I've often sat myself down and thought I was letting people down by not going to college. College life is good for those who can handle it. I am not one of those. And I realized that if I had gone, it would only have been to make other people happy, but I wouldn't have been. I always worry about what other people think of me and I don't spend enough time thinking about how I see me. You can ask people where they see themselves in five years and they'll know. If you ask me, I can't see that far into my future. I never find myself looking, realistically, that far ahead.

Later: I'm sitting alone at a McDonald's service station somewhere in New York off the 90 west interstate thinking of absolutely nothing yet thinking of everything at the same time. Being very early morning, I'm not quite sure of anything that surrounds me right now. What is real? I find myself asking. The light takes on a different tone, shimmering lightly above my head; it dances on the paper and shadows come at me from every corner. I am tired but on I will go! I'm ten miles from Utica, NY.... And realizing I have a long way to go.

SEPTEMBER 21, 1999

I arrived in Fairmount, Indiana today! Home of THE James Dean! It was totally, completely, and utterly amazing knowing I was driving down the same roads that James Dean had. I can't even begin to describe the feelings I had/have. It all seems very surreal to me. I can't believe I'm actually here. When I saw the "Welcome to Indiana" sign, I started to cry because I was so happy. It's been a dream of mine for so long to come here and I'm not used to having my dreams come true. What an amazing feeling. Tomorrow will be great!

(2014: My first trip to Fairmount, IN. My first foray onto the open road. I didn't realize that it would cause a fever. The fever to travel. The fever to leave behind traces of myself as I hit the open road giving me the opportunity to feel free. Fairmount holds a special place in my heart. Not just because it's where James Dean grew up but because it afforded me the chance to make friends from all over the world. As the years pass, each trip I take to Fairmount is more special than the rest. I sincerely do believe it is my second home).

OCTOBER 3, 1999

Why is it that nothing ever goes according to planned? You can have everything worked out to a T, but when it comes down to it, you somehow get thrown off course. Just one disappointment after another, that's what it seems to be. Life, always throwing you off course until one day you snap, you cry, you scream, you fight, then you give up and go to sleep and wait for a new day to begin. New days always bring new hope but halfway through the day, that new hope gets washed away like a bad cup of coffee and you're faced, again, with life's sublime pleasure of making you miserable. What to do? What to do? Go drink another cup of coffee and try to get through the day always looking for tomorrow. You can't plan for the future when you're living in the past.

Let go of everything you know and try to live life by surviving the moment.

Sometimes I feel as if I could just burst. Literally burst, split right down the middle, exposing bone and blood and nobody would give a second glance. No one would notice. Then I wonder: Do people see me? I mean, really see me? Do they know who I am? I feel like an apparition much of the time, like I could walk through the halls and no one would see me. But I am very much real. I'm alive. I have blood coursing through my veins this very moment, yet people have a tendency to disregard.

Then there are times that I feel like bursting open just to see for myself if I do exist.

Mentally, I'm a train wreck waiting to happen. Maybe I'm the aftermath: a confused jumble of twisted scrap metal. Most of the time I can't find my way out from underneath the heap of steel, but I can sure as hell feel the weight of the train sitting on my mind.

Then of course comes the most common question of the moment, which could be any moment; am I crazy? Simple truth: yes. But do crazy people ever ask themselves that? I wonder. And my answer is: no, they simply second-guess themselves four or five times. That's me. Simple diagnosis: I am crazy. And you know, I'm ok with that. To be brutally honest, I'm liable to go totally mad at any moment. But philosophically speaking, aren't we all waiting on the edge?

Do you ever just want to get away? Dumb question, I know, but you know what they say, "There are no stupid questions, only stupid people." Yup. That's me. Occasionally anyway. Sorry, right now I'm in a real self-loathing, mentally bashing kind of mood. It's late. I can't sleep and I'm not even home right now. Back to my question. I feel that I need to get away. All of the time, I feel like I should be running away but from what or who, I'm not sure. There's something inside of me that keeps ticking – like a time bomb and if I don't find that place where I'm supposed to be, I'll explode. But I'm running on empty most of the time. No matter how far I run, my destination seems to get further away and the emptiness of not knowing why expands across the horizon. And there's not a map in the world that can show me where to go.

DECEMBER 1999

THE WOUND THAT HAS been closed for so long reopens itself time and time again, redefining the agony each time. I can't keep it closed. No matter how far and fast I run, it's always waiting for me at the end of the road. I feel helpless, powerless against this monster and time doesn't seem to heal this gaping wound. Maybe I'm impatient; maybe I rush and leave things unfinished. Unfinished business is the torment of restless souls. Spirits who never cross the boundary to the restful World. I've no idea where I'm going. At times I just want to be left alone. Isolation is the key to finding oneself yet extensive isolation can turn one into a diabolical tragedy. I long to be distinguished; to have a sense of accomplishment. To persevere through all the odds, stumbling fool or not. Obstacles were made to be overcome if one only has the tenacity and fervor to attempt the arduous task. I long for the Utopia of the soul; my own Shangri-La. A dreamland of majestic beauty and enchanting ecstasy. If one is capable of achieving this feat while still in the world of mortals, I shall be infinitely envious. My concern lies within my disquieted, foreboding panic; my debilitated sense of logical rationale. I fear I will be the cause of the retaliation of my senses against my most steadfast alliances. I'm already beguiled by my own stream of consciousness. My trepidation is that of becoming the essence of sardonic cynicism. God may allow us the choice of what path to pursue but the deciding factor lies within the depths of our hearts. Those which are plagued with an already desolate heart become the barren souls of hopelessness. Who can be sure of which path to follow? Is life just that – luck? Chance? Or can we retrace steps already forged in the sands of Time? Complicated journeys lead me to the opposition; counteract the very beliefs I have and view life from all angles. I want a path that leads me to a charmingly simple, unspoiled, Arcadian lifestyle. How many roads will I have to tread upon to reach this heavenly kingdom?

Weep not for the memories. How can one be so cold? Unfeeling? Insensitive? Mayhem and mischief instead of compassion and love. The young, beautiful, talented; struck down with the force of two worlds colliding; blindsided by corrupted rage. Venomous poison drips from the heart where rage and fury reside. The devil's den – Home of the vulnerable and unguarded souls that are easily, quickly, and quietly manipulated by contempt and vengeful fantasies that corrode and fall apart if not ventilated properly. Just your average, garden-variety, uneducated fool, strapped down with the belief they are the more powerful being; more important than anyone.

To look evil in the eye, one only needs to look at themselves. It's there, waiting and watching. Most are stronger than these destructive urges, some are not. The weak minded, gullible, vulnerable – all susceptible to tragedy – both becoming it and providing it. Lost souls who die for a lost cause. Evil only caters to the devil. We have to want it – to want things to get better – to relieve the future generations of our mishaps and senseless violence that has caused so many to shed untimely tears. Those we've loved and lost, taken from our world by the hands of injustice. Angels cry with us as we remember; remember our friends, our families, and the friends we never got the chance to meet for they were pulled from our grasp at too soon a time. Memories are not better than the real thing yet so many must settle for second best. To touch, to feel, to love; turn to misery when one can no longer hold the hand of a loved one but must settle for the touch of a visionary apparition. They are here with us, our lost ones, forever by our side and in our hearts. We can no longer touch nor feel, but we will always love.

(2014: I used to often sit and contemplate the fate of the world and all those in it. I had a very macabre sense of thought. Death fascinated me. People fascinated me. The unknown enticed me with an insatiable thirst for knowledge. Having experienced the loss of a friend early in life, I think, set the course for my ponderings of the afterlife. I lost my grandmother two weeks before my 8th birthday. And when

I was 12, I lost a friend to murder. I've realized it does not matter how much time has passed because when you lose someone, they do not vanish completely. Their memory resounds within the mind. I think the unjust nature in which my friend died is one of the reasons I continued this macabre train of thought. Death, violence, evil; I've spent many days dwelling on these things instead of experiencing the positives in life. Through the years, the pain may lessen but I still sometimes find myself in that frame of mind. Thinking, contemplating what it all means and ultimately trying to figure out what it all means. When one stays in that frame of mind often, it can be difficult to move ahead. I realized it's beneficial to focus on the positive memories, not the loss. When you lose someone, it will always hurt but in order to cope, one must remember the good. It sounds simple enough but, as is evident from my journal, it takes time.)

I think I am in love; in love with an idyllic beauty; with the conception of a pristine world; in love with an apparition, a mere figment of my imagination. To want to be loved means to love. When one cannot love, who is to love them? My wishful dreaming has led me nowhere. To the end of the world and back; over the same barren streets, same listless décor, and the everlasting existence of immoral monsters. I don't know how I've survived all this time, in this cold and inane world. We must learn before we can vanquish all the hate in this world. A long and tiring battle, but we must strive for the best. Help each other and take one step at a time in order to achieve the balance the world has not seen for centuries; since the first unjustified bloodshed occurred. The vindictiveness that devours the savory, uncorrupted hearts of the young and unguarded. A tooth for a tooth; an eye for an eye; the age old justification of redemption. Retribution for these evil spirits should be eternal damnation; to go through the throes of pain and suffering that their unsuspecting victims have lived with and will continue to live with for the rest of their hollowed out lives. Yet, I am no one. No one who should preach their idealistic musings on those who don't want to hear it and would probably choose not to listen as it is. So I shall keep my feelings true to myself and die a thousand deaths every day when corrupted souls surface and claim the life of another innocent.

DECEMBER 14, 1999

OLD FEELINGS COME SURGING back into me with a newfound life of their own. Out of the blue, for no reason at all other than there must be a greater force at work here. I don't know what it is inside of me that makes me empathize so. I day dream these atrocities and I can't shake the images out of my head.

Are memories enough to sustain someone throughout their lifetime? I find myself asking this question more and more lately. I'm not sure why but questions like this bother me to no end. I'm getting a morbid curiosity.

DECEMBER 15, 1999

THE BLOOD IN MY veins runs as cold as the winter air blows. Sloshing about inside me like a monsoon, it crashes with such force that it's no wonder my heart is breaking. Worn down, like a boat being sandblasted for smoothness. Soon there shall be nothing left. Empty. Hollow. Dead. I've no idea what's in store for me. No plans, few dreams, mostly fear and a feeling of abandonment. I have been left, forsaken by those who meant the most to me. I cry inside myself and at times I am flooded with this tempestuous rage that drowns me. The current is strong and I am weak. Whatever it is, I will not fight. I will go silently and willingly if only it would come. Then I'd be sure of at least one thing in this world. Everything I thought I had known has become clouded with mystery as to what went wrong, what happened, and why. I am being stubbornly vague for a purpose; one of which I will not reveal; one of which I cannot reveal. Though sometimes I want to; to desperately cry out into the icy black night and have my savior arrive to carry me up to the stars. The stars are too far away though. Distant worlds, windows to other galaxies; Wish upon a star. My wishes have run out for none have come true.

Tired and weary, I want to lie down on the frost-bitten ground and be swallowed whole. Warmth from the ground that will hold me tight and won't let go; suffocate me at will.

The imitation of love is so strong sometimes that one is blinded by the outward guise it appears as.

DECEMBER 22, 1999

STRESSFUL TIMES ARE UPON me. Not just stressful but agitating and painful. Not pain, pain but more like the pain the heart feels when friends turn their backs on you, which is exactly what's been happening lately. "I'm beyond it" – that's my self-help mantra of the week.

DECEMBER 29, 1999

I FEEL I SHOULD reassess the importance of my life, or lack thereof. I've been waiting patiently for nineteen years for an indication of the significance my life is to deliver. One thing is certain; the human body is frail; delicate; it can be snapped in half like a twig; bones break; the body bleeds. Torn apart; skin that mends itself back together. My heart cannot mend itself back together; it's been broken far too long. Ripped apart, bleeding internally, falling to the floor of my soul; only to be swept away by the constant cleansing my mind brings. The continual lies I tell myself in hopes of forging the pieces back together. The only success I've ever known is disappointment. I rarely fail in that category. The human heart can only take so much pain and suffering before it's unable to fight back with hope. Human frailty is a vulnerable thing.

2000

The loss of a friend
enhances the despair
of a life lived in the
constant glare of
isolating sadness.

HAPPY NEW YEAR!!

FEELS WEIRD TO WRITE 2000, but here we are. We made it. Just another day. It's about 12:03 AM. The ball dropped three minutes ago in Times Square. First initial feeling about the year 2000? A dark and somber year is what I predict. Despite my ominous prediction, let's hope 2000 brings some luck, hope, and love back to people.

JANUARY 10, 2000

WHAT LASTS FOREVER? Is there anything? Does love? Friendship? Or even loyalty? I'm not sure there is such a thing as forever. Something eternal that doesn't change seems too elusive to ever find. Forever is an illusion, it's a fantasy created by someone's mind that hopes that moment they are in never ends. Moments move by so quickly though. Lives pass and love loses its fervor. In the beginning, something can feel like it will last forever, but before you know what's happened, the feeling is gone and you end up wondering how it passed so quietly and quickly. Like a phantom that passes through the night, we never see or know forever. It's a hunger that is never satisfied. It's a catered lie fed to our hearts and minds to ease what little bit of disappointment we can. Change is the only constant that our hearts and minds know. Nothing lasts. Everything can be torn down, ripped apart, and forsaken. Everything can be lost, and when it is, that's when people want to grasp the concept of forever. But you can't hold onto something that's not there.

2000

I LAY THERE TODAY in the conforming warmth of the water. It surrounded me, held me in its currents; comforted my disillusioned mind. With my head beneath the surface, except for my nose and eyes, I listened. What I found was not quiet. I could hear my heart beating, pumping the blood through my veins. Muffled by its internal surroundings, it was faint but persistent. My eyes quivered with every beat, subtle but vibrant. I stopped breathing for a moment, but my chest still rose and fell. My heart beat against its barriers, trying to break through the cage of my soul. I envisioned my heart leaping from my chest; jumping from that which holds it hostage, taking the plunge into the waters that surround it; lying cold and lifeless in the currents. I touch my skin and feel nothing but coldness; a surprising contrast to the warm waters that hold me. The hole in my chest, where my once beating heart remained, mends itself together, leaving everything hollow inside. My heart lies beside me, no longer beating in its fervor. It escaped from that which it loathed yet, without that cage, it had nowhere to go. But still it beats inside of me now while I contemplate its motives. It is trapped inside my soul as I am trapped inside my mind; both prisoners to this life that leads us nowhere but under the water.

JANUARY 13, 2000

How I LOATHE BEING where I am. How I despise myself for not being able to do anything to change it. The only anger I feel is towards myself. Towards my own dysfunctional being;

my erratic emotions of elation and sorrow. Do I pity myself, you ask. Am I that self-indulgent? I can only speak in vague terms; perhaps. My illusion is that of the life I lead. My fear may be my own creation yet my hesitations are innate. My ability to forgive myself for my debilitating rationale is no more. Forgiveness is not in the hand I play. I must fold to the honesty of what my life brings to me. I must not hide beneath the cool exterior; I must allow myself to drown in the ocean of tears we all cry. I can hold my own, I suppose that's the way to say it. I can, without a doubt, resist the urge of self-destruction.

The mishaps I've delivered, those to myself and unintentionally to others, play with my mind. Corrupt my thoughts into regret; never let me rest in peace. My dreams are clouded by haze and get lost somewhere in between the truth and my own foolish aspirations.

Are choices really left up to the individual? Or do we only live out the course of our lives that has already been planned? That has already been written in the heavenly stars? What does life hold for each of us? We all believe that the end is death. When, how, and where are left up to fate. Fate that is predetermined for us? Or do we hold the key to our own?

JANUARY 2000

WHAT EXACTLY IS THE purpose of life? To work and work and work until you finally build the foundation of the life you want – then die? You realize that you've worked for the largest portion of your life but what have you worked for? The greater good of man? Have you fought to better the world in any way? Have you ever given a second glance to those who are less fortunate than you? I heard something once that said, "What do any of our lives mean in the long run? It won't be how many people know your name when you die that matters; it will be whether or not you touched the lives of others that will be remembered".

Morning:

Another sleepless night. My mind has stopped working altogether, J. Give me guidance; give me direction; and give me life. Breathe fresh unspoiled air into my lungs. Let the skies be blue and the sun burn bright. I want the moon to hang so low that I can latch on and ride through the celestial sea; tossing wishes here and there to the stars that will fall for only me. Grant me these things and I will be forevermore indebted. Just to get this continual weariness out of my head would be a start. I am oh so sleepy, dear J, and the only thing I cannot seem to do is rest my head upon a pillow to find the dreams I dare to dream. Though the feathery pillow that lays upon my bed looks inviting enough, it's hard as a rock when the time for sleep rolls around. I wrap the blankets tightly around my body and huddle underneath in sheer darkness; afraid to look out into the night for fear of finding myself. I'd rather spend eternity in darkness than be a coward and succumb to that which wants to destroy me. Am I a contradiction? Probably. I am a lot of things and a contradiction isn't going to destroy my life. In time though, it may be the end of my mind.

JANUARY 15, 2000

I CAN FEEL THE chill in my bones every time I think of what may have been. I stand in the open air and scream out to the night, for all the injustice that my heart can no longer bear. When my mind spins in fury, I must take a moment for myself to wallow in the contempt I felt towards the unfairness. My life has led me to this! To cry to the black night so no one can hear my pain, so no one can attempt to console my breaking heart. To let no one in, I risk the fate of resting alone, yet I gain the upper hand of never being let down. But aren't I the only one who is responsible for always letting myself down? I give myself no chances of forgiveness, but I always lay the blame upon my shoulders. Dear J, can't you save me? Can't you pull me out from underneath this wreckage that is my mind?

I am getting tired of waiting for you, why have you not found me yet? Why have I not found you? How many miles reside between your heart and mine? I am full of these unanswerable questions that keep my mind reeling in the confusion of what I desire. I know not what it is that I crave. My clarity has become unclear, and my mind left in pieces of you. An unsolvable puzzle is what my mind is. A maze that has no end; it's a trap with no escape. Blindsided by that which should make me whole, my soul has dispersed from my body and floats somewhere in between life and reality. My own purgatory of sorts, I am caught in the web that threatens to leave me where I am; hanging limp and bloodless while the strong prey on my weaknesses. Immobile as I may be, I still search for the reasons of why? Why am I here? What is my purpose? I strive to learn the answer and I

search over desolate lands and climb the isolated mountains; chaos bashes my head; I ache with the burdens of every day.
Seek and thee shall find.
The search never ends does it?

JANUARY 16, 2000
2:34 AM

SOMEONE PLEASE HELP ME!
No one came and no one comes. Perhaps I wasn't loud enough. I could probably scream and scream until my lungs burst through my skin and still I would be alone; alone and lost in the midst of a forest tangled with weeds. I fight and fight but never get out; that is my prediction.

J, you ask me why I have such a dismal outlook on life, the answer is simple; nothing has happened to prove me otherwise. If something good were to happen in the world, I would probably be so astounded that I'd go into shock anyway and miss out on it. Spend the rest of my life in a coma with a listless look on my face? I don't think so. If that situation ever arose, just pull the damn plug, flip the switch, whatever it takes.

We never really die because we were never really born. Everything comes back time and time again.

JANUARY 2000

I DRAW, I PAINT, I write, I laugh, I talk, I love, yet I am so unsatisfied with my life. What I have is more than even some dare ask for yet I under-appreciate myself, and can find no joy in the little things. The necessities of life have become everything, it seems. I have more than enough, more than I need, more than I really want, and yet I still crave more. Why is this? What has the world become that we must rely so much on materialistic items.

JUNE 2000

I CAN STAND IN front of the mirror and not recognize myself. I'll see a girl who doesn't look anything like what I perceive myself to be. I can look in the mirror once and see someone smile, someone with clear, green blue eyes; someone with a look of hope – happiness??? Then I look twice; and see myself as I really am. My eyes aren't green and blue, they're dull, listless; bloodshot. Dark circles surround my eyes that haven't had a decent night's sleep in ages. The weariness just exudes from within the eyes; they are the window of the soul after all. You can tell a lot about a person from looking in their eyes. I'm tired, weary, forgotten; in a constant state of uncertainty, searching, searching, always looking for something, ahead or behind, never sure of where to go or who to see. The view can constantly change but it always looks the same. All around, the same bleak skies, the same setting sun, the same darkness that surrounds, envelops all the light, all the life. My mouth misshapen, conforming to a twisted smile that radiates neither happiness nor sadness. Now or never, nothing on this earth lasts forever. Deeply searching, behind the shadows of my soul, the weakness accumulates, deadening this translucent desire. Thick clouded, glazed over with the improbability of aspirations that fall through all the open doors. New rooms, different corridors, all leading to the same vaulted door. The combination to unlock is still kept a secret; coded dreams never realized, just remain as fantasies in my mind.

JUNE 6, 2000

THERE SEEMS TO BE a somewhat fascinating correlation between writers and suicide.

Looking up Sylvia Plath; and an even more enthralling captivation is the association of manic-depressive illness and creativity. It's been asked before: does some fine madness plague great artists?

I've read that studies have shown that creativity and mood disorders are linked.

Do you not also find this fascinating? Or is it my own twisted mind that relates to these subjective theses? I suppose I have a desire for these conjectures to be proven undeniably true, so I have some sort of proof that my work is justifiably mad; that I may have some hidden talents that contrast and compliment my own maddening mind.

Are genius and insanity entwined? Do they coincide in some sort of habitual remorse? Perhaps my journey will be more accomplished than I initially anticipated.

The Text will not be in vain.

How can one person impact your life so much? How can just one friend make you see the truth of things? Make you see the beauty of life; the love of friendship? What is it that makes us admire someone so? What attracts us to one another? Personalities? Similar interests? Or just a simple common ground? An appreciation of the same things; an appreciation of each other.

Friends influence each other so greatly but do they ever tell each other just how much they have changed their lives? How much they appreciate each other? How much they love, respect and admire one another? Do they ever put their love into words or do they express with actions; a simple touch, a simple laugh, a kind word during a hard time? A hand to hold a hand, a shoulder to cry upon, a smile to brighten a day, and a heart you can always rely on. True friends are the most precious gift God can give us.

JUNE 27, 2000

MY LIFE DOESN'T REALLY even amount to a damn does it; certainly not in the grand scheme of things. Simply one more life wasted in this vast, unruly world where nobody really listens. Not to your heart anyway. They may hear the words that tumble from your mouth, sounding out fleeting feelings that carry themselves as echoes through open doors but they don't hear the silent reveries that harbor themselves deep within your heart. Though it beats so fervently sometimes, you wonder why no one is listening to it. You wonder why no one is doing anything to ease the reverberations felt with regret and sorrow. You wonder why no one helps you;

why no one understands you. Then you realize: it's because you push people away, always, always, always hold them at arm's length – distance yourself to feel safe – which is ironic because it only accomplishes the opposite.

JULY 4, 2000

THERE'S ALWAYS THIS FEELING of making promises I just can't keep; that none of us can keep or, let's put it this way, that none of us can be sure of keeping. We always say that there will be plenty of time to do the things we all want to do. We always think that things will turn out the way we want it to be, the way we planned it to be; that we'll always have TIME, but time is short, people need to realize that so they don't let moments slip through their fingers; so they don't have any regrets once the hour is up and time is out. I can *feel* it, you know. But do I ever follow my own advice? Hardly. I can dish it out but I can't follow my own words of 'wisdom'. I'm surprised anyone else does. Why can't people learn to follow their own advice? When they're in the same situation that someone else had been in and that they had given advice about; why can't people remember what to do? Always do the wrong thing – always, always, always. I mean, just look at my life; everything about it came too late. I mean, when I'm in a situation to do and say what I want to, to someone else, I never know what to do until the moment is gone. Then I say to myself, "Oh, why didn't I say that?" or "why didn't I do that?"

Regret comes so easily that it doesn't seem like regret at all but rather a magnified form of idiocy.

I replay in my mind what I should've done and then I curse myself for what I did do. Just forget and forgive and let go. Those are the hardest things to learn how to do. If we forget, then we don't learn. If we forgive we always second guess ourselves for consenting. If we let go we fear that we've lost something. It's all so complicated sometimes, but should it be? Why can't life just be life, not worries and heartaches; not categorized or labeled; not distinctly different. LIFE IS LIVING, so why can't we just live it; not worry about it, agonize over it; why can't we just live side by side in a mutual understanding that life is simply living and caring for one another and taking care of each other the way we are supposed to.

I feel like I'm a tourist in my own life. I sit back and watch all these things happening, not quite believing that they're happening to me. I take pictures of memories that I don't want to lose, snapshots of friends fill my mind, replaying over and over the moments when things were right. I feel so helpless most of the time that I walk around with a camera around my neck just so I know that sometimes things go right; that once upon a time, I had someone in my life who meant something to me and who I meant something to. I live my life behind a shutter lens and f-stops, always looking for the right amount of light to get something good. Always adjusting and focusing to conform to my surroundings but never letting what surrounds me, conform to me. I'm always the one behind everything else, looking for a moment to show myself; never really in the picture but off to the side, just out of range; always taking pictures of someone else's life, someone else's memories just so I can say I was there even though sometimes I wasn't seen; walking behind the curtain of my life but never stepping out in front to confront the crowd; living behind locked doors, drawn shades, and shut windows.

My camera may capture moments of happiness but most are not my own. I wonder if there will ever be a day when I take that step in front of the camera, when I let someone take the pictures of me; when I say to myself: I'm not a tourist. I belong.

I'll just be sitting down somewhere, or driving, or be anywhere, anytime, doing anything, and suddenly I'll remember the oddest of memories and I don't know what triggered it. It's nice when you all of a sudden remember something that had once been so much a part of you; that you did, or said, or thought, or just a moment shared with someone else, you'll remember that moment in time and think to yourself how great it was. You'll remember every little detail, every word spoken, gesture made, and every laugh shared. You remember the good things in life just so you know that once upon a time you were part of something special, even if it only lasted a moment or two, there's some things in life, some people, who you can never forget, because they touched you so deeply; or they made you smile just once; or laugh at something silly; or just because you did something nice for them. People remember those things. Or at least I hope they do. I know I do. I remember the good and the bad; the laughter and the tears; the love and the loss. They all become part of you, they are what make you whole and they are what can tear you apart. There are some people in this life that will always remain with you; that you'll always carry a special memory of; no matter if you've known them a minute or for thirteen years. It doesn't matter how long or how well you know someone; the only way you will remember someone is if they have touched your life in a way you'll never forget. Your heart can't be judged by how much love you have given but rather by how much you were loved by others; because if you were loved by others, that proves how true your love and friendship was to someone; it proves your heart was pure. That you were giving of love, and because you gave love, you received it as well.

2000

EVERYONE IS SOMEONE'S FRIEND. I can't imagine my friends not being my own but being someone else's; someone that I don't know. And this brings me to the question of how people can be so judgmental of one another – of these friends never met. They could have been your friend if you had lived where they do. It's strange how that works. We all end up somewhere but why do we end up where we do? Why was I chosen for this life in Maine and not Arizona? Why was I born to this family and not someone else's? What am I doing here? And why do I want to get out so badly? I know if I ever left that I'd want to come back here, to Maine. We all have roots, heritage, and history in the places we were raised and it's as if the land itself wants to hold you in its grasp, plunge you in its soil to grow roots of your own. The universe is an expansive place to say the say the least, and to be pinpointed to this life, in this town, to this family, on this Earth, is an amazing thing to ponder over.

JULY 2000

DEAR J,

How do you be 'real' in a world where everyone pretends? How can you be honest with yourself, and others, when you're never sure if people are being honest with you? First impressions are always false, it's only after the first impression that someone's true colors start to shine through. Some people that I've known almost my whole life are complete strangers to me now. They'll say or do something 'out of character' from what I perceive them to be and I'm sure I do the same. But is it all those little 'surprises' that make life tolerable? If everyone were to be what everyone thinks they are, what's the fun in that? Besides everyone has a different perception of the same person. What I think of someone isn't necessarily what you would think of them. We have to form our own opinions, not be told. But what do you do when you find yourself questioning those you've always held to be true? Honest? Sincere? How do you dig deep enough to uncover the 'real' person behind the façade?

People harbor too many dark secrets and when they don't let their frustrations out, it grows into hate, anger, and even violence. The thing is, I don't even know the real me. I don't know who I am or even who I want to be. I want to be a good person, someone people are proud of. I know enough about myself to know I'm a good person, relatively speaking. Modesty is key. Although I do have my moments when I'm not so good; but I'm not out there in the world hurting people. Not intentionally anyway but people's pride gets hurt, their ego bruises; there's always emotional turmoil but sometimes that can't be avoided. You can't love one person without hurting another. I just wish it were easier to love the person you want to love without getting hurt in the process. You are always on one side or the other. You love someone, someone loves you, but who you love isn't the one who loves you back. Isn't that the way? Maybe I'll just love everybody and not worry about it.

When I talk about love, there are many different things I mean. There's romantic infatuation love, there's friendship love, and love in general: caring about people and actually giving a damn about what happens to the world around you. Maybe if more people decided to care about the world, it would be a better place. Stop racing around trying to fix things that need no fixing: new technology when the technology we have is just fine. Stop trying to better all the materialistic things in life and start focusing instead on what really needs to be worked on; our own hearts, minds, souls.

Mankind is a violent species; capable of mass destruction. We build all these things, all these weapons, with the notion of war already on our minds; the nuclear holocaust, right? We are constantly in preparation for a battle with guns, bombs; violence and death. Why can't we live with the notion of peace in our minds; preparing for a holiday when the whole world can rejoice together and not worry about war? I'm sorry if I'm living in a fantasy, J, because I know the world as a whole is not capable of maintaining such peace. If a single country can't unite itself, how can the world become one?

JULY 16, 2000

TERRIBLE, TERRIBLE CHEST PAINS. It feels as though I'm having a heart attack. Something is wrong inside of me – just twisting and turning and squeezing and strangling the life out of me. Pain shooting its way through me like a knife slowly plunging into my flesh, deeper and deeper, cutting and slicing through skin, veins, muscle, and the raw meat of my existence. And it doesn't go away quickly, rather, it bides its time, taking every jab ever so slowly, to make sure the pain is measurable by waves of agony. I claw and clutch at the place where the pain resides, but I can't reach it. It's inside of me, not on the outside. It's not visible; no one can detect it but me. I just clench my jaw and grimace until it goes away. Show no emotion, let no one know, that's the way it goes. It's subsiding right now, though every time I take a deep breath it's there again, waiting to tear through my heart and cause imminent pain. I wonder what it could be.... And what it means.

JULY 19, 2000

I HAVE DECIDED THAT I'm going to go to Massachusetts in the next two weeks; either this weekend or next. I might just persuade someone to go with me because I don't have the money myself. I want to go to Amherst to visit the grave of Emily Dickinson. She's my hero. I'm very inspired by her and feel a deep affinity with her work. I will go out of respect, reverie, devotion, love and inspiration, and I'll make the pilgrimage in honor of her life. You know who else I'd like to visit – Sylvia Plath – but she's a bit too far away. I love to go and pay respects to the people who have inspired me in so many ways.

JULY 20, 2000

I GET TO SEE Emily Dickinson's house!! I'm ecstatic! I can't wait to go. Imagine it: I'll be walking the same halls she walked – looking out the same windows she looked out – I'll be *inside* her house; where she lived so many years! I'll be in the presence of one of my greatest influences and most revered personas. It's so exciting to me! We called and made reservations today. August 5th is when we're going. It'll be a preview tour of the Evergreens and a bonus tour of the Homestead. It's going to be amazing! Just think: EMILY DICKINSON!!

Then we'll go to Concord so I can see Alcott's Orchard House. Luisa May Alcott, one of my favorite books is Little Women. That is going to be quite amazing as well. Not to mention Ralph Waldo Emerson.

And Thoreau – On Walden Pond.

I'm most excited about Emily Dickinson though.

After Concord, it's off to Salem!! I've been studying the Salem Witch Trials of 1692. It makes me so sad. Has our society really changed from those horrible days when people were persecuted for circumstantial evidence, most of which wasn't even tangible? I fear our society has not come too far. Look at all the corruption around us. Look at all the accusations and lies. Where has the truth gone? That's too serious to talk about now.

JULY 22, 2000
3:30 AM

THE THUNDER ROLLS AND growls as if it feels my anger; silent as the moments in between, when lightning flashes across the sky and through my eyes. Brilliant spectrums of color get lost within the gray mist that closes upon the world, covering the traces of humanity with indignation. Bitter resentment falls, as the rain outside, inside my mind. Corrupting the earth below, pellets of rain fall as bullets through the soil; manifesting emotions from one extreme to the next. Anger – sorrow – fear – hatred – regret – despair – grief – all come to their final resting place inside my heart. What the world thinks it knows is nothing more than its own perception. Events take shape, take form and happen without consent, but stands firm in its place of history. One day you wake up only to read the headline that you never wanted to see. You try to turn away from the article that you don't want to read – but your sight is drawn to the fine black print and you devour every word that is said, whether you want to or not. Temptation is strongest in its weakest form: despair. Looking for that silver-lining, the fine print between the lines; but all you find are empty shell casings on the floor.

AUGUST 11, 2000

BEING IN ANOTHER'S PRESENCE for me is like being enclosed in a prison cell. I was born alone and that is probably the way I will die.

What's a life without love? Friends? Family? I can't say it's a life at all. But somehow, in its own way, the prospect is appealing. To get away from the constant bickering, the constant annoyance, the ongoing resentment; to just get away, be unsheltered, live among the trees, by the ocean; live anywhere but where I am.

Survival is a key element in life. Not survival of a tragedy or an accident, but survival of our lives, of our everyday battles, our internal struggles to find some sort of conviction in this downtrodden world. To survive adolescence unscathed is a rarity but so many succumb to these outward pressures and these internal battles that they never make it out of adolescence. I've always been afraid of not making it out of my own youth.

AUGUST 2000

Do I LOOK AS dead on the outside as I feel on the inside? If I do, then it's a wonder people can actually still look at me at all. Everything I feel is turbulent and irrational. A deep seeded mystery sits inside my being, waiting to be discovered, waiting to be tapped into so it has to conceal itself no longer. If anyone knows what this mystery is, don't you think it should be me? Yet I do not know and I merely speculate on the causes for my diminished lifeline.

I have become increasingly diligent in my avoidances of nearly all interaction one can participate in. I've hidden myself away. Caged myself in a dark abyss and thrown away the key. I feel like a frightened creature, standing in an open field in broad daylight waiting for the trigger to be pulled.

Waiting for the bullet to penetrate its way through my body; ripping, tearing, and destroying the life inside me.

The sun has become too bright. My eyes hurt and ache at the mere thought of the burning star. When I do venture outside, my heart pounds, my head aches, and everything in my body tells me to run to the darkened shadows to hide from the light. I hide beneath the canopy of my hat, willing the strength to come into me as I take each step forward, feeling that at any moment, my knees will buckle and I'll fall to the ground burning and incinerating from the light. I veil my eyes with dark lenses as I try to move forward to the confines of a structural familiarity. My skin tingles as my pores absorb the heat, cradling it beneath my skin in a cruel twist of fate.

And at last I am back. Back in my own darkened cage where I control the amount of light that burns and singes its way into my flesh, branding me with the ongoing fear of what awaits me outside. Until the sun goes down, I will wait patiently. Then I can emerge from my shadow and cloak myself in the endless dark that awaits and welcomes me.

I am home.

AUGUST 17, 2000
12:06 AM

Do you ever wonder what it is that makes you the way you are? What was it in life that contributed to your personality? How did you end up where you are now? And was it all your choice? Or was it all a pre-destined star map? Why can't I change who I am? Have you ever actually tried to change yourself? Well, I have, and I can tell you that it is no easy feat, J. Not for one like me; and if anyone out there says that the power is mine to change my life, I'd tell them that I used to dole out the same advice, but as for the reality of it, it's not that simple.

AUGUST 2000

I SEE IT ALL too clearly now. Everything that was shrouded with blackness illuminated itself against my will. Now it confronts me; the finality of all things stands before me and tempts me with its own mocking beliefs. The convictions I've held to are losing momentum to this piece of mind – as I am losing momentum to this life. There is one dark circle that hovers around my head and bids me the opportunity to step inside. This encircled faith is not what I crave. I crave boundless restrictions that lead me to a graceful fall. I do not want to be the stumbling fool I so often see behind the glass refraction. I don't want to lose my balance and consequently lose my place in this world. I want to be in one place, at one time, without my mind wandering to another place – a place that is unnatural for my being; for I am meant to be here, where I am. I am meant to live my life for as long as I can. So what is it that constricts me with an intangible rope?

Why rationalize everything when it seems as if everything is in disarray? Why not just throw my hands up and surrender to the truthful glances cast my way? Why hide behind a cool exterior and a seemingly endless charade of false intentions? Why care anymore? Because caring is all that's left to be done; all that's left to hold onto. I don't want to become the monster that I sometimes see staring back at me. I don't want to shield my face from stares or shield my own eyes from my own scars. Everyone has scars. Some can't be seen, but some are visible to the world. I have both.

SEPTEMBER 2000

WHERE IS PARADISE FOUND? More importantly, what is paradise? Is it simply a place that manifested in our minds to fit our own idealistic conformities - or is it a place that sits inside our hearts and souls, waiting for us to discover the secret map and take the Journey? Does paradise exist? Will we find it on our own, or will we need guidance from a Being who's already seen this unsurpassed and unparalleled locale? Are we so naïve to think that what we have right now, is all we deserve? Is it all we'll ever have? Or is there some greater glory waiting for us on that secret oasis of dreams and beauty? Do we even deserve to go there? To find this paradise lost? Or is it lost for a reason?

Tumbling inside my mind like lost reasons on the wind, these questions deepen my quest to find the salvation I've lost. In my mind, it takes shape and form; it becomes a place of reality. But where it is, I can never tell for sure. The map is unclear, and the sun burns so low on the horizon that not enough light is shed upon the desolate shadows of the land. Mountains, majestic in their own humbling way, outline the sky like barriers to a lost world; shielding us from what – peace of mind? Or protecting us from danger? Are they meant to keep us inside a conforming cage or do they keep the others out of our beautiful world?

Everything in this world of ours can be sidelined to the contradictions. Consistency affords us the comfort of knowledge but it's a knowledge we created; we did not learn. We will never learn. The mountains will continue to barricade us with its lessons and we will continue to dwell inside the secret valley waiting for the rocks to crumble away so we can find our way out to the sacred city of blessedness. We must realize that we've been trying to find our way out for thousands of years. And still, we are here. We've advanced ourselves in technology – in the race to achieve the greatness in society's maddening convictions that we need to improve our standards of monetary living. We do need to improve our standards but it's our standards in our faithful convictions that need the tending. Not in computers – not on Wall Street – not our man-made structural significance; our souls need tending and our hearts need faith; then our minds will direct us to paradise.

Paradise can be found in your heart, soul, and mind. It doesn't matter where you are as long as you're where you want to be. That's all it is. The great secret, the mystery, the map to paradise – is written in the stars and only your heart can decode the message. Find the place where you know you belong; find the road that leads you where you want to go, and live in the dreams that you always wished were true and you will have just discovered…. Paradise Lost.

SEPTEMBER 3, 2000

SIXTEEN MORE DAYS UNTIL I leave for Indiana!!! I haven't bought my bus ticket yet. Perhaps I should do that sometime soon. I was going to get it Thursday but I will probably go Tuesday, or maybe even tomorrow. Not today though. I don't much feel like moving today. What else is new? This trip is going to be an assault on all my sense, I think. It will attack and destroy all the nerve and strength I've built up on the first night. It will be scary, but it is something I have to do. If you don't ever take chances in life, it's not really a life worth living. To be able to do what you've always wanted to do is an indescribable feeling. It brings freedom and peace to a restless soul. No longer will you have to wonder if you can do it because it will already have been done. You have to live while you can, right? No time like the present.

SEPTEMBER 5, 2000

JOURNAL,

I feel liberated today. I went out this morning and bought my one way ticket to Marion, IN. no more worries, no more cares, just throw caution to the wind and be swept away by uncertainty. Two weeks from today, lucky number 14, I'll be on my way to Indiana with a backpack full of life and a mind full of dreams. September 19th is getting awfully close. I have a lot to do yet I don't know what! I've gathered up what few things I can but Peter hasn't dropped off the tent and backpack yet. I don't know what else I'm going to need or how much I can bring. I don't know what I'm doing to be quite honest. I'm kind of throwing myself into this. I haven't planned it at all; I'm just going day to day with whatever comes into my head. It's all good though. I'll find my way. Wonderful things can happen to you when you least expect it. Of course, it also goes the other way; bad things can happen without you expecting it either. But they won't. This is my deal, my trip, my dream, and my life and nothing is going to stop me in my pursuit of self-freedom and a wild adventure. I will be fine. That is, unless of course, I just completely jinxed myself right now and some horrible misdeed occurs and leaves me paralyzed with insecurity, fear, and regret. No. I will be fine.

(2014: The year 2000. I decided to travel back to Fairmount but this time I didn't have enough money to drive myself. So I bought a bus ticket. I packed a hiker's backpack and tent. I didn't know what I was doing but I thought it would be an adventure. Not knowing anyone out there, I foolishly thought I'd be able to survive with only a few items of clothing and a tent. I never thought of where I would pitch the tent to find sleep. But the adventurer in me said, "Do it. Let's go. It'll be an adventure". Looking back on my decision to travel this way, I can't believe, at 19 years old, I thought it was a good idea! Lucky for me, I was taken in by some very hospitable people and didn't have to worry about finding a place to pitch my tent. Little did I know, however, just how much of an assault on my senses this trip was going to take).

How much am I willing to sacrifice? How much can I afford to give up in order to follow my dream? My heart? My faith? Everything? How can I survive without what I love? And why does it always seem that the one thing you love, is the one thing you can't have.

Someday I'll find out. I'll throw myself to the truthful fury that rages inside my soul and I'll listen instead of pretending not to hear.

Enjoy life for all its worth while it's here. It's a hard thing to do because a part of you is so blind that you believe it will always be here.

Trying, trying, trying to fill that hole inside but it just keeps growing. You spend your whole life trying to fill the emptiness that sits inside of you, you try to grow something there, to breathe life into it, but it remains a silent reminder that there is nothing out there to fulfill you anymore.

Some have had it, some never find it, and most lose it before they are ready to let go.

I'm not sure where I fit in. Have I had it? Has that emptiness in me ever been satiated? Even in the slightest moment? Or has it always been a gaping would than cannot heal?

I can't remember.

SEPTEMBER 8, 2000
10:30 AM

Last night, as I lay down in bed trying to fall asleep, it felt as if my ribs were trying to breakthrough my skin. It felt like someone was stabbing a needle, burning at the tip, deep into my heart. I was attacked by this seizing pain that thrust me to tears. Though it lasted only a few minutes, it felt as if it were forever. I couldn't breathe. I couldn't move. I could only fall into the pain.

I've come to accept pain as a means of living. Without

pain there is no life. Without suffering there is no way to learn. And without knowledge, there is only an emptiness that dwells inside of you; there is an eagerness to understand: to comprehend the tragedy of life, all one has to do is live. Perish for your own sake, for your own well-being.

Live only to die. A little lamb led to the slaughter.

SEPTEMBER 8, 2000
11:30 PM

MY GOD JOURNAL – Katie just died. I can't believe it. The accident was a few hours ago. I heard the sirens; ambulances; police cars; I heard them go by the house. It was just up the road, right before Broadview Heights. Right there on that turn, that corner. Her car rolled over, flipped over. Oh god. Not Katie. Oh why did you have to take her? Today was her birthday.

(2014: I remember clearly the phone call received that night. The phone rang just past 11:00 PM and my dad answered. I heard him say, "No. Oh god, no." So I went halfway down the stairs and said, "What's wrong?" He said, "The accident. It was Katie." I was puzzled for a moment and then asked, "Is she ok?" He just looked at me and said, "She died." And my heart felt as though it would burst through my skin. I was too shocked and bewildered to say anything. I literally crawled up the stairs, into my bedroom, shut the door, leaned my back against it and cried. I cried for days. I still cry on occasion. The pain is indescribable when you lose someone. In time we manage our emotions but in the beginning you're only plagued with the question "Why?" A question without an answer to satisfy).

SEPTEMBER 9, 2000

JOURNAL,

It's 10:30 in the morning as I write to you now. I've yet to sleep. I'm on my 25th hour. It's been eleven hours since I first heard it was Katie. I'm still afraid to go to sleep. I'm afraid to wake up and realize that it's all real. I can't bring myself to acknowledge this is real; that she's gone. Still the words "She died" run through my head. They haunt me with their presence; their repetitiveness inside my head. They attack me with the harsh truth I do not want to hear. Why did this have to happen?

I feel lost. I keep praying for the realization that this is all one horrible dream. I don't want to fall asleep because I know I'll eventually wake up to realize nothing has changed. It will still be the same. Katie will still be gone. Everyone will still be hurting. And I'll still be crying.

SEPTEMBER 11, 2000

I HAVE TO GO to visiting hours for Katie today. I don't know if I'm strong enough. With this, comes reality. I'll have to stare truth in the face.

Later:

I just got back from visiting hours. It's 9:19 PM right now. I was there for seven hours.

I cried and cried until I thought the tears had run dry, but one look at her in the casket, in her pictures, the mere thought of her flashing through my memory and I couldn't hold on.

SEPTEMBER 12, 2000

THE SERVICE, THE CELEBRATION of Katie's life today, was beautiful. The church was packed. I expected no less though. Lindsay and Amanda came to my house, we went up to the accident site, and then to the church. Saw a lot of familiar faces today. After the service, people were getting in line, when people were filing out of the church, the three of us waited until all the pews had emptied and then we got in line. I just placed my hand on Katie's casket and whispered, "I'll see you sometime, kid. I love you." Then we moved along the line to see her parents and brother.

SEPTEMBER 13, 2000

SOMETIMES I WONDER WHAT the future would have brought.

Would it have been living if I followed not my heart but dared instead to follow my dream?

What one said, the other denied.

What one thought, the other kept silent.

When one hurt, the other agonized in the grief.

When one smiled, the other followed not in suit, but rather strayed too far.

Synchronized to keep one another distracted; never believing the same view.

Consistent only in confusion.

SEPTEMBER 19, 2000

WELL J, THIS IS it. I'm off to Fairmount, IN in about six hours. Yes, I decided to go. Katie's mom told me I should.

OCTOBER 5, 2000

THE TEARS THAT ROLL down my cheeks right now coincide with the rain that quietly falls from Heaven above. I don't know how long I'm going to have to do this. There's an emptiness that just expands more so every day. There's an aching, a hurt, and a yearning to understand something that seems to have no logic or reason.

It's the unpredictable tragedy that sends everyone on a soul searching quest for the answer why; sends them searching for the truth; but everyone ends up at a different truth. They find an answer for themselves; an answer that makes them feel better; secure; and comforts them with a certain ethereal sense of peace. I've yet to come across that. I live each passing day in a constant struggle between my faith and my own conscience. They continually contradict one another. What my mind believes, my heart does not. What my heart feels isn't complimented the least bit by what my mind tells it. Uncertainty is what eats away inside – expanding the emptiness – the hollowness with no truth.

How can I be so filled with emotions and love but feel so hopeless and empty at the same time? Do I feel too much?

You know, all I really want right now is an answer; an honest, truthful answer to my question of Why? I listen to everything around me, inside me, everything that surrounds me. I strain and lean into the wind hoping it carries the truth. But it just passes through me, affording me no peace of mind.

There is only an empty field where scattered memories are our only truth.

OCTOBER 8, 2000

TIME IS A MONSTER. I've come to regard 'time' as the destructive force of our lives. It eats away at our purity, becoming the cynic of our soul; and it slowly etches its markings upon our faces and bodies. It destroys moments and takes the things we cherish most.

But time can also be a blessing. For all the time I've spent with you, I wouldn't trade the world. Time can be precious when spent together. But time can be lonely when all you have is gone and all you want, you can never have again.

Perhaps time is only what you make it.

OCTOBER 14, 2000

THE SUN IS OUT today. The sky is a soft, metallic blue. The air is crisp, but not cold; it's fresh. There's life in every corner, in every shadow and every open sunlit place; and I am getting ready to go to Katie's burial. The world is full of irony if one will only look for it. How am I feeling right now? Still stuck in that disbelieving state. I drove past the cemetery last night and saw the little mound of dirt that was covered with one of those green throws; a hole in the earth where the remains of our friends' body will be laid silently down, becoming one with the earth. It's a sad day. I have a headache just thinking about everything. It's about time to go. Later, J.

I think it's only about 7:30 PM, but it feels as if I've been up forever and a day. Just how long is forever? Infinite. Went to Katie's burial this morning. It was surreal, like I expected it to be. We each got a balloon, a rose, and at the end of the song (Martina McBride's "There You Are") we all let go and the balloons grouped together to form an almost mystical appearance in the sky and they floated towards the Heavens above. It was beautiful. I felt the irony of a metaphor contained in this simple action of 'letting go'. It's easy to let go of objects but to let go of her life and accept what can't be changed isn't quite that simple.

Seeing the small box that contained her ashes, sitting there silently among bunched roses, with a blue velvety blanket draped upon it, was a vision I couldn't comprehend the meaning of. In a way, I found it was easier to look at this small box than it would have been to view her casket there.

OCTOBER 23, 2000

WHAT DO YOU DO when you don't like the person you've become or when your actions control you and your mind is left with the guilt and regret of something you never meant to do, say? Who do you turn to when there is no one you can confide in? When there is no one you *think* you can confide in?

The real trouble starts when there *is* someone you can trust and confide in but you don't.

You hide yourself away; deep within your own mind, within your own guilt and regret, and you manifest a shield that surrounds you that, to others, seems impenetrable. You want to let someone in, but you can't find the door.

All around you is a solid form; a substance that seems so real you wonder if you'll ever be able to find a way out for yourself.

For someone to live a life without love, by their own choice, is the most foolish thing one can do. But what if you don't trust yourself? You don't trust yourself so you constrict yourself to a life of solitude; heartache; misery. And the only thing that reinforces that feeling you created is the fact that you seemingly have no control over Life. When you think you're in control, when you think you're doing what you want to do, need to do, are supposed to do; it's not you that is in control... it's a fate that has been written in the stars for longer than you can imagine. There are no coincidences; there are no accidents... there is only trial and error and Life.

Am I testing my strength, my mentality, by seeing how long I can go, how much I can handle without breaking? I guess the funny thing is: I'm already broken... I just haven't fallen apart yet.

NOVEMBER 25, 2000

Isn't it sad when someone with so many dreams never accomplishes anything they set out to do? They ground themselves with the past; never really living in the present; and seeing no hope for the future; they give up. They idle along in the mainstream; in the monotony; the presumptuous opinions they hear are only their own text read through thoughts that convey everlasting failure. When so much has gone wrong, it's hard to believe in anything anymore; especially yourself. There are people out there who constantly put themselves second; they help others even when it hurts them to do it. So why do they continue? Maybe because they begin to think that by doing this, they have something left that's worth fighting for; if they give themselves enough time, it will all work out and they'll believe in themselves again. And it's a tough position for these people because no matter how much encouragement they get; no matter how much praise and how many compliments they receive; if they can't believe in themselves; they're still not going to get anywhere. It's a waste. It's meaningless when you have the talent but you don't use it. Certain people were given certain gifts and it's up to them to utilize them. But there are so many more obstacles for individuals to overcome these days; and some days, it hurts them to even breathe; to even acknowledge their own existence is something that they sometimes would rather not do.

There are people out there who feel all alone in this world. They can be surrounded by many people; friends, family; but still they feel alone; no one understands them. No one wants to take the time to listen. But what do you suppose these people would say if given the opportunity? Would they be honest and answer the questions truthfully? Or would they simply tell people what they want to hear? Would they hide their own feelings; try to disguise them so maybe they'll forget them too? They wonder: is it possible to fool themselves; to pretend to be someone else; live someone else's life; if only for one day, be someone else. They daydream and fantasize about what it would be like to be that girl; or that boy – the one that seems so happy; seems to have all the luck; their lives in order; their future bright. And they sit back and look at their own lives and they don't see the optimism that lives there. They've already killed that; buried it deep enough so no light can ever find it.

There's people who live in the constant, blinding glare of grief. No matter who is hurting; no matter where tragedy strikes; there's people who feel it deep within their heart – hoping to take their pain away; these people wallow in the grief; the hurt; the pain. They swallow it down, choking out the sobs, drowning in their tears. They purposely look for pain. Why? In some twisted form, they think it will make them feel better. For all their life, they've known hurt; so they continue to look for it. It's not hard to find in the world today. The trouble is, these people just don't see anything but the pain; the tragedies; and so they turn their own lives into tragic tales – ending in hurt; pain; and grief. They wind the days, months, and years into a countdown, knowing that one day – it will all be over and they won't have to worry about anything anymore. They will be free.

If only they knew, right now, at this moment – they are free. They can do anything they want as long as they want it bad enough; as long as they have the drive to make it there; to push through the barriers that we all face no matter if we're born in luck and wealth – or if we're born in poverty of all the senses of the word. If you want something – go after it. Look for the beauty in life – not the pain. There's heartache all around us; there's pain in words; grief in tragedy; there's a hurt we all live with; that we all have to live with – but we have so much in front of us... if we only look; if we choose to see.

Take the plunge into the View; the vision of your future is in your hands and the present is merely the first step in trying to get there.

There are people in this world who go about their lives feeling empty. If only they knew, right now, that they could feel whole, if only they give themselves the chance.

DECEMBER 16, 2000

LIFE DOESN'T SHED ITS skin. It regenerates day after day, layer upon layer. The thickness of its skin expands; conforming to what was put before it. Different shades of color can be seen sometimes, but the horizon that looms ahead is always black, dark, and ominous; leering at you with hungry sights; ready to swallow you up into its blindness until you find yourself sitting at a computer one day, realizing every day is just a copy of every other.

The predictability of my life seems quite obvious. Talking to these people, day in and day out, the same people, the same faces, the same jokes; nothing ever changes and I'm tired of the monotony – the predictability – the never changing, never-ending 'customers' of my life. Putting myself on display, where the world, my world, can make conjectured opinions about me; can laugh; can imagine. I don't like the position I am in; the display case I'm shelved on. I want to keep moving, just keeping out of eyesight, out of their range. I want to move and move and move until I find a place that can stop me; where I can see the beauty of every day and every day is something new; not the same as the day before; where the sunsets always keep their luster; the sunrises always give their hope and rain doesn't cry, it only falls.

I was thinking the other day, right now at this very moment that I am writing this, someone out there in this world, in this country, is receiving the worst news of their lives; someone is crying; someone is weeping in grief, in despair. Someone just lost someone they loved with all their heart – and I wonder – are they alone? Are they sitting in their room crying silently because no one can hear them? Someone out there right now is contemplating suicide; thinking there's no one who loves them or thinking their life isn't worth living and if they were gone, no one would really care or miss them. And at the same time this is happening, there is someone else out there who just put the gun back in the safe, realizing there's still so much life inside of them. Someone is bringing a new life into this world – someone is getting married – someone is at a funeral – someone, somewhere, is sitting in a cemetery next to the headstone of a loved one. Someone is being hurt. Someone is being murdered at this very moment; someone is being raped. Someone is thinking of someone else, longing for them, wishing for them, dreaming of them. Someone is missing someone – someone is meeting someone for the first time. Right now, two people are falling in love – or making love. Someone is fighting, hitting, angry at the world, at this life. Someone out there might be thinking of me right now – or you. And there is someone out there, at this very moment, who needs to be held, who needs to be loved, and who wants to do the same. Someone is alone.

There is never a moment in Life when something is not happening – something good – something bad – it all coincides. Someone receiving the worst news of their lives – someone receiving the best news of their lives; at the same exact moment in time. It's all a grand scheme – this Life. Nothing happens without something happening in return; trying to maintain a balance that we can't see – but that is there.

When you think about things like this, it takes you to a whole new level of mentality; realizing that you're not the only one in the world who feels as you do; realizing there are people out there hurting at this very moment you're wallowing in self-pity; and knowing what they may be going through, you can empathize – and you want to put an arm around them and say, "I understand. It's alright to cry. I'm here for you".

There's a whole world out there, living, as I am living – at the same moment – feeling the same emotions. We're never as alone as we think we are. Emotions can play dirty tricks you know, make us *feel* things that aren't real. Right now someone is dreading to go to work just as I am. Someone is as unhappy as I am being stuck in a place they do not want to be and don't care to go. There are people out there who feel as if they don't have any options and that they have to keep doing the same thing over and over again, every day, just like me.

This balance that the world maintains teeters so violently on the edge sometimes that one wrong move could send us all into a haphazard dishevelment. We'd be lost – somewhere that is not ours – something that is not our lives – not our World. If we lost this 'balance' we'd be thrown even deeper down into the darkness than we think we are. We don't know the rules of the game, we can't see the instructions or know the objective – the outcome – all we can do is Live. It's hard to keep up sometimes. Sometimes I just wish the World would pass on my turn – throw the dice by me – skipping me over – and give me time to think.

DECEMBER 20, 2000

WASTING AWAY IN THE vastness of a dream so high among the clouds, I wonder if I'll ever be able to soar high enough to realize. Idleness in this contemporary world – where slogans scream at you with a voice so loud you wonder why you can't hear it – why the words somehow get lost becoming a dyslexic version of the alphabet – a monstrosity of vowels – a howling apparition of a once, long ago, Genius. Simple melodies and jargons ring inside my head; insight and continuity get shoved aside. New phrases I see, I hear, become the essence and objective of my own being. I easily discard the old to begin, to try once more, with the new. Hoping to better myself in ways I haven't yet grasped. The obvious correlation between my life now and the life I've already lived is that most of each has already passed without my completing the one simple goal I put forth in front of myself. The one true, idealistic fantasy that sits as a broken seashell in my mind; waiting to be found; to be picked up, brushed off; to be molded and transfixed to some fine artifact becoming a priceless treasure to the one who wants me; to the one who sees me and loves me just the way I am, saying, "such beauty is rare to find these days". And they'll keep me, locked tightly in their firm grasp; holding forevermore, me to their side. Polished off after the years, made to look new, bright; to bring back some of the luster I was first born with – to find the pearl inside. "A pearl of wisdom" – they say; implying what? That a treasure can be found in each of us; that we hold, inside ourselves, a priceless entity of unrealized Wisdom? What good is that if we never find it? It merely sits on the bed of the ocean, decaying, wasting away in the vastness; in the grandest dream one can fantasize about; never completing its sole purpose of invention; trapped in the whirlpool of its own survival, thinking it's alone.

DECEMBER 21, 2000

READING THE CHAPTERS OF another's life and intoning the emotions, actions, and individual objectives into my own, brings about, in me, an insatiable need to feel the closeness. It's the intoxicating presence of someone like you that keeps you hungry for more; if only to feel the connection and to not feel alone.

How many years have been spent sitting here, staring pensively out the same window whose view has never changed? The same tall trees, long branches, and shady interior hide the opposing threat of the world; shelters me with only isolation it thinks protects me. But it only shrouds me; encloses me in its vine encrusted sanctuary; blocking me from seeing what's on the other side, what awaits me beyond this wall of false protection?

There is a World out there I've never seen. I've only dreamed, fantasized, and longed for the one journey that would take me to an un-located beauty. Is there a place that has not been tarnished by the touch of man but still exists with only the touch of God? Is there a place that has not been soiled by the blood of martyrs? Of men? Or is this world growing on our own faults; our own blood seeds the land and our sweat toils out the non-endearing existence of society today.

A final sunset; one last setting horizon blazing across the sky in brilliant spectrums of color that invoke our spirits to become an entity of light; of devotion. Such beauty exists somewhere, I'm sure. Such devotion occurs now and then and is illuminated in the eyes of tragedy.

DECEMBER 2000

IT'S NEARLY TIME FOR the New Year, 2001. I can't help but feel, deep within me, that 2001 will somehow be etched in stone. A magnificent awakening will occur and my once tired soul will open its eyes to a different world.

Later:

The stars were shining brilliantly last night. No clouds floating aimlessly alone; no sign of a bad horizon. Only the stars; gloriously aloft a black night sky. I stood there in a moment of indecision; looking at the stars, breathing in and out, watching my exhaled breath take form and silently disappear into the atmosphere. What to do. I felt hands entwined with mine; hands of someone I love yet someone I don't want to be with. Pressure. Temptation. Just to end the night I gave a simple kiss. Two pairs of lips, hot, moist with anticipation, contrast with the frigid night air; a simple kiss – meaningful to one – obligatory to another. It may be the last time, I told myself. Yet I didn't feel anything this time; no real emotion on my part, just an obligation to conform to temptation. What happened to those feelings I once had for him? Being held beneath the sky, wrapped inside warm arms and feeling no comfort. I only wanted to be alone with the majestic night – searching the sky for the one – the only one. Lost somewhere in my mind, my imagination, my own thoughts; yet there I was, trapped in an omnipresent indecision. Will I never learn?

(2014: A boy and a girl, unrequited feelings. There was a boy who said he loved me. He always said he loved me. I uttered the words to him once too but it was not meant to be. My state of mind was far too unpredictable and I couldn't give all of me to him. I loved him, yes. But I couldn't love him because I couldn't love myself. I couldn't get out of my head long enough to give attention to his needs. So I thought it would be better to say farewell. I used to think, "If I can get beyond this, if I can move ahead and away from this damaging frame of mind, maybe it could work." But no one waits forever. I didn't feel worthy of love so I would not let him love me in the capacity he wanted to. I suppose we all have lost loves in our lives. I think back on that time with no bitterness or resentment. It was young love, perhaps a glorification of lustful feelings. That was the last time I saw him too).

2001

History Becomes Etched In Stone

JANUARY 1, 2001

LET ME START BY saying: HAPPY NEW YEAR!

I am typing this with one eye open because if both eyes were open, I'd be seeing double vision and speaking in a language that no one would understand. Really though, I haven't had that much to drink. Only three Zima's, four white Russians, and I nearly finished the bottle of Hot Damn! But it's 2001!!! A completely new year. Hopefully things will get better. Thank god for these little red lines beneath misspelled words or else no one would be able to read this entry.

JANUARY 9, 2001

MY EYES HAVE SUNKEN into my soul. Looking around the blind corners, the Faith resumes. God save me! Save me from myself as I retreat, cowardly, back into the old habits. As I unwittingly invite the old feelings back into my veins, urging them to churn the blood; to boil the crimson river inside my heart, scalding me with the pain of failure. Failure to succeed in aspirations; failure to communicate with fellow peers, with whom now is too late; save me from the blinding vision of tears and the searing sensation of grief that consumes a being whole with a fiery haze and a conflagration of tragic loneliness.

I am that girl; the one who is afraid of herself; who longs for reassurance but is scared to ask for it. I am the one in need of guidance; wanting to be led in the direction of my predecessors but who doesn't have a compass to show her which way to go. Lend me your hand and lead me to the right path; towards strength; towards freedom; towards you. I have not given up. I will not lay down my sword and surrender. I will fight, for all I am, for all I believe. I will continue to fight my way through the demons who lurk amid my mind trying to coerce me into the Temptation. I am stronger. I can make it through another day – and another – and another – and another until it is time for me to go; time for me to lead someone else. Until then, I will continue to keep my shield up, my armor on. But I am scared.

Save me from my own sacrificial offering – save me from myself.

JANUARY 25, 2001

I'VE BEEN ILL FOR the past week with a throat that would've felt better if cut by a guillotine. Every time I swallowed, the image of razor blades slashing through the thin lining of my throat invaded my mind.

To study something, to prove a theory, you need both a controlled and an uncontrolled environment which, in and of itself, seems ridiculous because control is really an illusion – it's a mindset we humans have because we believe we are the most powerful, intelligent beings – but really we're just living an egoistic fantasy. We think we're controlling the 'study' when, in actuality, we're probably the ones who are the test subjects; thrown together on this world, trying to make a living, trying to make a life for ourselves, hoping to succeed, doing our best to learn and all the while we're being watched by our predecessors; and they're watching us to see if we do what we're supposed to.

We've been set up in this controlled environment where everything seems chaotic and out of place. It's a complex system. It's like we're in a controlled environment and we make it uncontrollable. Even the things that seem to have no logic or order, things that, at one point, seem out of place; even those things have a larger meaning and set the course for what happens in the future. For example, take that cup of coffee I have this morning; that sets the course for the rest of my day; because of that cup of coffee, I may be late to work or I may decide to drink two cups and be even later. And on my way there, something could happen, I could go off the road, hit a deer, hit a car and I would be thinking to myself 'if I hadn't had that cup of coffee, I would've been on the road five minutes earlier and that car wouldn't have been there. I wouldn't have gone off the road'. But because things happened the way they did, because I did drink that second cup, because I was late for work, I happened to be on that road at the exact moment when the other car was; the exact moment that the deer ran out in front of me and because of that cup of coffee I went off the road, I hit a tree, maybe I died. And it could go the other way. A normal day when I have coffee, I decide not to so I go to work early (not likely to happen) and because of that, because of that one variation of my day, something happened; something good, something bad – it's hard to say.

They say that sometimes when something bad happens, it's a blessing in disguise. I guess that makes sense because we're always learning from something, some event, some tragic tale. We're learning, growing, gaining knowledge and insight into our own lives, our own spirits and our souls are expanding; loving. And you begin to think, if I didn't have that cup of coffee, would things really have been different? Would I have avoided that car? But because things happen for a reason, the scale would have tipped differently and the person in the other car, or the deer in the road, would have altered their 'controlled' environment and things still would have been the same.

You only do the same things every day because it's a routine. You're used to it. But you also do it because you feel the safety of something familiar. You figure, if you keep doing it, you'll keep being safe; you'll stay firmly in your place of safety never thinking that just because you do things the same way, it doesn't mean that the other person in the car did. Maybe they were the one late to work; maybe it was the variations in their environment that caused yours to alter so drastically. Control is completely out of your hands. Routines don't offer safety; they merely offer the familiarity and illusion of having your life firmly and safely in your own hands. But it's either your time to go or it isn't.

All the things that make our Journey so bittersweet at times, they're out of our control. We're the specimens, the guinea pigs of this 'controlled' test subject world. Our life is our choice, and all our lives, together on this world, become a spectator's sport. Predecessors watch us unravel the riddle we set for ourselves. This world is an experimental place, there's no denying that, we're all here experimenting, trying new things, trying to perform our own legacy, trying to build our own awareness; and Heaven awaits us like a salvation; the reward for a job well done.

It's like the mouse in the maze: the mouse knows that at the end of the maze, when he gets to where he's supposed to be, there will be a prize for him; there will be a reward;

a big, hefty hunk of cheese, a delectable treat to his senses. And our lives, our Journey, is like a maze; leading us around on different paths, closing doors on us, dead ends around corners sometimes, but at the end is that sweet salvation. When we make our way through finally, we'll be rewarded with our own prize of eternal life. While we 'mad scientists' scurry around and place these little mice in mazes trying to guide them through by promising a treat at the end, so too are we the mice, being led around the mazes of this world, being promised the pot of gold at the end of the rainbow, being lured with knowledge and tempted with the safety of a familiar Home.

FEBRUARY 9, 2001

I MUST BE LONELY. Why else would I do such a desperate foolish thing? Drudging up the past when it would be better left buried. I'm resurrecting something that, by all means, is dead and should remain so. Such feelings are transitory, they mean nothing. But desperate times call for desperate measures, foolish or not. But I think I have a tendency to do stupid things when it comes to relationships, in friendships and love. Another aspect of my ongoing commitment phobia. The thing is, 99 times out of 100, I don't feel lonely. It's only on those days, those particularly devastating days, when I'm reminded of what is missing from my life. I don't want to be with anyone and yet it's the only thing I want at times. But like I said, it is better left buried, those feelings. It would be foolish of me to go out, shovel in hand, and dig it up again. So here I'll stay, squelching any deep rooted desire I may have.

When the sky falls down, warns Chicken Little, it falls hard.

FEBRUARY 18, 2001

HOW DO YOU WRITE; how do I write? Become the character – breathe life into a lifeless form, a shapeless entity. Inhabit characteristics, develop mannerisms, and accentuate the obvious. A mind wanders, and a character is born.

And how many different people have I been? My role-playing, my manifesting characters; is this simple tactic the reason why I don't know who I am? Why I'm constantly running, why I'm a different person every day? Or am I a different person every day because I don't like who I am? Because I want to be someone else.

APRIL 17, 2001

STANDING OUTSIDE TONIGHT, LOOKING at the stars, seeing the impossibilities once again shining bright but realizing the stars hold no special power, except their brilliance. They can't grant wishes when the fall. They can't offer any real consolation; they're just there, gleaming through their unawareness. And you think of their beauty, you see their burning desire, and you wonder if it's the last time you'll see such beauty, you wonder if the next star that falls, will be yours.

You can pick one out, you can look at it tonight; but if it were gone tomorrow, you wouldn't even notice it's gone.

There won't be an obvious hole in the night sky; there won't be a vast empty space – there will only be others. And that's all you'll see. Your eyes will adjust and focus on what's still there not realizing that one more star has fallen. Because the star you look at tonight, the star you fall in love with, might not really even be there; it may have never existed within your lifetime, but you can see the afterglow of its glorious life still hanging in the sky; its light still glinting off the clouds. All it is, is an apparition of its former self; holding on to what it hasn't got any longer. What you see tonight, what your vision beholds, what it takes to be true and real – might just be an illusion. And when the moment catches up to itself, the star will fall, and its light will be gone.

You can always try to recapture the star that has already fallen, but with no light to aid you, you fade into the backdrop of the night and the darkness that blinds you, absorbs you within its realm and keeps you there until you can find it in yourself to realize that it's really gone.

APRIL 2001

PEOPLE SEEM TO BE under the impression I'm made of stone.

Earlier this evening, my pal and I were getting into a 'discussion' up at a friend's house and she called me "Ice Queen". I try to take it all in stride but sometimes it burrows so deep underneath my skin that I can feel it crawling through my veins. They seem to think I can brush aside the casual accusations almost as if they were never really spoken. It all just goes to prove that no one really knows who I am; that no one really understands me.

To have someone to confide in, just once, to tell them everything about myself, everything I've had to keep to myself in order to sustain this 'perception', would be a great unburdening. I am not as strong as they think I am. I'm susceptible to insults and subtle insinuations just like everyone else. Just because I choose to keep my emotions to myself does not mean I don't fall to my knees and weep on occasion.

There is an underlying impression I made so long ago that seems to be the definition everyone reads me as. I fall easily into temptation too; sometimes it's the wrong temptation. I have secrets that no one else knows; secrets that hurt; secrets that whittle away peace of mind.

I have indelibly marked upon others a perception of myself that it is almost impossible to shatter. If someone were to be let into my mind, to view all the thoughts, ideas, dreams, heartaches, and secrets that keep their hours within the confines of my heart and soul – they would come into contact with a stranger; with someone they do not even know nor recognize. There's more to me than what meets the eye; and no one has been let inside my world far enough to truly understand what I'm all about. There is a confidence that people see in me that is only a disconcerting illusion. I have created myself into someone who is nearly unattainable for me to keep up with.

MAY 16, 2001

YOU KNOW, IT'S TRUE: when you don't sleep, nothing is real. The life of an insomniac is that of a life living in a world that the mind fixates and forms through its own perceptive illusions.

I look at my hands, my wrists, and arms, scrutinizing every detail, every scar, every vein that runs the perceptible length underneath my skin and it doesn't look real. I form my hand into a fist and can see the subtle variations underneath this external flesh when my muscles contract and stretch, and my bones move beneath my skin, disrupting the relaxed elasticity of flesh. I move my hand backwards and on my wrist I notice the brightening of veins underneath – I can see where their lines run, how they part left and right; I can see the blue blood as it runs its course through my living body. If one were to cut deep into the flesh, letting this air infiltrate beyond the barrier of skin, the blood would pour out in a crimson river. We are all different colors, but it's when we bleed that we are all the same.

MAY 28, 2001

YOU CAN ONLY BE still for so long until you have to move; it becomes a necessity for your survival; it becomes an involuntary obsession to never be still again; to never idle along in the conformist society. There comes a time when you have to move for yourself, no matter who's in the way – you have to go around them in order to get past yourself; to keep moving along towards your own ideals. I'm increasingly aware that my time for moving is approaching. I've idled in this stagnant pool long enough. I've maintained this conformist lifestyle of complacency for too long now. I've got to move for myself before I forget how to do it; before I become paralyzed in this moment in Time; before I can't go anywhere because I've forgotten how to walk away. I could walk away right now. Hell, I could run until my breath gives way to a euphoric suffocation. But I won't. My feet are shackled together and I can't take those long strides towards my own freedom yet. I'm constantly living someone else's life because I can't stand to be in mine right now because of these unpredictable whims of contradictory emotions that take hold of my mind and twist it around until it cannot untangle itself from my soul.

JUNE 27, 2001

AT LEAST ONCE WE'VE all done something we preach against; we've set aside our morals and made at least one mistake. No matter how big or small the misdeed of conscience was, we've all been there. Can we make up for it? Sometimes.

JUNE 30, 2001

I FEEL I HAVE been slighted; jilted to the very core of my being. I feel every pang recoiling inside of me. It pains me to think of this hasty lack of judgment that is being performed against me but I dare I cannot lay the blame upon anyone but myself, as is usually the case. Far be it for me to throw accusations around when, like a boomerang, they will just head back home and cut the determination I have set for my goal in half as if it truly were nothing but air. I am not so inclined as to think the course of my narrowly engaging road will suddenly and most inexplicably widen itself to the likeness of an eight lane highway, but I am not completely disinclined to think that it won't. As the sun must rise each morning, I have tomorrow to look ahead to with anticipation of rectifying these discourteous misdeeds that have been marked upon my own heart just as I have, undoubtedly, marked the same slights upon theirs at one point or another.

It is a painful acknowledging, for both myself and others I imagine, that we can be so impudent with one another. Should such disrespect be graciously disregarded by those dearest to us? Should we forgive easier for knowing of past occurrences where it was the opposite who invoked such a fracture of trust? And if the trust should never fully mend itself together again, what of that? What could be said, what could be done to repair such dishonest tact?

There is not a surgeon in the world with such steady a hand as to mend the tear of a soul. For it is in the soul where friendship blossoms, where love is contained and trust is learnt and accepted through the honesty of such relations.

The heart is nothing more than a muscle, just as a liver or small intestine are nothing more than what make our bodies properly function. Without the heart, our bodies are no more, but we do not die. For if love, friendship, trust and all else truly were sentiments of the heart, once the heart stopped beating, all would be forgotten that were once so entrusted inside. But that is not the case. I can only say that I believe that all the importance of life lies comparatively aloof and separate from the heart and is contained in the soul of oneself. It is not an uneducated guess to which I have alluded. Our bodies are nothing more than flesh, bone and blood, and how could anything so dear as love and friendship be contained within the currents of blood or the marrow of bone, or the easily scarred flesh?

Whom we are, whom we choose to love, and whom we hold close as dear friends, are not sentiments of the heart. They are the embodiment of our soul, which is a far greater commendation to one than the over expressed feelings of the 'heart'.

JULY 16, 2001

SOMETIMES I THINK PARENTS wish their children never learned how to speak. How many glib remarks can one toss out during the course of a day? I've not lived up to my potential yet, nor do I aspire to ascertain that bittersweet victory. I earnestly do try to not be so annoyed by people but the harder I try to tolerate their little idiosyncrasies, the more agitated I get. I am a very high strung person as it is. I'm always stressed out, over the littlest things too. I don't sleep well. I'm on the line every single day trying to not fall off and kill myself. I can be a very difficult person. I'm well aware of my shortcomings and downfalls and I try to overcome but some days I just can't find my way out of this dark cave that has me lost inside most of the time. I'm pretty blind.

Have you ever felt like you were on drugs when you know that you're not? You see the things around you in a different light – a different tone and texture? It's almost as if you can see straight through things – like they weren't even there and if you reached out your hand, your fingers would penetrate through the nonexistent fabric of time. When you walk outside, you can taste the smells around you; you breathe that air and it feels heavy on your lungs, weighing them down but not filling them up. You can taste the humidity as it rolls in through the sky and burns you inside. The tingling sensation your skin feels as your pores absorb the rays of sunshine that are deceptive in their torturous right; they make you feel warm and safe but all they're really doing is destroying your life – they are burning you – charring your skin until you begin to notice the heat – and then you realize you're incinerating – you are cooking – and if you stay out long enough, soon, over time, you skin will become hard and coarse – like leather. This excessive ruin just goes to prove that we are dying every day. We continue to die as we go through our lives, but how many of us continue to live as though we weren't dying?

AUGUST 1, 2001

HERE WE ARE, LITTLE girl, in the month of August already. In the month when the pursuant dream will have its chance to breathe and as your dream takes flight, so too will you have the opportunity to breathe; to feel alive once again. Today is only the beginning. There are many nameless days just ahead; many profitless days to endure before obtaining the ultimate goal. You are not afraid of this, are you? You are not afraid of leaving behind that which is most cherished and precious? You cannot be afraid. You know how fear weakens desire; how it undulates inside your soul and infects all the peaceful reserves you once enjoyed being able to step inside of. You know. But without the fear, what will there be to overcome? What would be the real purpose of striking out on your own if you were not the least bit afraid? What would be the real accomplishment there? A little bit of fear is good. It feeds the insatiableness power of the mind.

What I fear most about taking this journey, is returning. What will be here when I drive back across the state line and down this driveway? Will I be any different than when I left? Or will none of my questions have been answered. I'll find myself back in the same hole that's been expanding around me for nearly a year.

How is one supposed to live after life throws you down in the trenches? Dig, scrape, and claw your way back up from Hell and try to see the sun before it falls from the sky? Try to breathe in the air without breathing in the dirt, mud, and muck that wallows around you and pulls you back down just when your hand reaches the open air?

I was driving earlier and was coming upon an intersection and thought to myself, 'wouldn't it be great to just chance it all and hit the accelerator and drive straight across without stopping?' perhaps 'great' isn't the word to describe it, but it was an inner compulsion that directed me to that thought. There was this sudden desire, this reckless craving to keep driving, to not stop, to just see if, maybe, luck was on my side. Of course, I didn't succumb to this foolish action. I applied my foot to the brake and slowly brought my car to a halt while I contemplated in my mind, why I even thought of that in the first place. What could possibly be my reasoning for having that thought cross my mind? It's not the first time that thought has come up. There's a craziness that accompanies me sometimes; one of those spur of the moment impulsive thoughts that crash through the barrier of logical thinking and good common sense.

AUGUST 2, 2001

YESTERDAY WAS A DISPARAGING day. I have those days now and then where I really am convinced that this is Hell that we are living in. How many times have you felt like not wanting to cope anymore? Felt like no matter what you did, it was always the wrong decision and you backtrack in your mind and say to yourself, "why didn't I do *that*? That would have been the *right* choice." And you mope around all day in a lethargic state, not wanting to face the huge, overbearing world with your own wretched presence. You sit, all day, in a pensive state trying to correctly estimate the worth of everything in your life and you come to regard most necessities as the cause and effect of your own poverty stricken soul. It's a sickening cycle that twirls around and about your mind that twists and contorts your memories into either a regretful absence or a fool hearted existence. Characteristically, you are no different than the rest of the world, but you distance yourself and you purposely seek out those subtleties, small as they are different, you amplify them until they echo throughout the entire Arena and it's all you can focus upon. And soon you find yourself alone and separated, seated in section H, row 666, of this great Arena we call the World. You built yourself this Hell, you know.

SEPTEMBER 11, 2001
HISTORY ETCHED IN STONE

"FREEDOM ITSELF WAS ATTACKED today by a faceless coward, and freedom will be defended" –President George W. Bush

America has been attacked. Our Nation has been thrown into an upheaval of sorrow, despair, and most of all, disbelief.

Terrorists commandeered four commercial airliners by force and deliberately attacked our Nation in a most cowardly and malevolent way. Taking these large 767 airliners, they steered the planes and crashed into the World Trade Towers in New York and the Pentagon in Washington. A fourth plane crashed in a field in Pennsylvania, suspected to be en route back to Washington.

Terrorist hijackers, identities unknown, are suspected to be linked to known terrorist Osama Bin Laden, who was indicted for the 1998 US Embassy bombings.

There was an estimated 10,000 to 20,000 people in the WTC towers when the first plane crashed into the North Tower. 800 people are feared dead inside the rubble of what was the west side of the five sided Pentagon building.

Each of the four commercial airliners had civilian passengers who, unknown to them, boarded the planes that would take them to their final destinations. 266 people died on the planes.

Thousands of people are purported to be dead.

Our Nation is thrown into mourning.

But we are the United States of America.

Our Nation will prosper. America will overcome this tragedy and we will fiercely defend our compatriots and our fallen brothers and sisters and we will redeem our pride and our freedom. Our patriotism will never be extinguished and will rise like a Phoenix from the ashes and Americans will face this tragedy with the steadfast determination and resolve we have shown in instances past.

America will retaliate in a fashion to defend our God given freedom which was unmercifully attacked with the intent to be taken away.

We will not go quietly and hide in the shadows like our deadly assailants have crept away from us to wallow in the darkness which consumes their hearts.

America was faced with an act of war today.

And if it's a war that America is faced with, it's a war that America will win.

OCTOBER 10/11, 2001

WE BLEED. WE ACHE. We cry. We grieve and mourn. We despair and question. We lose ourselves, moment by moment, in the heartaches. We traverse along the road of pain and tragedy.

But we breathe through it all.

The smoke clears, the skies turn out once more, and we breathe in and we breathe out. Second by second, we regain our hope; our despair gives way to inspiration and perseverance.

We get lost all the time, every day – but somehow we manage to find our way back home; to that place where we can feel love and feel that we just may belong.

NOVEMBER 2001

WHO DOESN'T DESERVE THAT kind of raw, uninhibited, contented, impassioned love? That emotion that drives you to the corners of all enamoring exaltations; that emotion that elevates our mundane, terrestrial beings to new heights of extemporaneous affection. Don't we all deserve that in our lives? If only just once? But I am sometimes a fallible judge in this primal game of searching for a companion. It's the comely attributes that first encamps the eye, is it not? It's almost a pitiable reliance we have on others. I suppose you can fight it all you want, all your life (as inexorable as it is). I am too inept at relationships. The equivalent of me being capable of maintaining a relationship is that of a fish being able to live out of water. I am an inefficient, most intolerable and impatient person when it comes to this degrading game of dating and falling 'in love'. Whatever that supposition means. I am about to declare a mutiny on my entire existence – rebel and rise up from the grave again. Stand meekly before my presupposed headstone, and take the sledgehammer right to the engraved life. My life is not carved in stone yet. Changes can take place. Brush the dirt off my shoulders, shake the bugs off, and begin again.

I like the saying, "I am from beyond the grave. Really. And out of work". – *Illuminations*, Rimbaud.

It's an extremely unwholesome outlook I have for my future. I have found the only one I am looking for but without my own reliable conscience I can't foresee the outcome being that of a winning one. I am an abashment to myself sometimes. I have a frailty of mind that complicates simple matters into unsolvable dilemmas. I am my own frenzied adversary.

Life is about love. There is passion, jealousy, envy, spite – all because of this intangible emotion that we can't define, categorize or describe in any certain terms. It just *is*. And the trouble with that, again, reverts back to the agitating, ubiquitous query, that all of us skeptics need, at least, a semi-conclusive answer to: why? Why do I feel this way? Why does so and so feel this way about me? Her? Him? People kill for love. Of course, it's not pure, angelic, blissful love that one kills for. It's the resentment of love. The indignant, egotistical side of love that drives itself to such an injurious result. And then there is love; the kind that sends two people on a soulful journey of hope, faith, and companionship; the kind we all want. Little girls who dream of a man, a lover of whom they know will never leave them or hurt them. And they can wind down in the categories and they can find the qualities he will possess, the job he will hold down, the contours of his face and body, and even the sound of his voice. Little girls who grow up believing in the fairytale dream they had as a child and realizing that life, instead, holds heartaches and cruel twists of unruly fate. And if we are lucky, if we are really, truly lucky, we find someone who we can at least tolerate for the rest of our lives. And even then, there's always divorce.

Not knowing exactly what love is, or why, creates an obstruction of order for me. I need to know the how, when, where, and why of things. That is why I go crazy. Why I neurotically emphasize the importance of such futile questions – futile because most of the time they cannot be answered. Not satisfactorily at least.

Why do I love you, why, why, why?

Are love and hate really opposites? I find myself able to both love and hate the same person, the same day, in the same moment. But I dare question, do I really hate this person or do I hate that I love them? I have two hands to try and balance this out. Two hands; sturdy, able to juggle three things at once, but unable to find the strength to hold up these heavy, yet weightless, emotions. I throw accusations in order to free my hands of this troublesome despair. I lay under the stars, seeking out the beauty in their simplicity, yet at the same time knowing how complex their configurations are. As are my configurations; life's configuration for me. They say mathematics is in every aspect of life. So is my life merely an uncalculated equation thus far? (I never was good at algebra). It's not the act of calculating that frightens me; it's the solution that is the problem. What is that one, unidentified variable going to stand for in my life? What is going to be the calculated solution to that unknown? I have the intelligence to figure that Love is a Demon. Hate is a Monster. And the line between the two, is often as blurry as the motive for either. The demon that sits in want, in each of use, yearning, longing, feeding ourselves the fantasies of illogical realities, is the worst of love.

There is another side of course. Love can be a beautiful thing, a once in a lifetime occurrence that proves itself too good to be true (often is). With this outlook on love, life, and hate – is it really no wonder? …. Hate; that is the monster of all monsters. That is the virus that infects our entire entities, eating away at our insides, blackening our hearts and destroying our souls. You see, love can be jealousy, envy, and spite. Hate is also jealousy, envy, and spite. It's an intricate thing, isn't it? The wonder of it, of not being able to define it with any certainty, makes it a mystery. It's annoying as hell for some people though (me).

I am one of those who are not happy unless they are miserable.

DECEMBER 2, 2001

I'M CONFLICTED, AT ODDS, yet again, with myself, my pride. My belief of who's to blame, perhaps. But you know, when two people, friends, suffer a rift, it doesn't matter who's to blame. If you are truly friends, someone has to say something. Someone has to pick up the pieces and try to fit them back together to see how they were able to fall apart in the first place. You can't be so stubborn. It's why pride is one of the seven deadly sins – pride gets in the way of friendships and kills them. People can't let that happen. So why am I so conflicted? Why do I hesitate on taking the initiative in these matters? Because I don't know what to do or how to say what needs to be said. But that's just it: if it needs to be said, you absolutely have to say it. No excuses. Friends drift apart – that is a fact – but friendships last forever. It's just another relationship that needs to be tended to, that's all. It's all so simple and logical when I'm sitting here talking to myself but put me face to face with someone and my words are as stunted as a dwarf's height.

DECEMBER 16, 2001

TWISTING AND TURNING OF my insides contributes greatly
to my diminished energy. My energy has been diminished
for the past three years. My ambition has prided itself to stay
independent of my being. It has appropriated the right to hide
in continuum, and I oftentimes cannot seek. No energy, no
ambition, can you blame me? My ambition has taken on a life
of its own, but it is stagnating here. It can't be resolved here,
and so it sits in wait, and it sits in want. And my imagination
feeds it; my imagination is the fuel thrown upon the fire; the
burning desire I have to see it through. I have not felt this
passionate for one cause concerning my own dear life for
quite some time.

Nonetheless, such useless time squandering to worry
about such things right now.

I'm in a fluttered state of uncertainty. What to do, what
to do. Can there be no easy answer, no easy way to get an
answer? It is trials and tribulations. You can't succeed if you
don't try, but you will always fail if you don't try. It's worth
a shot, I think

2002-2003

Trying to find coping mechanisms in all the wrong places

JANUARY 7, 2002

AND SUDDENLY I HAD a vision – a vision of things to come – and how solitary it was.

JANUARY 8, 2002
11:14PM
EVIL

WHAT DOES EVIL LOOK like today?

Evil is a double barreled Savage. It's cocked of steel and smoothed by wood that runs along its side. It's grained with suppositions, it grates along the skin and hides behind the Sight. Evil is a trigger-happy fool that doesn't care about its Aim. It has no aim, in the Face of God, every man, woman, child is game. Big game too, what could better satisfy Evil than the destruction of itself; mankind. And you can't hide your head from the Sniper's view.

So what does Evil look like today?

It could look like me, and it could look like you.

JANUARY 24, 2002

SO NOW THAT'S IT, eh? Poured some dry gas on the two hundred page fictional biography and lit a match. Bye-bye. What encouraged me to do such a thing? Contempt for the past. Sheer disdain for what was. Tired of the reminders, the remembrances, and the objectivity of 'before'. Before what? What, where, and when was the exact point of 'before'? Where did it start going right? Wrong? In what direction am I pointed? Besides West. Sometimes I get the feeling that I'm not pointed in a direction, I'm just twirling about this world in a disorganized aura of emotions, with my arms stretched out at my sides, I twirl and twirl, round and round in circles. My eyes focus on absolutely nothing because I'm spinning so fast, every sight meshes together in a nonsensical tapestry of visions. That is what confusion is. That is what I am. That is my life.

MARCH 13, 2002

THE PAIN IS BACK. Not physical, just anguish. I gave in to the moment. What else can you do? Such vivid memories, such intricate mind relapses back to a moment you want to forget. Maybe forget is too strong a word. I don't want to forget any experience that I've had because I draw upon every experience, and I rely on every experience, to get me through the next one. It is a moment that is better to not be focused upon. And how it happens to come about, for no reason at all, I don't know. Oh god, I just don't know what to do sometimes. I don't know what to do with myself, I don't know where to go with myself, I don't know why I suffer myself. If I could have one day of absolute clarity, maybe that would help. But one day is never enough as soon as the next day comes. As soon as another day comes, that one day becomes yesterday. And all that would happen then would be my longing for another yesterday. I am tired of longing for yesterday. I want to look forward to tomorrow. I miss all that was when things were right. But when was that?

I don't want things to worsen. I don't think I voluntarily contribute to it, but it happens nonetheless. Because I can't let go. The pain of that day, those days, those numerous, nameless days that have marked themselves in the calendar in my head. They've marked themselves so I would never forget. I don't want to forget any of these things, but I want to look back upon them without feeling so helpless and so anguished still.

MAY 15, 2002

I HAVE BROKEN INTO Pandora's Box. I was presumptuous in congratulating myself on my three month sobriety. I am still sober, don't think of me as a fall down drunk right now, but I did taste alcohol tonight. I couldn't resist. When temptation is stronger than will, what is one to do?

JANUARY 22, 2003

FOR SOMEONE WHO APPEARS so grounded and level headed, I sure am a pushover. How easily I get wrangled into things; it amazes me that I have not yet grown a backbone to stand up for myself.

FEBRUARY 6, 2003

I AM AT THAT stage again, J, where the murderous tendencies of self-annihilation seem a formidable route of escape. It's not so much a despairing depression that captures me at this time, but more a lingering sadness. That same sadness that has undoubtedly accompanied me throughout the course of my own twenty-two years. It's a sadness that I don't believe is even rooted to just one cause. It just is. There seems to be no way around it, no way to hide from it, and no way to confront it and come away with the upper-hand. It's not something one is able to control with any certainty or pull the reigns in on at any time one chooses. It's there at its own will, it emerges in its own time, and it complicates life at its own pace. Is it all out of my hands?

What made me think that this time would be any different? There is a familiar pattern that keeps emerging in my life: I get too close to someone and then I unintentionally sabotage the relationship by pushing them away from me at the same time as pulling myself away from them.

How long will I continue on this path of self-doubt. What will the morning be like when I wake up and can finally give myself a chance? Will the sun be shining and shimmering down on a clear and hot summer day? Will the breeze gently roll the clouds through a deep blue sky while the answers are whispered to me through the air? One would think that would go hand in hand with an epiphany. Who would want to spend such a glorious day of awakening on a dark, dreary, rain filled day of somber tidings and melancholy skies?

I've just had a day today. I had a day the other day too – a day that I can't even remember. I think it was Monday but can't be sure. All I know is that I wasn't quite myself. And the next day I woke up, I couldn't even remember the previous day. It was distant, as if it either happened to someone else or happened so long ago it was a hazy recollection. I guess it was because I was so despondent that day, so depressed and in such utter agony within myself that I blocked it out. It was a night to which I had desperately wanted to disappear; a night where I felt my existence to be too burdensome to others and especially myself. I was away, living with a mile-high shield around me.

MARCH 2, 2003

SHE WAS LOOKING AT me with a somewhat sad, yet bemused, smile on her face when she said, "You are so afraid to be happy". It was like she was just seeing that for the very first time; like she had solved the underlying mystery of my discontented soul. And she was right. I am afraid to be happy. You know I still have my secrets, J. Grave secrets I call them, for they shall follow me there.

MARCH 17, 2003

I feel enslaved by a gripping panic. It immobilizes me in a moment of fear. It feels inescapable. My chest is tight, breathing comes only if I tell myself to do it. My lungs do not expand in invitation to air, it rather rejects the infiltration of oxygen. At times I feel it would rather be breathing carbon monoxide in – to temper down the rhythm until only a flat line stretches across the screen. That is only the murderous demon talking though. The one that sits in the back of my mind, whispering to me all through the day, the benefits of such a tragedy; to overcome would be such a joy. Would really be such a miracle, but to overcome, I must really face it first. Have I been doing such? To you, maybe every now and then I drop a hint or two as to what whispered thoughts are traveling through my mind, but to come outright and say it directly, I don't think I've been that honest or truthful to you or to myself. It's so easy to justify it all in my mind but when I step outside that box, that rapidly enclosing trap, there are no justifications that can be deemed reasonable. I guess that's because once you reach the point of no return, there's nothing left to reason. That's why people kill themselves, right? Not because they're sad or unhappy or depressed; but because there's no reasoning left. One can always live with pain, unhappiness, depression, but one cannot live without reason. Once you lose that, there's no turning back.

MARCH 23, 2003

I WONDER WHEN I'LL stop making my life such a mess. Does it really have to be so bad? Why must I agonize so? Why must I tear myself down and relinquish the right to any self-contentment or possible joy that may come my way? Do I honestly believe that I don't deserve such a thing? And I sit here trying to count: how many breakdowns have I had in the past week alone? More than I really want to acknowledge. I get so worked up; my blood pressure skyrockets and all

I do is cry. I start to feel violent. I want to lash out and hit something. I want to take a knife and cut my skin open until it bleeds, I want to bruise my face, my hands, my arms, my legs; I want to take on any physical pain I can in hopes of distancing myself from the emotional pain that terrorizes my soul. It's an anguish that dwells inside my being. It sits there, patiently, like a tickle on the back of one's throat; it's there, you want to cough it up, but you can't. You can't do anything. It's there on the inside where you can't reach it, can't kill it or numb the pain and irritation away. You can only wait. Wait until it either goes away on its own or your body reacts violently and pushes it out of your system. And what kind of violent act would have to take place for me to rid myself of this mental torment? There shall be no easy way.

MARCH 26, 2003

TRY-OUTS ARE OVER AND done with. The teams have been formed and now I'm left alone with a JV softball team in my hands. What am I going to do now? I ask you often, J, how is it that I get myself into these situations? Of course, every question I ask you is a rhetorical one so I'm no better off now than when I asked. So now I have my own team. How am I ever going to get through this? I wonder if my natural hesitations are going to hinder my attempts this season. I would imagine so.

JUNE 15, 2003

Journal notes:

- Fact: I'm a screw up and that's never going to change. You can clearly see that I'm back into the self-hating, loathing, personality I so despise about myself. But when one screws up as irrevocably as I have – what's not to despise? The fact I've worked so hard to remain in control and keep myself in check – to be good, true, someone respectable and likable, and in one instant, I throw it all away. I have a hard time even saying what I did because I hate myself so much for doing it. Hate myself to the point of wanting to run away from all I've ever known or killing myself to rid the world of my stupidity and irresponsibility. How can one be a role model or a good influence when they make the kinds of mistakes I always seem to make? And I got myself into something so deep this time – I don't know how I'm going to get out of it – how I'm going to repair what I've done – how I'm going to face anyone again. That feeling that comes so often – that cliché – wanting to crawl into a hole, curl up and die – just disappear. I feel like I'm ruining my life – day by day. I've been having a breakdown for the past three days. Panic attacks, crying fits, bouts of maniacal suicidal thoughts – a desperation to leave – to get out – to run away. And what holds me here? What are my reasons for remaining in this shame and guilt – this unabashed self-loathing? What's my reason for remaining? Friends – Friends/family = one in the same.

- Things had been going so well for me then I make a dumb mistake which jeopardizes not only myself but my future and my friends – my family.

- Instead of merely rambling on and on, maybe I should get my nerve back and try to tell what I did that I'm so ashamed of. Hester Prynne comes to mind – though I'm not having an affair and this 'tale' doesn't involve sex in any way (thankfully, because the mistake I made certainly could have ended up that way) – I only say I'm reminded of Hester Prynne because of the shame and fear of others judgments of her. And I can't handle being less than what everybody else perceives I should be. But I am less than what they think I am– I am not who they think I am – and, try as I may, I am not who they want me to be.

- I am fallible. I am human. I make mistakes. Why does it feel as though I am the only one who does make these bad choices? Why do I feel like I can't handle anything? I feel as though I am losing control. Nowhere to go. No one to tell. Secrets. More secrets that I must keep vaulted up inside of me. I've got so many, some I have not even confessed to you and I think they are killing me. Slowly suffocating my life away. Bleeding me dry. I thirst for the sanctity of truth, to be free of this tormenting reminder – the guilt of shame – but I cannot utter the words that would set me free because that would mean facing a truth I have fought for so long.

- And my past flooded back. And it hurts. It's a pain that has always dwelled within me – it's origin, at times, unknown. There is a dull, persistent aching that has always resided within my heart and this past weekend – that dull aching has become a fervent reminder of what kind of pain I've always endured. A reminder of why it hurts so much to live.
- Why it hurts to breathe.
- Why it hurts every time my heart beats.
- Why every day is just a painful reminder of why I hate to be me so much.
- And it all came rushing back to me this weekend. Everything I've fought for the past few months – everything I've struggled with forever, reared its ugly head and came back for me once again. And it sank its venomous teeth into my flesh and its poison fled through my veins and blackened my heart. My heart is sick and dying. I can feel it letting go – wanting to let go – but I won't let it. It has been weakened – but not yet defeated.
- But I can't face the world with my mistakes.
- Is it really the world I can't face or just myself? It's nice to sit here and write all this out to you, yet I feel it's useless to keep pondering over.
- Something must be done.
- And I must be the one to do it.

JUNE 16, 2003

I HATE MYSELF so much I leave and go to the bar. I start with a Medori Sour – 1 turns to 2 to 3 to 4 plus a shot of something and some other drink. Too many. Small talk with two men from MA – Tristan and WB. Even though Tara told me, "Don't do anything stupid", against my better judgment – I left the bar at 11:30 PM and went back to their cabin. They could've been killers, rapists, anything – but I didn't care. I was self-destructive. Tristan turned out to be my Angel though. We talked until 2:30 in the morning. He listened to me, gave me advice, let me read his journal; was everything sweet and kind that I needed.

The evening had a few more ups and downs because of my unsteady temperament and unpredictable mood swings but the evening ended with me getting a date. Tristan and I hit it off that inebriated night and we're going to go out.

See how things work out.

If you don't try too hard to orchestrate fate, things work out for the best (or at least the way they are supposed to).

I'm very neurotic right now.

JUNE 17, 2003

I HATE THE SHRILL ringing of a telephone. It's like a nagging old hag, cackling in the early morning hours, obnoxiously thinking that anyone cares of her opinion. The phone rings – the image of an old gray-haired, musty woman with a worn face of lines and crags cut deep as if they had been hand-carved and etched on her skin, pops into my head. I hear the ring – and my heart leaps to my throat; it catches in my throat – a blockade for my breath. Air does not move in and air does not move out. I am still. My heart seems to stop as time seems to freeze around me hanging in a moment of panic-induced intensity. Do I answer – do I let it ring? Who is on the other end? Who is calling my home? Who wants to speak to me? Who called for the sole purpose of hearing my voice? And I wait, wondering if my heart will begin to beat again. Depending on who is at the other end of the line, I don't ever know if I want my heart to start again. Don't know if I want my breath to come again – or keep it trapped inside my lungs until they burst with a sickening pop of bubble gum – with the outward tearing force of a gunshot.

Who is it?

JULY 7, 2003

I CAN UNDERSTAND WHY people kill themselves. Most everyone I know says, "I don't see how someone could do that. I don't understand how they could do that". It's so simple really. What they don't understand is simply what they don't want to understand or acknowledge; that it could be them. They've known hopelessness and desperation before – but it had been merely a fleeting pass, nothing more, nothing less – easily forgotten – or, perhaps, more easily stored away in the part of the repressed consciousness. Who in their right mind would honestly want to acknowledge to someone that they know what it's like to want to kill themselves – to tie a noose from the nearest tree limb or rafter – to load one bullet into the chamber of a gun and put the barrel in their mouth – to OD on prescription drugs found in the medicine cabinet or drink a glass full of bleach. No one would admit to having seriously thought about these things. No one would want another to know that hopeless, weak, pathetic person hiding just beneath their skin. They wouldn't want anyone to know that person because they don't really believe that person exists.

SEPTEMBER 12, 2003

I FEEL SO ASHAMED. On so many different levels. And I don't know why I should be ashamed of who I am. I'm not terribly bad – I'm not hiding any real secrets – except for the secret that I hate myself. But is that a secret? Why do I hate myself? I told you that I had been reading that book the other day, the one about bulimia and anorexia. Actually, the book that grabbed my attention was a book called, "The Anorexia Diaries" and I felt that I could've been writing those diary entries if only I was as honest with myself as I often claim to be. Truth is, as this girl wrote and as I have even written in the past, to write down the truth – makes it real. When it's still just swimming around in my head, it's still safely tucked way into a recess where it is visible to no one. But when words are put onto paper, it gives them life; substance; truth and reality. Visible. There is still that fear of being seen. What seems to have been happening all this time is that I've inevitably placed myself in a catch-22. What I want is what I fear and no matter what I do there will be a consequence I don't want to face. It seems almost deliberate on my part – an unconscious effort to remain hiding where I am. You do realize, don't you, that one of these days I'm going to break free. It's not bested me yet and I feel strong enough to say that it never will. Another irony. I put strength in those words and rest on hope but I am so weak that I can barely stand, can barely think. I guess it's different because the strength isn't physical and it isn't really mine. I don't find the strength within myself. My only strength, I guess, comes from friends and family.

You know, I ate a donut this morning, a plain one, and I don't hate myself for it. I actually feel better for having eaten it and kept it down. I didn't want to throw it up (Ok, I did, but I didn't!). Anyway, I ate it and I don't even feel sick. I did last night, I told myself yesterday that I'd had it, that I wasn't going to put myself through that hell anymore and I was going to eat something. Well, I did eat something and I got so sick afterwards. My stomach was recoiling with seeming disgust at the food that sat within it. And I felt absolutely horrible. And then I got really scared because I said, "If I can't eat anything without feeling this way, this sick, then I'm just not going to eat at all". Well, that's a sure fire way to kill myself, isn't it? Don't want to do that, really, so I've got to start off really small. I managed to eat that donut this morning and keep it down and I don't feel sick, so that's a start. I sat here in my room last night and wondered at how I got to be where I am. Talk about issues, man. What ailment haven't I dealt with? Ailment or mental illness? Personality disorder. Depression. Eating disorders. And I'm still afflicted with all of them, but I realize it, I recognize it, and that's how I've been able to not cave in to it completely yet. Or have I? I suppose I have my moments. One way or another, it won't last forever, will it?

OCTOBER 3, 2003

INDIANA HAS BEEN so good to me this year. I met a great new friend, Jesse. I met one of James Dean's former flames (not to mention his classmates and family again). The other day when I stepped into the Gallery, I was overcome, as I always am, by James Dean. By the familiarity of a man I never knew in life. By the comfort and ease to which I feel at home here. Perhaps it's the camaraderie that accompanies us 'Deaner's' upon first meeting. But Jesse, whom I was talking with last night for over an hour, said to me, "Why don't you come down to the diner with us. You can ride with me. Arlene is going to be there. And Pam. And a bunch of us. You should come hang out with us." So of course I said I'd go. It was awesome. I feel like I've made some great new friends. Jesse is just a rockstar. She and I exchanged numbers, addresses, and emails. I look forward to seeing her again. I'm glad we met.

(2014: It was in 2003, when I traveled to Fairmount, IN, that I met Jesse. We instantly connected. It was a year or so later that found me asking her, "Do you think I should go to Graceland since we have a few days before the memorial?" She of course said yes! So off I went to the home of Elvis! I would often take off during my travels and go somewhere that had not been my real destination. Whims would often take hold of me and I couldn't resist. The temptation of travel, seeing new places, was too tantalizing for me to ignore. It was Jesse who gave me the go ahead I was seeking and I had a fabulous time and we talked all about it when I returned to Fairmount for James Dean's memorial. I had been traveling to Fairmount since 1999. I still consider it my second home).

OCTOBER 7, 2003

I WAS STANDING BEHIND a young girl in line a few moments ago. She ordered a tall WCM, with a shot of vanilla and a scone and an over-sized peanut butter cookie that she asked to have warmed up in the microwave. Then she changed her mind and asked to nix the shot of vanilla, replacing it with chocolate. I was annoyed because all I was going to order was a regular coffee and this was taking far too long. It's the coffee drinker's ailment of impatience that sets in every now and then. Luckily, my mind and somewhat continually bemused demeanor never allows them to see the impatience that is wallowing just beneath the surface of my tactfully displayed cool exterior. At times I am absolutely livid, but no one is the wiser. In a way, it's a menacing attribute to have in one's arsenal. I think to the cold, unfeeling eyes of a psychopath. Surely they must be able to hide and conceal things much the same way that I do. Fortunately, I have no violent, murderous hidden agendas.

The girl I was standing behind got her plate of food before her drink was ready. She dove into the peanut butter cookie as though she hadn't eaten in three days and was dying of malnutrition. She wasn't but she took her plate of food and her drink and sat down at the bar. As I prepared my regular cup of coffee, I was envious of her. I sat down at the other end of the bar and began my routine. Out of the corner of my eye, I watched her as she took large bites of the scone and the cookie and washed it down with a gulp of her WCM. She ate freely, as if she didn't have a care in the world. And I envied her this, also. She wasn't counting calories, she wasn't worried about the fat calories. She didn't have any nutritional agenda on her mind, she was merely enjoying her food. She looked content and happy. And I knew that if I were to sit down with that very same plate of food and the drink that I'd worry, agonize, and curse myself for having enjoyed such a feast. I allow myself no leeway for enjoyment. I am constantly punishing myself for no good reason. If I were to really think about it, I know the reason why I am doing this. I am not as good a person as others think I am. Of course, people rarely are. There are numerous facets that people hide about themselves. No one can truly know another individual. If we did, there's probably no way that we'd like them. To catch a glimpse of their hidden thoughts, desires, ambitions; to know what they really think when you ask them a question, we don't want to know the truth of these things. Even when one answers a question in a truthful, honest way, in their head is another little voice that ad-libs dirty little words and ideas that no one would ever dare speak. And people who deny having these unexpressed thoughts, in my opinion, are lying. I have those kinds of unprovoked thoughts about everyone. Even when I hold no ill-will towards a person, no resentment or anything, still those little thoughts creep up in my mind and when I try to push them out, saying to myself, "How dare you think that! Why would something like that even come into your head? Where did these thoughts come from?" I don't know where they come from; originated, but I cannot deny their existence.

Each human being has a certain, culpable amount of violence in them. Even if it's dormant, never expressed, there is a seed of evil that dwells in each of us. Only in a select few does that seed blossom into a full-fledged hate. I'd like to think that those evil thoughts are not my own at all, but where else would they come from if not my own mind? Has another planted them in my head without my knowledge? Or have I consumed so much violence while growing up that it became a natural course for my thoughts to take? I am not a mean, hateful, vengeful person, but that does not mean that the thoughts don't sit in my head every now and then. I hate myself, most often, when those nasty thoughts do pop into my head, but it's uncontrollable on my part. The more time I spend trying not to have those thoughts, the more persistent they become. If I gave it no thought at all, the thoughts would merely come and go, passing as quietly as a swift wind through a wheat field, but it's when I stop to say, 'why would I have such a thought' that it lingers and stays with me.

OCTOBER 14, 2003

I ASKED MYSELF A question today. I said to myself, "who are you doing this for?" I was standing in front of my mirror after having just taken a shower and I was thoroughly disgusted with myself and my actions. I keep telling myself that as soon as this wedding is over and done with, I won't worry about it anymore. I won't worry about my weight, how much I eat, what I eat, if I eat. One step at a time is what I'll take and I'll get over this obsession soon enough. This bingeing, this purging, this abstinence, this totally disgusting and pathetic way of life that has done nothing but bring me down even more. I'm not going to ask for anybody's help. I'm not going to cry and tell my little sob story to another soul because I don't want them to think ill of me. I don't want their pity, their abashment, their lectures, their sorrowful, tearful looks or their degradation. I don't want them to know my weaknesses, most of all. And seeing as how I am most reluctant to even tell you about them, why would I tell another human being? The only reason I am reluctant to tell you about them is because you already know (me). But to write it all down brings everything to life and I don't want it to be true. This is not who I am. I keep telling myself that, but how did I ever become this person? I hardly recognize myself as a person anymore. I feel soul-less. I feel I walk around but I'm dead. Inside is hollow, devoid of everything.

OCTOBER 29, 2003

THE ONLY REASON I got out this lap top to begin writing was so I had an excuse to chatter away some of these thoughts into a visible form for my eyes to feast upon. As for right now, seeing as how it is nearly midnight, I am wondering if I should just go to sleep or do some more exercise to punish myself for my bad behavior and terrible eating habits, which I punish myself enough for anyway considering this perplexing psychological problem I am having with it all. I cannot get past it and am beginning to believe that the texts in those books are accurate when they say that this is a disorder, a problem that does not go away quickly but in actuality can take months to 'cure' even though there is no real way to cure it – except maybe just a dogged determination. An almost rabid, dogged determination. I shall overcome because I must. If I don't – then I will die. It's as simple as that. It's a slow, painful, wearisome death and I'm not looking to intentionally kill myself right now. Besides, this way would take too long.

NOVEMBER 1, 2003

I HAVE A QUESTION: why is everything in our culture, our habits, and our social lives, surrounded by the premise of food? Lunch dates, dinner dates, snacking while conversing; we can't do anything without food around us. Or maybe this heightened sensitivity towards food is because I've been neglecting the right nutrition since June or July. It is the worst decision I have ever made in my life. I am not happy. What I am, is hungry. I feel like I could devour everything in sight and there have been times when I've done just that, not that it has stayed with me or anything. Why, how, when did I become this person? This obsessive, compulsive, neurotic, paranoid, insecure person! I can't even allow myself the smallest, most delightful treat without shouldering a weight of guilt that drives me into the ground. The cost of (supposed) beauty. And the compliments only add fuel to the fire. I rebuff most compliments by saying, 'it's really not worth the upkeep', and they say, 'what I wouldn't give to be that thin'. They throw words around like 'beautiful', 'gorgeous', 'thin', 'skinny', and I cringe with every mention of my weight. Now they've all got me so terrified of putting on weight. What was I before if only now I have caught their attention? I know I'm being absolutely insane about all of this – but the rationality I once possessed, as small an amount as that was to begin with, has plummeted into the dark waters. My rationality was an albatross to begin with; utterly doomed to my overpowering neuroses. I am raw inside and I am nothing inside. And I have to wonder: how long can I last? I'm trying to fight, trying to overcome, but like most other things in life, it is difficult to accomplish alone. But you know me, I seek no assistance. I ask for no help. I refuse to appear weak. I am the only one who knows what I am doing to myself and I can't make sense of it. I don't know if it's possible for me to attain for the longer term. It's hard when you don't like yourself to begin with, how can you ever expect to be happy?

NOVEMBER 12, 2003

MY BIRTHDAY WILL SOON be upon me. 23 years old. I know I do not feel twenty three years old. Most days I feel older and yet younger at the same time. Younger, I believe because I am naïve about so many things still and older because I am weary and drowning in this cesspool of despair more so every day. I seem to have lost all control over what I do and what I don't do. It almost feels as though the real me – the person I was close to becoming once – has been shoved back to the dark recess of my mind and soul – I know she's there somewhere but she can't see and can't escape. I only hear whisperings of her long ago screams – echoing through this empty chamber I embody.

This me – the one who has taken an insane approach at control, condemns and tortures the real me. I am split. But I am split into more than two. I am not half of anything. I am whole but more than one. I don't truly believe I have multiple personalities but different aspects of my singular personality are so contrasting that it feels I am waging war between multitudes of personas. In a way, I suppose I am.

I write what I feel but what I feel I cannot always write. Its torture, is what it is. These mind games and arguments are a torture to my mentality. Onward we must go; forging through the heat, the wind, the rain and snow, moving forward with every step –but still seeming to get nowhere; or always seeming to fall short – to backpedal. I never knew it could be this bad.

I remember the days when I thought it could get no worse but of course even then I realized that once you say that you must know that things can always get worse and more often than not they do. Well they have. And I am fighting, fighting, fighting to get myself under control again. And people have no idea. That's what gets me. They have no idea what I'm going through right now. But, again, that is the way I want it. Why must I always do things the hard way (alone)? That is how I was made. I have tried to create for myself a different mold – but it is who I am and I have accepted it but the acceptance does not tell me where to go next and it does not inform me how to survive.

NOVEMBER 15, 2003
1:33 AM

I JUST HAD THE best birthday ever! (In recent memory that is) and I know it's not really even my birthday yet, but tonight something was reawakened in me that had been dormant for so long. Long lost friends coming back into my life. As you well know, last night was our bowling night and the excuse for going bowling was, of course, my birthday. All week long I had be waiting and looking forward to going bowling. I wanted to better my score from the last time we went. I knew that Christine was going to be there because mother had told me that she had gotten in touch with her so I was looking forward to that with immense anticipation. All week long I had been thinking about Amanda and saying to myself 'wouldn't it be nice if she were to come Friday. I wonder how to get in touch with her'. But I had no idea how to get in touch with her so I just brushed aside the thought, a little anyway. But who should show up to the bowling alley with Christine but Amanda! I hadn't seen her in over a year – she looks wonderful. Christine looks wonderful as well. And for as much of a surprise and treat as it was to see and be surprised by Amanda's arrival – I was on my toes all evening after Amanda told me that Sylvia might stop by. I thought to myself, 'how cool would that be?' – but it was getting late – nearing midnight and soon enough midnight had come and it was about five past midnight before we were greeted with the presence of Sylvia herself! I was so excited to see her again – she has just gotten back from Europe where she had been backpacking for three months or so. We told her that she looked really tan and she so nonchalantly says, "Oh, well, I just got back from Portugal", and all three of us, in unison, said in mock jest, "Oh, well, just Portugal!" Sylvia looks so good – she is absolutely beautiful. I can't believe that we're all as old as we are – all turning 23 this year. It was such a wonderful night! Seeing Christine, Amanda, and Sylvia was the best birthday gift I could have gotten. Speaking of which, Christine, the doll, brought me some presents and Sarah gave me a ten dollar gift card to B&N – WCM, here I come!

3:21 PM

Last night went by like a blur. It was a hazy night of recollections and memories, all streamlining in to a perfect evening spent in the present with gifts from my past. I've said it before: you don't realize just how much these people mean to you until you go months, possibly even years without seeing or speaking to them and then one night, out of the blue, you see them, you embrace, you smile and laugh and say, "What have you been doing!?" Friendship is the glowing ember that needs only one sweet breath of air to rekindle the flame. No matter how much time has passed it seems as though friends, the people you love and grew up with, never change, never age – they are more familiar for the absence.

NOVEMBER 20, 2003

You see how I have reverted back to the old ways, don't you? Try as I may, there seems to be no habit of which I can kick as of late. Every troublesome little thing keeps intensifying its grip on me until I am sure that I will no longer be able to tolerate such betrayals of my own desire. Everything has become a mass consumption upon my soul. I am agitated to the core of my existence as to my behavior. I realize I am destroying myself and yet I seem to have absolutely no will power or control over the matter. Mind over matter, is what they say, and I used to believe that this trifling little anecdote was useful upon nearly any circumstance one may encounter but when one suffers frailty of the mind and more frailty of the emotional state of well-being – what can one expect to do but succumb unwillingly to something that is of more power, strength, and determination?

Do I hold, in me, the power to negotiate these rough waters that I have flung myself into? Or am I to be swept away with the current? I certainly feel as though I have no control over anything anymore. Once, I remember, I did have control over these impetuous impulses – I could override the desirous want that sat in my soul, feeding my mind with its unbalanced yearnings. Now – I merely prolong the inevitable fall by trying to persuade my way out of such situations by using that tactical maneuver called, 'avoidance'.

It seems the power has slipped through my fingers. The last trace of control that I have known was many months ago. Everything is spiraling so quickly into the void – I feel the dizziness encapsulate me and I unwittingly fall into this demon's hands. Not of flesh do they hold me – they are scaled with corruptions and burnt with an amorous hunger for ultimate control – for condemned virtues and abhorred morals. I have lost this battle though I have not thrown the white flag on the ground by my feet just yet. I do not raise my hands in surrender nor bow before the false god. I will continue to stand stoic as long as I possess enough strength to stand on my own. When strength fails me, as I feel it must do on occasion, then I still will not bow and will only succumb fully to this demon if he swipes a sword across my knees and bids me to fall to the ground for his amusement. Other than that tragic downfall, I will not sway nor fall, though I will stumble with nearly every step. I will continue to stand tall as long as the one true God allows me to do so. Other than His urging to go with Him, I shall remain where I am, no matter how painful of situations find me.

DECEMBER 14, 2003

WHEN I WENT TO see Rose (about all the softball business this coming year) I walked through the door of her classroom and one of the first things she said to me was, "My god, you've lost a lot of weight, haven't you?" of course, I was very modest in my reply, saying only, 'a little'. And then I changed the subject as I do not like to talk about my weight (or lack thereof). Boy, if I ever felt self-conscious before about being heavier, though people would insist I was not heavy, I feel self-conscious now about being thin. But I really only feel self-conscious around my family because they look at me as though they don't recognize me – they look at me suspiciously with hard eyes. I don't like their looks, their glances, or curiosity. It annoys me and makes me feel as though I am under a microscope.

During the week I survive pretty much on bananas and low-fat chocolate milk. The weekend is what's hard because I'm home and always hungry and could very well eat everything in the cupboards but that would be a horrible mistake if I allowed myself to do that – so I refrain. Restraint is a learned thing – it cannot be taught without force. Self-restraint is one of the hardest things to foster. My self-restraint seems to migrate every now and then. Oddly enough, mostly during the winter months. I could probably do a study on the migratory patterns of people's habits during the different months. Self-restraint flies away during the winter months because there is nothing to do, nothing to keep in check, cannot go out and play and, most importantly, cannot avoid!

(2014: 2003 was a year which found me desperately grappling with the beginnings of an eating disorder and a damaging addiction to alcohol. Self-destructive behavior became even more omnipresent than before. I was trying to regain control of myself but in doing so I found myself trying to manage these disorders in destructive ways. I did not seek out healthy answers. I forged into a battle of wills with myself and nearly lost the battle. In truth, I still struggle with these damaging 'coping' mechanisms. But these afflictions are no way to deal with the real deep-seeded problems that exist. Eating disorders, alcoholism, smoking; they are all distractions. They are not solutions. And more often than not, they leave you feeling even more powerless than before. One cannot attempt to control something that is ultimately out of their control. When trying, it is often more detrimental).

2004

The suffocating
feeling of loneliness
can alter our
perceptions of self.

JANUARY 4, 2004
1:42 PM

"IT's SIMPLE TO BE saved". A piece of paper with those little words stares up at me from the floor. I could use a little 'saving' right now. It was a piece of paper I found wedged in the crack of my drivers' side door the other night after I'd driven to Farmington for no other purpose other than escape. When I came back outside, after grumbling, mumbling, and crying the entire evening, I found that little piece of paper in my door. "It's simple to be saved". What do I do now? Pray? I could pray for guidance but would I take it? If it doesn't come to me in an identifiable, easy-to-read instructional way, I will probably overlook it and wonder why no answer has come. I don't know, I looked at that piece of paper this morning as I lay in bed, unable to move, my head pounding, my stomach churning, my eyes still bleary from the night before. Everyone needs a good drink every now and then, someone once said. Maybe that's true but maybe it should always stop with that ONE good drink; maybe you shouldn't follow that one good drink with ten mediocre ones; but that seems to be the way it goes. As I made my way to his house last night, I told myself, "now, don't drink. You remember what happened last time, don't you? You said you wouldn't do it again. Do you really like to feel that way?" I gave myself all the warnings, all the little red flags were waving right there in front of me and I disregarded each and every one of them. Why? To loosen up? That is a very pathetic and pitiable excuse, but it's true. I wanted to loosen up because I've been wound so tight for so long I've forgotten what it feels like to relax.

Later:

I have to ask the obvious question: have I ever been relaxed? Needless to say, last night, in the midst of my drinking binge, I was relaxed for a little while... until I lost all control of myself, my temper included, and really let some people know how I felt about things.

JANUARY 14, 2004
11:52PM

EVERY DAY I HAVE looked at the calendar and chided myself for being so lethargic with my writing. "Tomorrow I will write"; I said this to myself every day since my last entry and it is only now that I have come to my senses and begun a new entry.

I forewent my yearly prediction for New Year's. I entirely skipped a New Year's entry altogether. Perhaps falling asleep at ten o'clock on New Year's night had something to do with the omission but more likely is the fact that I really just don't give a damn. Any good prediction I may have made would have undoubtedly been proven foolhardy and any bad prediction I may have made would have just as unjustly come to be. Perhaps that is the old monster of pessimism sprouting new wings upon my back, taking flight, and perhaps it's just the cold, hard truth of realism that has pounded its fists against my head for so many years that I have become deaf, dumb, and blind to everything. What have I been doing since last I wrote you? I daresay nothing too spectacular or significant, unless you count the procrastination that has accumulated me nothing but more frayed nerves and anxious agitation due to the immobility of my station. It is all my doing, this I know, and this I also cannot seem to correct, to overcome. It is the same old argument again and again and I can't' seem to come to terms with anything. I merely contradict myself, chastise myself, and berate myself into an unwitting acceptance of mediocrity. The tragedy lies in the fact that I know I could achieve so much more. The realism reiterates the truth that only I know: I am afraid of everything in this life.

I am afraid of the good just as much as I am of the bad. I am afraid of the happiness just as I fear the sadness and loneliness. There seems to be no middle ground for me to find footing. Either I slip and fall, tumbling down the mountainside and landing on my rear-end, or I ascend to such a height that I become fearful of the fall because it will hurt that much more. The higher I go, the farther I have to fall – that is where the line of reason blurs for me.

One accomplishes nothing when they are in fear of everything.

JANUARY 15, 2004
11:23 PM

ONE SURE FIRE WAY to warm yourself up in these sub-zero temperatures is… no, not that, but Tae Bo. Although *that* would certainly do the trick as well. I've neglected Tae Bo for a few weeks now. It tapered off after a couple weeks of working at school and then when the school job ended, I found it hard to get myself back into the routine. But after tonight's indulgence of whatever lay close by my fingertips, I decided I had better get myself back on track sometime soon, rather quickly, so what better way to spend my Thursday night, after my shows of course, than by exercising a bit. I've been neglecting it for so long it feels as though I have gained ten pounds, though I'm sure I haven't, but a couple of pounds here and there and it does not make me happy. Of course, most would argue that a few extra pounds on me would be a good thing. Everyone would say so, everyone but me. They just don't know what it's like and I cannot explain it in any certain terms. I may be able to explain it but the truth remains that I don't even care to try to explain it. Why should I try to explain away my irrationalities when I recognize how neurotic it all is? It would only generate more consternation and I don't want to do that.

I'm trying my damndest to keep a steady balance and outwardly I seem to be succeeding exceptionally well, but it is all merely an act, something I have perfected in my young twenty three year life – acting to play the part of whomever I am serving to their set of standards, to their expectations, as inadvertent as they may be, I still know they exist. I have yet to determine what my expectations for myself are. Do I have any expectations for myself? Realistically, I think I only have dreams, whether or not they are merely pipe dreams or truly attainable, I haven't had the courage to venture out and see. So many times people think, "If only I can have that, then I will be happy," and so many times thereafter they realize happiness doesn't work that way; it doesn't revolve around the acquisition of certain things, of items deemed necessary by want instead of need; and so often what we really need becomes what we neglect because, more often than not, what we really need are the things that we know have the potential to hurt us; love, friendship, guidance, honesty; it is so much safer to hide behind the veneer of these falsehoods of want – they masquerade in the guise of need but as soon as we possess those items of want, we realize that we don't need them, they are not essential to us, our happiness, our satisfaction and we go in search of the next thing, the next project, still neglecting the things that we really need. I suppose we neglect the things we really need more easily than that of which we want because it is so much harder to find what we really need. We invent so many distractions for ourselves, to keep our minds occupied with idleness in want instead of determination of need. I don't know why the sudden talk of all this need and want nonsense; perhaps it's due to the melancholy country music ringing in my ears – all the lyrics of love, trust, friendship, and honor – it gets my mind wandering and wondering: Where is everybody?

When one is adamant about the fact that they don't need anybody to get by, most often no one comes to their aid when they are in need; and even if someone does, that person has already contrived a lie to themselves by saying, "Well, it took them long enough to come to me. They must not really care. I don't need them." And they say to the person, "Everything is fine, don't worry about me. I'm fine". And on they go, trudging through day after day alone, in need, but no one comes to call on them again. That is – they don't call unless they want something for themselves. Have I become so jaded as to believe that is the way it really is around here? The truth is, or what I have convinced myself the truth to be: it's easier with no one else. Gram said to me the other day, as I was saying that I prefer to not get myself involved with all the family dynamics that are transpiring right now, she said, "That's our Katherine, off in her own little world." I said to her in reply, "It's safer that way". It is what I have convinced myself to believe in. Is it really safer that way or is it just lonelier?

The lonely have the indistinguishable air of confidence, self-assuredness, viability, determination mixed with the right amount of aloofness to appear in control and level headed. What it all really is, what it all really amounts to is an act to appear calm, cool, collected, and ambitious with a mind set on achieving a certain goal; and in actuality, the lonely are scared witless. Scared of letting anyone too close, of letting anyone in to their 'own little world of safety'.

It's not a world of safety though. It's a world devoid of the most necessary things in life. It all comes back to want and need. It can all be categorized so easily, the wants and needs of life. Life is so charmingly simple that we have to complicate it beyond reason. You'd think the human race actually liked being confused, unaware, and constantly at odds with something. You'd think we like all these complications we set out as traps for ourselves to fall into. When you really stop to think about it – life should be so simple – and yet it's not. So many obstacles get in the way of reason; of common sense. Our priorities are skewed across the globe – why can't we figure it out? Of course, I'm not naïve enough to believe I have any of the answers, I'm just thinking. Maybe no one else even has these same thoughts that I have but I'd like to think that somewhere out there is someone who believes in the same things I do. I wouldn't be so lonely then, would I? Many times I have said that I am not lonely and I don't feel lonely but I don't really know what I feel besides an undying and unceasing grip of fear that holds me hostage. I'm not lonely I'm just trying too hard to be what everyone wants me to be that I haven't turned into anyone yet. I can't seem to get my mind straight. Everything is so mixed up, confused; everything seems far too complicated when, in actuality, I know it's not. My mind tells me one thing and it makes perfect sense but I can't get any other part of me to obey. And in the meantime I become immobilized. After being immobile for so long it is difficult to move again. Am I going to end up a solitary monument for the rest of eternity?

JANUARY 18, 2004
2:00 AM

ON A DAY/NIGHT THAT I should be tired, I cannot find sleepiness. After exerting myself to the extremes today, I thought I'd be fatigued enough to go to bed at a reasonable hour and fall asleep but it just doesn't work that way for me. The more I do, the more physical activity that I endure, the more impossible it becomes for me to go to sleep. Truth be known, I am tired right now; I am physically wearied, no doubt from exercising too, and I would like nothing more than to lie down and sleep but every time I tempt my eyes to close, I find no rest. Is it any wonder that I am so irritable all the time? I bet lack of sleep accounts for this incessant nervousness and fear that holds me. It's all cause and effect though; it goes back and forth like a tennis ball. I will be so glad once spring is here and I am able to go outside once again, play, and get active. I absolutely detest having to stay inside all the time. I don't have to; there are no chains that bound me in captivity here, but one step outside, one slap in the face of that cold wind and air, and I'm right back inside again feeling as though I'm in lockdown; an unofficial house arrest.

Does it make sense as well that the less I seem to eat, the more energy I have? Why am I the complete opposite of normalcy? (Relatively speaking). I've eaten bananas and raisins today.

I truly hate the weekends. Monday is a holiday. It's a nice holiday to celebrate (MLK) but I hate that everyone is going to be out and about again. Sometimes I feel as though I want the whole world to myself. If that were to be, I'd quickly change my mind, I'm sure. But in those moments where I feel overwhelmed by everything and everyone, I fantasize about it. Who hasn't, now or then? I'm going to try to get some sleep because I'm talking about such ridiculous things it is beginning to annoy even me. G'night, J.

JANUARY 21, 2004
7:58 PM

So I ONCE AGAIN have to face the reality – the truth – the fact that I just don't like the way things are right now. I've oftentimes said that I feel lost – but never more so than I do at this particular time in my life. What makes this time so very different from any other time I have issued the same statement? Not so very much, I suppose, unless you take into accountability all that has transpired in the last month or so. Perhaps it's all merely an overload to my emotional stability, which was very fragile to begin with, but maybe the only way I know how to cope with my feelings is by trying, in vain always, to run away from them. I am not strong enough to face them head on. Just because I don't want things to be a certain way does not mean that my wishes will be complied with. Some problems exist without the ability to 'will them away'. I have many of those problems but refuse to believe that I cannot will them away if I so desire it. And if they are persistent, as they seem to be, then I reason to myself that I must not really want them to go away because if I did, then I would be able to easily overcome them all. But I realize that things just don't work that way.

Sometimes I think I'm living more than one life; a schizophrenic, perhaps, though I know I'm really not. Borderline personality disorder – maybe – whatever that is – I don't like the idea that I could be categorized in such a way; stymied into a definitive explanation for my neuroses. I don't think any illness is as simplified as that; something to look up in a PDR and say, absolutely, matter of fact – that is her problem and this is the cure. Perhaps no problems exist that I do not invent myself so therefore it really is all in my mind. Am I looking too hard or not hard enough? There is an overwhelming indecisiveness that stirs within me making nearly every aspect of life harder than it needs to be. Someday, someday – I always say – but why not today?

JANUARY 29, 2004
7:42 PM

WHY THE SUDDEN ATTACK of anxiety every time I come near any place that isn't a darkened movie theatre, I don't know. I daresay I am even more uncomfortable with myself than I usually am. There is nothing I find that I can mark in the positive list about myself. I don't know exactly what my problem is but only that one exists. I cannot deny this. I am very much afraid to face everyday people. And it's not the people themselves, really, sometimes it's just the day that I am afraid of. I am almost in fear of the sunlight. I would much rather just show myself during the nocturnal hours. It's a hard life, living beneath the horizon. I go through bouts of this; this, what would you call it? These temperaments, these fluctuations of identity; and it hits me hardest during the winter months, being cooped up inside. The fact that it is terribly cold outside with a whipping wind that lashes at my skin like a whip; I have not been warm at all this winter unless I am in the tub, water covering every inch of my body, steaming the room with hot moisture; but, inevitably, the water cools and I have to step out of my temporary sauna and into the chilly hallway finally making my way back down to the cellar that is barely above freezing itself.

We make our own choices in this world, so I'm told, but I seem unable to make even the simplest of decisions. The obvious choice for most becomes an agonizing see-saw battle of contradictions with me. I know I've stated these same things, over and over again, in these journals of mine, but I am no closer to finding a solution to my sorrows now than I was when I first wrote to you. Everything becomes more deeply felt as time moves on.

JANUARY 31, 2004
11:47 AM

WHAT DO YOU THINK the symbolic merit of this dream is: (one I had last night) I was on the Titanic with only a bucket; that was the main theme and while I dutifully scooped out water with that bucket, thinking it would make difference, the end result was still the same; but the whole idea of being on the Titanic with only a bucket? That really says it all about my life, doesn't it?

FEBRUARY 3, 2004
7:40 PM

I CAN NO LONGER tolerate staying at home. We've been through this time and time again though. I have to admit that it's very nice having my own computer here in my room again. For as much as I loved the laptop, and for as much fun as it was, I really wanted this one back. Maybe I'm sentimental. I don't think it's that inasmuch as having my own, stationary, computer here at home which allows me to have something to do at home without having the option of taking it with me and hiding somewhere else.

I've been trying to find a cave to hide in for the past few months. Sometimes I feel as though I have succeeded in finding one but when I open my eyes I see that it's only my little cell that I've found, or my car.

FEBRUARY 4, 2004
3:05 PM
B & N

IT SEEMS I ALWAYS want to come here but the closer to my destination that I actually get, the more I begin to have second thoughts and think that maybe I shouldn't be here at all. It always hits me about the time that I'm cruising down the interstate at sixty-five miles an hour (or a bit over) and I start to panic a little, thinking, "Why am I going there? Do I really need to go? What is there that I need? Someone there is going to see me. What are they going to think? Are they going to recognize me? Are they going to wonder why I'm coming back again so soon? Are they going to think terrible things about me or think I'm doing something I shouldn't be doing?"

I don't know why I begin to panic so but nonetheless, the feeling is there and it cannot be ignored because of its omnipresence. It is very strange though, how I can leave my own house, quite content with excitement at coming here and maybe getting a WCM and sitting down to write or read or whatever my intentions are that particular day. But then, from somewhere deep within my mind, this fear takes over and plays tug of war with my mind and rationality until hardly anything of me is left and I become a useless little rag doll trying to regain my composure. Severe social anxiety, would you call it? I'm close enough to the psychology section right now that I could go look it up – diagnose myself. But I've done that so many times. Maybe I'm simply a hypochondriac. A more subdued version of a hypochondriac because I really don't believe I'm going down with any ill-fated disease or that my body is being ravaged by an unknown virile infection. I'm more paranoid than anything else and a lot of that probably stems from the insecurity that grinds me down to the bone, consuming the marrow and my livelihood as it goes on sandblasting and whittling away.

If I could just learn to not take criticism as a personal attack then I should be alright.

But everything around me affects me to such an extent that I have a hard time dealing with something that may or may not end in failure for me. For some reason, I feel that if I fail one thing, I will fail everything I try. It's that damn old fear, isn't it? What a monster.

Once I begin something I don't find it hard to keep with it, really, but it's the starting point that makes me falter. I have no real motivation to actually start anything at all and if I never start it, I reason I'll never have to finish it. Simple enough, isn't it. That is really no way to live though. Someone could look at my life and say, as an example to a young impressionable kid, 'that is no way to go about things. You see that it has gotten her nowhere, and if you follow suit, that way of life will get you nowhere too.' I guess it's not all bad though. I have done some extraordinary things, met some incredible people, have fallen in and out of love so many times it's hard to count, but in the process of all things, I have never fully surrendered myself to anyone or anything. Maybe it's a fear of putting my entire heart out there on the line and having it unceremoniously returned to me on a platter.

MARCH 20, 2004

WAS WATCHING ANGELINA JOLIE'S new movie, "Taking Lives", and suddenly got an intense craving for a clove. For the past couple of weeks now, I have not been able to rid myself of this desire –this self-destructive indulgence. Though I have not yet gone out and bought a pack of cloves for my smoking pleasure, my refusal to do so, to give in, has nearly been a fight to the death. I was so near to buying a pack this past evening, so near; I was in the store and could see behind the counter at the pack of cloves that seemed to beckon to me, albeit beseechingly, for I know the dangers and risks involved, especially with a person such as myself who has the pitiable curse of becoming addicted to any form of self-destruction. I have fought the battle with a smoke filled mind once before and I have fought the bottle more often than anyone knows and I am currently in a battle for my life with this eating disorder that has plagued my very existence. The name of this disorder is so ugly I refuse to speak it. It is so menacing that I cannot bring myself to acknowledge the fact of it.

With any luck I will not give in to this temporary and fleeting urge to saturate my being with smoke. For so long now, it seems that my survival has depended on my own will power and my own strength; two things of which I am always almost certain to be without but that always seem to prevail in moments of crisis. Besides, there is none who destroy me more effectively than I do myself. Believe me, J, it is something I am still working on.

MARCH 23, 2004
11:12 PM

I BELIEVE MY SLEEPING problems started in eighth grade, possibly seventh. Through the years it has progressed into sporadic bouts of insomnia which can last days, weeks, or at the worst, seemingly endless months where an hour or two of sleep in a couple days' time is all I seem to procure.

I have run myself into the ground today though, only eating one small 79 cent package of Twizzlers all day, doing Tae Bo on top of that, and drinking coffee, Diet Coke, and Chocolate Milk. That is not exactly running myself into the ground, really, but I figured the less I had to eat and the more energy I expended, the more tired I would become and I'd be able to fall asleep sooner. I don't know if that little scheme is going to work though because as of right now, I'm wide awake and seem to have a little extra energy to go around, though I am not entirely sure where it came from. I suppose its adrenalin, released from my exercising, and it hasn't yet turned its course through my bloodstream. Once that's gone, I think I'll be able to lay my head down upon my pillow and fall into an easy sleep. That's what I hope for. Of course, as I sit here gulping down a cup of coffee, I'm not sure that plan will work at all.

Today found me procrastinating even more. How is it possible, you wonder? I do too. I keep telling myself and promising others that I'm going to get my life in order pretty soon. I'm going to start something and finish it. I'm going to be responsible and committed to something that will both benefit me and better me on the whole. And yet I've not taken any steps in a forward progression. I've not even begun to backtrack – I've just remained; I've just solidified. I have bouts of inspiration and when I do, I begin to tackle something with a fervor, anything I set my mind to, I drive myself into it, and then just as suddenly as I'd begun the project, I stop. I fear the finality of completion, so everything in my life is half done; started but never finished; begun but not furthered. I annoy myself with my inadequacy. My shortcomings stand tall in my eyes. And every day that passes I fear I am becoming farther away from the starting point. When the starting point vanishes, when the opportunities dry up, then I'll really be lost. It is too late in the evening to get too deep in thought. I am in no mood for philosophical chatter, for serious ponderings. My motivation lacks will-power and my will-power lacks motivation. So tell me what to do about that.

Why does my mind make me believe I am a certain way when, in reality, I am not? What dysfunction lies therein that makes it so? Is it society that has so influenced my deranged self-image? Are my own ideals and expectations getting in the way of my health? Am I buying into all the model behavior that is splashed across the billboards and magazine photo montages? What is it that distorts reality for me? I don't know. I'm not a therapist and even if I were, I could not psychoanalyze myself (even though a therapist differs from a psychoanalyst – you get my point).

One cannot deconstruct their mind into different aspects of neuroses. It takes an outsider looking in to determine what is invisible to oneself. You think? If I could afford a psychoanalyst, I think I'd go. If nothing else, it would give me someone to talk to, someone who is paid to be impartial while listening. Someone who is paid to not inflict their own personal judgments on you but rather offer sound advice from an occupational standpoint; most importantly, someone who is bound by a confidentiality contract. I'll never tell.

APRIL 14, 2004

I HAVE NOT EATEN in 10 days now and I have sustained myself with liquid nutrients, chocolate milk being my most indulgent besides coffee. Neither of which is very good for me. Well, milk is good but only to a certain extent.

It's a bit strange now though; it's been ten days since I have eaten anything, since any form of solid food has been consumed by me, and yet I am not hungry. I have not wanted for anything and I have had energy to spare. Perhaps that is the caffeine taking over; perhaps all the coffee has fueled me with only temporary and fleeting energy. Perhaps it's all in my head. Am I wasting away without even realizing it? I have noticed no change in my appearance and I suspect that if I become too gaunt, too sickly, then it will be brought to my attention by someone else; by someone whom I wouldn't expect it to come from. Those observations, the ones from people who normally wouldn't notice, are the observations that strike a chord deep within. I begin to think, "Well, if they noticed then something must really be apparent. I must not be hiding such and such a thing so well". One problem at a time, I tell myself.

Right now I am dealing with being thrown out of my house – I am dealing with a new sense of heightened anxiety. I would say that it has reached its fevered peak now. I am dealing with money issues, as I always seem to be doing. I am dealing with hesitation, once again, of having to go to the doctors and explain away symptoms that I cannot seem to articulate into words of substance but I promised a friend I would so I have to.

So maybe I am actually dealing with more than one thing at a time. This whole eating thing though is probably the one that I should focus on for right now as it really is the life sustaining force that keeps me in the here and now but part of me just doesn't care. If I can feel this good without eating, why should I eat? If I have this much energy, which seems to be more than when I was eating, what's the problem? Until I truly become skin and bones, I don't see the problem. Until someone 'outside' notices the problem, I'm not going to do anything about it. I have already become accustomed to the fact that the adults around me think I am too thin and what not, as they've been saying that since September, but I don't seem to have lost any more weight since then, so maintaining this balance seems to be working for me. Is it enjoyable? Well, no, but eating is not enjoyable for me either. Once I go to the doctors and talk about my anxiety and, presumably, lie about everything else that is wrong with me, I'll figure something out. I've already fallen a bit more down into this endless rabbit hole. I have given into temptation; smoking (cloves), and having the occasional drink. It's in my unfortunate nature that I easily become addicted to things – many different things – not just alcohol, not just cloves, but I have some form of OCD and I become obsessive to the point where I realize it's unhealthy; they're phases, or they seem to be. They become really, almost unbearably, intense and then it begins to fade away and something else takes its place and eventually it circles back and the process begins to repeat itself. It's an endless cycle. I overcome to the point where I feel almost triumphant and then I fall back. It gets irritating after a while.

I've got all sorts of problems and I have to wonder if it is I who create them just to torture myself; just to make my existence more of a burden. Why can I not seem to have even one day of normalcy; of peace; of relaxation? Do I need to invent all of these different problems for myself just in order to feel as though I have a constant excuse; to feel pity for myself; to be burdened for no other reason than to occupy myself and avoid what really needs to be done? Do I really even have a choice in the matter?

I feel my life spinning out of control and I have this illusion that I'm really in control of it but I don't think I am. I think I lost control, so many years ago, that one moment in time when I lost myself and my innocence and became corrupted by someone older, stronger – corrupted by someone more devilish than I have ever known. Maybe all these problems are an escape from facing that truth; the truth of who I was; am; and why I am that way. What was done to me, I cannot face it and it feels as though, when I think about it, that it happened to someone else; it was not me. I have not spoken of it but in vague and nebulous terms; words veiled in mystique so deciphering them is not easy. I do not speak in outright terms because it is all too ugly; it is despicable and the words that would be used to describe the situation are too terrible to invoke on paper; they would come alive, to write the absolute truth would be to breathe life into something that I have tried to kill for so long and I am not willing to do that. I am content (laugh now at that statement) to let the memory retreat and recede into my head as far as it may burrow where it will remain a burning ember of a long ago moment. It happened to someone else anyway. Someone that was lost long ago; someone that remains on a lonely mountaintop, screaming into the wind, her words lost and carried away by a force greater than she. And she remains perched atop that mountain, elevated higher than Everest, unreachable by mortal hands; untamable but by God Himself; living in that unfavorable light of truth while trying to find the shadows to hide within. But what shadows can be found on the tip of a mountaintop? Where is there to hide? The only thing that keeps the truth from being obtained is the fact there is not enough air; if she shared the air with the truth, then one or the other would die. And she would sooner the truth die than herself. She would rather watch the burning ember fade to nonexistence than she would feel her lungs implode from lack of oxygen. She wants to kill the truth, to cast it away from her and watch it tumble down into the shadowed depth. And maybe then she could fly away. Maybe then she would be able to descend from her lonely mountaintop and plant her feet firmly on the ground again. Perhaps then she would be able to breathe and the truth would not threaten her any longer with its honesty; with its ugliness. She'd be able to move on. And, really, that's all she wants.

I have so many things to say and sometimes the only way I can say them is by unleashing a torrent of creative e writing; an outpouring of emotion that is contained to the page. But to me, it is so much more than that. It's not a containment with words, it's a verbal release, even if vague to others, it's perceptible to me; it's tangible to me; I can see it, feel it, hear it, all senses come alive when the thoughts are with me;

when the memory is lit within my mind it becomes a living, breathing entity within me. I am almost split in two with the memory, the thought. I have been trapped for so long inside my head. I have been screaming so loudly, but its fallen silent on everyone else. Few can perceive the trouble that wallows beneath my eyes; few can glean out the emptiness that sits within my soul. It's such a contradiction. I feel hollow, empty, but at the same time, I am so full of emotion that I can barely contain myself.

APRIL 17, 2004

SO WHAT IS TODAY? Day fourteen or thirteen of my 'not hungry' scheme? I ate a banana on day 12 and that's all I've had. Sustaining myself on coffee, chocolate milk, and DC still. I live such a surreal lifestyle. Outside appearances play it up to make everything ok. Only select few know of select problems. I have a feeling that no one would want to be around me if they knew the full extent of damage that has encircled my entire existence.

I cannot seem to regain my footing. I take one step forward and fall back a few strides into old habits that I thought I had overcome. Things just aren't easy. I wish I could land on some solid ground somewhere along the line. I am just at a loss. I don't know what to do, say, how to act or how to speak. I have no voice but a generic one; feeding people the lines they want to hear. Where am I? Where have I gone? How did I manage to become so lost? I'd like to know the exact moment in time when it all became too much – too real – when I became too far gone to recapture any real semblance of a 'normal' life. I look at people, I envy them. I know they all have their problems but I wonder if any of them face the same things I do. It's not as though I could ever ask. I would feel so ashamed.

I don't want people to know how entirely screwed up I am. I can laugh and talk and make jokes (sometimes) but it's all a façade; all a shield to mask the insecurity and incurable sadness that dwells within my being. It's as if my soul itself is crying in despair. Maybe it is. What repairs a soul? God? Faith? Friends? Family? Or a combination of all of the above. Why can't I regain the life I once had? I am a shadow of my former self. I never thought I'd want that girl back but compared to the one I am now at this moment, it wouldn't be such a bad thing.

Once upon a time I knew how to have fun, I knew how to act crazy and foolish and be silly all at once. I knew pure laughter and joy. Maybe it wasn't constant (because I know, for a long time, something has always been amiss within me) but I really used to be fun. I am nothing but a drag now. I bring no real fun to any activity I enter myself into. What do I give? Why would anyone want to be around me? I just bring everybody down don't I? And when I am able to make people laugh it is only a defense mechanism I use (jokes, sarcasm, and self-depreciating humor) in order to divert attention from the real problems that lay just beneath the surface. At times I wish I could just scream out and tell the world why I feel the way I do (why do I?). I wish I could cry and fall into a friends arms and be held and consoled. I seek comfort in all I do, but I don't afford myself the luxury to let it be known. I act aloof and distant, appear laid back and 'cool', but inside I am in turmoil. I am in constant discomfort with all that surrounds me. I wish I could tell someone all of this without fear of their judgment, without fear of their reaction, but I am in fear of everything.

I can't seem to get a grip. I can't seem to get firm footing or find solid ground or hold my head up high with confidence and self-assuredness. I look to the ground, my eyes intentionally avoiding all others, my feet shuffling along the ground, shoulders hunched, longing in my eyes, longing for a friend to simply put their arm around me and say, "Everything is going to be alright. Maybe not today, maybe not tomorrow, but you're not alone and we'll work this out together". And, yes I realize I have friends who have said these words to me and for as many times as they've told me this, for as many times as I've heard it, I am the unfortunate type of person who needs constant reassurance. I need constant reassurance but I rarely ever ask for it. I rarely ever ask for help and it seems that the only times I really do ask for help are when things have broken down so completely that I fear for myself and the hopelessness that seems to capture me in the moment; and I breakdown, and I cry, and I lose control, and I lose that little ounce of light inside of me that keeps me going with the promise of tomorrow. In those instances, I feel I have nowhere to turn, nowhere to go because I don't want to call someone and burden them with my problems. I seem to make my life into a catch-22 because no matter what my options, I always gravitate towards the unfavorable consequences that await me. I never see the bright side. The glass is never half full, to use a cliché.

I wonder why I am the way I am. I wouldn't trade the friends I have right now for anything but it is not fair of me to continually seek them out with only my distress. I would love, absolutely love, to go to them with happy, bright, sunshine-y news, but the problem is; nothing that good ever really happens. The only good things that do happen involve the times that I spend with those certain people, those particular friends. And it's not as though I could go back and write them a letter and say, "Guess what wonderful thing happened to me?" because it would only involve me telling them, "I got to see you" and they'd wonder, "Is that all". I got to see them but we didn't do anything particularly 'special' or even that memorable. It just comes down to: I got to see them. I got to spend a few moments with them. And that gets me through. And those are the only good moments that I can come away with. Those few, fleeting, seemingly insignificant moments when I get to spend a few seconds of my time with them, brings me such joy and sadness. Joy and comfort comes with their company, their presence, and their smiles. And the sadness comes a moment later when we're separated again. I am in such desperate need but I don't want anyone to know. Why? Because I hate the fact that something is wrong to begin with. Do I just want to keep on pretending like this? I cannot go on like that forever. I am so afraid of loving people because there is so much pain involved in that. And yet that is the state I find myself in. I love my family, I love and adore my friends, and for some reason, it hurts. I don't know why.

I think what it comes down to is that I need therapy. Like I'd pay for that though.

APRIL 30, 2004

THE SKY WAS BRUSHED with soft pastels tonight. I went for a walk around seven o'clock this evening. Walked to the stop sign and back, the sun setting in an orange burning glow, slowly sinking below the horizon, my line of sight; the sky was painted those soft Easter hues of pink, orange, purple, blue and yellow. It was lovely.

What are not so lovely are my incessant worries and panic attacks. I thought being on medication was supposed to calm me a bit but I'm all hyped up still. My heart still beats faster than it should in commonplace, everyday situations; so mundane are these tasks I do and these errands I run, I don't know why I fear doing them. My moments of peace are few and far between. And on top of everything else, I have guilt, I have worry, and I really have no one. I reach out for help every now and then but in the end it always ends up that I'm alone and I'm trying to work through it all alone. And really the only thing I want to do is cry and fall into someone's arms. But I can't do that. That just wouldn't be acceptable. I would never allow myself to do that anyway. It's not who I am. Maybe I just wish that I were that vulnerable, that I had that kind of a relationship with someone where it was possible that I could do that. Maybe I just want to have the option of doing that but I don't feel comfortable enough with anyone to do that. I am not comfortable with myself so how can I expect to be comfortable with anyone else?

MAY 1, 2004

MAYBE I JUST DON'T want help. I don't honestly like feeling this way but what it comes down to is the basic problem of all anxiety cases – fear. I'm afraid of everything and everyone so why not be afraid of help too? I'm too insecure – I'm too self-conscious – I'm afraid of everyone's opinion – I'm afraid of their acceptance as well as their rejection. How can anyone live like that? How have I managed for the past twenty three years to not kill myself? Because, deep down, I don't really want to die – I want to live – I'm just afraid to really put myself out there and do it.

I went to school Wednesday afternoon and my friend said, "Where's the other half of you?" Meaning, of course, that I have lost weight and I said, "Oh, she's gone. Got rid of her." Wishing all the time that I really had. She still lingers like the ghost of my Siamese twin.

MAY 3, 2004

ONE CAN SIT AND contemplate all night long about how they got to be where they are but will it ever make sense? Does there ever come a point in one's own life when it will all make sense? I envy those who, at least believe, their life makes sense. I envy those who have gotten to go where they wanted to go and are who they set out to be. Is it possible, in this life, this world, this time, to ever be satisfied? How could I, someone with a reasonably sensible head on her shoulders, someone with ideals, dreams and morals; how could I have become the sad, pathetic figure I am today? The insecure stranger who would rather swim across a leech infested swamp than risk the potential embarrassment of saying the wrong thing, doing the wrong thing, or not doing anything at all, in the presence of others? How did I become afflicted with all these problems? These disorders? How did I get to the point where all these things control my life and I am submitted to their mercy? My life is not my own. God is not in control of my life. He is, most presumably, disappointed with my lack of stability, will power, and susceptibility to all the demons of the world. Demons in the sense of bad habits, habitual procrastination, a weakness and vulnerability for all things that one can become addicted to. I am so weak in so many ways and strong in only one: that being I have not given up completely. I have not entirely given up on myself, though I've come close. Most of all, I have not given up because I am always thinking of someone else. Am I here for me? No, I don't think I am. If I had the choice – if God were to send an Angel for me right now – an Angel to ask me whether I'd like to stay or go – I'd take flight without hesitation but only if it wouldn't cause another pain. But I don't have that choice and am not going to have that choice anytime soon probably. So I have to ride out this predestined cruise for as far as it takes me and hopefully, in the end, something will make sense and something will have made all this pain and trouble worthwhile.

I can sit here and say I suffer but I am stricken with so much guilt by that thought. What do I really know of suffering? I am not starving (except by choice), I am not homeless (sort of), I am not alone in this world though I feel I am, I have not been beaten beyond recognition or on a continual basis. What I have are mental disturbances, I suppose. I'm a head-case, pure and simple (though, really, not so simple). I've had many things happen to me that I wish had not happened to me; I've gone through many experiences that I wouldn't wish on anyone else, but it hasn't been constant – it's not an everyday occurrence. But when moments do arise, I cannot shake the memories from my head. I relive moments over and over again in my head, in my dreams, in my thoughts – in every darkened corner there lurks a distant memory; it hides there in the shadows and only emerges when I'm alone; it steps out into the light and rears its ugly head. I close my eyes but am still accosted by sight, by remembrance. One of these days, something is going to have to get better, don't you think? I hope.

MAY 14, 2004

MOMENTS ARISE THAT MAKE me rethink the whole 'medication' thing. I swear to you that it doesn't work. Perhaps it's more psychological than anything else. Perhaps if I had the mindset that it was going to work, that it was working, then it would. Will it to happen. But I have never put much stock of belief into medication. I have a fear that all the pill really is, is a placebo, and doctors always prescribe them and then laugh behind your back. Paranoia is a side-effect of anxiety, isn't it? Paranoia and fear seem to run rampant, from time to time. I was very pleased that Lynn turned around and spoke to me today. Maybe that's all I ever want: acknowledgment. I feel bad for being such a cop-out with softball this year but I just cannot face people now. I'm tempted to just run away forever. But I'll only end up making the same mistakes somewhere else. One can't really run away from a problem because, more often than not, the problem that exists is simply a problem they have with themselves and, try as one might, no one is able to run away from themselves. I believe I've already tried that.

How many personalities have I tried on? Nothing fits. I am destined to be a misfit forever, I suppose.

JUNE 13, 2004

EVERYTHING HAS JUST BEEN going downhill this year. It has been heading in that direction for quite a long time – a few years to be exact. Though something was always wrong, it never used to be this bad but I'm really in deep now. I'm finding it difficult to claw my way out of this freshly dug grave. I am trying though. I have not lain down yet. Just don't give up on me. That's all I really want to say, don't give up on me.

JUNE 27, 2004

I CAN'T EVEN BEGIN to fathom how much money I have just cost everyone (with the tooth, abscess, surgery, near death, etc.); my trip to the ER and to, seemingly, all the dentists in the immediate region, the emergency surgery, the medication, the mounting cost of yogurt and sorbet sales. Of course, they've been good to me and have told me not to worry about it, that money doesn't matter as long as I'm alright, but I still feel bad. I have such a complex about money – mainly because I know I don't make nearly enough money to sustain myself and I feel guilty about that. I am not responsible, I'm not nearly grown up enough – as I should be at 23. I still feel like a kid just out having a good time (only I'm not actually having a good time). I like traveling and doing all these things and I already rue the day that I'll have to settle down into a steady-job, unless I find something that suits me just so and gets me excited just thinking and anticipating the next day. Something that I wouldn't say was a 'job' but a 'living'. I don't know if I will ever find that niche where I belong. Is there one? Or must I continue to create my own?

They say you should have variety in your diet, though I'm sure they didn't mean just ice cream and yogurt. I had Thai food the other night and an entire pizza the next night after that and that was pretty much the last time I had 'real food' in me. It's a wonder I haven't gained twenty pounds. I've also been living off soup. For the past three nights I've had soup for dinner, around seven PM. I'm not too nutritionally bound right now.

Besides, I think I may have mentioned this but I saw a picture of myself a few weeks ago and it scared me because my arms looked like twigs. I keep telling myself that a few pounds would probably do wonders for me – give me some more energy – enable me to do more – be more active – though it's hard to get more active than I have been. But I haven't been active off energy – I've been active off sheer will and determination to lose weight – and you know what? I don't really need to lose any more weight. I've been to the danger line and back – to see if I could manage it – and I did and there's really no need to do it anymore. I can say this to myself but getting my body to respond and act on it is another thing entirely. The power of my mind doesn't always seem to overcome the fragile self-image I have of my body. I am a split person. I am beginning to think I have some personality disorder. The medication I'm on now, the Prozac, doesn't seem to be doing a damn thing. I'm convinced it's not working. I don't feel any different. But I'm also afraid to go back there and find out something worse about myself. I know more than I tell and I don't have to tell all – and I probably never will. Though it all might make a great, sad, memoir someday but for the time being, I'm going to forget about most of the things I've gone through. Someday, J, someday I'll let you in on a little secret but not right now. It's still too painful to think about.

I was going to write to you last week and start off by saying "I am in a very Sylvia Plath mood today". I don't feel quite that way right now but last week I did. I went out to the trunk of my car to gather my book of Sylvia's journals. Sometimes it's a bit disturbing when I get into those moods and Sylvia's methods begin to appeal to me – the method of sticking my head in an oven and gassing myself to death and out of misery – in order to not have to face anything ever again. But I'll persist and march on because it will all eventually be worth it. When I stop believing that, I'll really be in trouble.

JULY 5, 2004

WHY AM I so god-awful tired? I have been so fatigued for the past few days that it's difficult to even sit up in bed. I am tired all the time. I was watching a documentary on

MSNBC last night – "Dangers and Diets" - it was called and a doc on the show said, "When we force our bodies to try and maintain a weight that it doesn't want us to be at, bad things are going to happen." You think?! Maybe I'm trying to maintain a weight that isn't conducive to how my body needs to be. Then again, I've known that for the better part of a year now. Another girl was on the show, she used to model, and she said, "My god, if I gained half a pound, I thought I was fat!" and I'm like, 'I know exactly what you're saying.' I worry about everything that goes into my body and sometimes I eat just in spite of myself – but then I worry so much about the effect that particular food is going to have on my body that I feel myself inflate at just the thought of gaining a pound or two. I've become so obsessive about it and I don't want to worry about it anymore. I want to be able to eat what I want to eat, enjoy the things I used to enjoy, and, dammit, most of all I just don't want to be this damn exhausted all the time. It's not as though I'm not eating at all (anymore) because for the past couple of weeks, since recovering from near death, I've been shoveling the food into me, or so it seems to me, but to someone who has persistently avoided food for so long, any amount that actually goes into my system and stays there seems like an all you can eat buffet.

How do people become no neurotic? So obsessive about such superficial things? Why does something always have to be wrong for me to feel right? Most of my life, things have been wrong, so the thought of things actually going smoothly and easily and my way is a foreign concept for me to grasp. It's like trying to communicate in a foreign city when you don't know how to speak the language. You try to relate to people with gestures, body language, with your eyes. You forgo speaking because no matter how loud you yell or scream, they are not going to understand you and you just end up frustrating yourself even more in the process of trying to explain. What's the use? You say, and eventually give up. Will I ever get it together, J? Ever?

JULY 6, 2004

WHY CAN'T THEY JUST let it be? I'll find my way on my own (I say as a little voice laughs at me from inside my head). I was reading yet another article about the plight of Mary-Kate Olsen yesterday and it stated that she began to substitute coffee for lunch and when I read that, my mind immediately made the connection between her plight and mine. How often has a WCM been substituted for a meal for me? Whenever I had one. Some days, that would be all I'd have.

You see, I know I have a problem and as of late I've been doing well to correct it on my own. However, reading about her made it make sense to me, how coffee is such a stimulant and essentially an empty 'filler' for a starved stomach. The comparisons are so easily correlated but, again, no one knows. It's not as though I don't eat at all now. Last night and through most of the day yesterday I seemed to fill up on anything and everything that was within my immediate grasp. I hate doing it (eating like that) but there comes a point when my body screams ENOUGH! at me and I lose control. And control of something is essentially what I crave, isn't it? Control of my life, which I seem to have none. Such petty trifles in the grand scheme, you know.

Anyway, on the eighth is when I go back to the facial and

oral surgery place in Augusta and get checked out again. Am feeling no real pain now but every now and then there is still a twinge in my jaw when I open to take a bite out of something. All seems to be well for the time being though. And I'm not dead, so I guess that's a good thing.

It's funny for me to think about how close I was to actually dying. Well, in truth, I was dying, but how close I actually came to an actual demise of body is something else. Only a couple days and I could've been in the ground. I'd have been in the ground by now probably. The funeral would have been over, the headstone erected, the cremation ensued; the ashes divvied up and spread and I would cease to be. I wouldn't be sitting here writing to you. I wouldn't be sipping a Diet Coke, typing on a computer, my feet propped up and resting on the desk while taking side glances to my left where my peaceful little Jett is soundly sleeping. I wouldn't be half-heartedly watching Star Trek on the television. I'd have no more worries. I'd be free from all this constraint. But I would probably have ended up being one of those lonely lost souls who don't cross over to the other side but rather linger through the ages watching people come and go and move on while I remain in the present-past. Restless in life and restless in death.

Yes, it certainly is a 'funny' thing for me to think about. For all the hours I've spent dwelling on death and the meaning of it as well as of life - there I was; on the cusp of discovery, and my body battled back on its own, not willing to give in so easily, fighting for its own survival. Natural instinct kicked in – it was as though a panic button had been depressed and my body overcame my mind and fought its own physical battle while mentally shutting down any opposition my mind may have tried to think. Pain overrides most all my senses and survival became the ideal while my secondary nature of curiosity backed down and said, 'not just yet'. Who doesn't ponder over such a vast unknown, wanting to be the one to unlock the secret and venture into the hidden depths of the next step? There are so many things that I must do. Why can't I seem to get started? Fear has such a paralyzing effect.

JULY 28, 2004

J, JUST ANOTHER DREARY day. Too much time to sit and contemplate all I want and don't have, all I should do, I don't, all I could be, I'm not. Don't you love these days when all you can think about are the things that you seem to always fall short of. Why must that list be so long? Why do people gravitate towards the negative more than the positive? Why such a gloomy, glum outlook on things? What is it in our society, our culture, our nature, our very souls, which always seem to seek out the worst instead of searching out the good in all things? Because it's so much easier to spot? So much clearer to find? Or is it because we are all innately self-destructive to a degree? Maybe it's a combination of all these things. Maybe that's why Prozac and Zoloft are the drugs of choice for this generation.

These days just keep passing by me and I find myself growing older and staying the same; nothing changes. It is my fault, but I feel it's not my fault because I feel paralyzed by fear. I just can't figure things out, J, don't you know that by now. It's been how many years I've been writing to you about the same things. You'd think I'd eventually learn to seek out help in some way, shape or form and though, perhaps, I have, every now and then, there is nothing that has stayed with me to help me in the long run. Everything that helps is just on a temporary basis. It vanishes nearly as quickly as it came. I continually work myself up over these useless things. I am going to have to find something to do or else I will truly go mad. But what am I here to do? I feel so useless, like I can't do anything. The simplest of jobs seems too much for me. I really don't believe I'm cut out for anything too spectacular and will continue to live this banal existence never realizing the potential that really does dwell deep inside me. I sometimes do not give myself enough credit. But at other times, I revolt against the very thought of congratulating myself or complimenting myself for anything because I know that I don't deserve it. Why don't I deserve it? I don't think I do because, basically, I just don't like myself.

I wish I wasn't so inhibited. I want to go a little crazy sometimes and I just never let that side of myself out. She used to be there, I used to know how to have fun but that girl seems to have died a long time ago; either she's dead and gone forever or she's in some sort of induced coma and I don't know how to wake her up. I wish it were as easy as snapping my fingers and having everything be the way I wish it to be. It's not as though I'm afraid of the work it would entail, I'm just afraid of the failure that I see as inevitable but I'm intelligent enough to acknowledge the fact that I'm only going to fail if I never try. They say the first step is always the hardest, but I don't even know where the first step begins or where it will lead to. I still have no direction.

AUGUST 4, 2004

I JUST CAN'T SEEM to figure things out, J. It seems the more I try to avoid the issue (eating disorder, depression, anxiety, etc.) the more I tend to dwell on it. I can't even seem to say things outright to you. I don't know why unless I'm merely afraid of the acknowledgement that it means I'll have to face. I just don't understand what happened. Don't understand why I'm constantly seeking the approval of other people when what I really should be doing is working on the approval of myself. I don't measure up to the ideals I set for myself. On top of everything else, I just don't feel good. I am tired, deathly tired, all the time. I have no energy to speak of. I won't give myself a break. I cannot shut the pessimism and harsh self-criticism in my mind up. I don't enjoy anything like I used to. I have no friends that I see. No one that I feel comfortable with anymore.

It's like the guys I date that I'm attracted to. I meet these really great, nice, sweet guys that most any girl would love to be involved with and I only see them as a friend. I can't get romantically interested in them or turned on by them. But then I go out with guys who are into all the wrong things who don't know how or when to say the right thing; are basically interested in only their gains, and I'm attracted to them because, inside, I know it won't work out; I know there's no future in it so I can do what I want and then be done with it all.

It's almost like a drug addiction I suffer from but the drug in this case is disappointment and/or failure. It's not good for me and yet I can't keep myself away from it, from unintentionally seeking it out and sabotaging myself without direct intent. It would seem that instead of having a self-preservation button in me, I have a self-destruction one. The fault, really, only lies in me. Don't I have the choice? I do. So why do I continue to make the wrong choices? It's not that I even make a choice at all – it's more that I avoid the situation entirely, not even making a choice, just letting things ride and waiting on everything and everyone else. I have no initiative in me; no motivation, no confidence, no guts, no belief. Am I just a coward? I don't stand up for myself at all and I let the simplest little criticism eat away at my thoughts until I become so insecure and self-loathing that I want to do nothing more than crawl off into the woods somewhere and die miserably and alone. I'm like a wounded animal – crippled to the point of being defenseless where all I want to do is hide. I stand up for other people, won't let anyone say anything bad about any of my friends and yet, where are they? Why do I continue to stand by people who do not stand by me? And why do I feel it's my fault that they want nothing to do with me? How do I continually manage to drive people away from me?

Sometimes all I want to do is cry and ask for help, but I never do. I smile and act nonchalant while my soul is cowering inside like a beaten child. It plagues my thoughts, what people must think of me. The mistakes I've made and have come to regret; the moments I let my guard down when it would have been more beneficial to keep the mask on tight, never take it off; stripping my skin away to expose all the flaws, demons, and imperfections that I try in vain to hide.

I am a raw nerve; exposed to the world; vulnerable to side glances, hard stares, whispered criticisms, leering glares and opinionated 'conclusions'. I am just paranoid and insecure to the point of immobility. I thought I'd have been past it all by now but it keeps getting more and more intense. I'm still taking the prescription, the generic Prozac, but I still say that it is not doing any good. The only difference I have been able to identify is the fact that my heart doesn't feel as though it's going to burst through my chest quite as often as it used to. On occasion, it still beats to the point of exploding, it still pounds so hard in my head that I can't hear anything, but it's not as bad as it used to be. Everything else about me is in the same dastardly state. Sometimes I believe things are worse. I have no energy now. I'm tired all the time, like I've already said to you, and I still have all these pent up insecurities that make themselves known by my complete isolation. Other people take my isolation as a sign of independence and just the fact I'm not a real social person; more of an intellectual – an introvert who would rather be alone than in the company of anyone else. I think I've made myself believe that's how I should be. It's who I am. But I am just a lost, lonely little girl no one knows.

I don't really want to face myself and everything that is going on and going wrong. If someone were to press me into making a list of the things going right in my life, the things I like and enjoy, I don't know what I'd put on it. The only thing that really makes me happy is spending time with my cat. If most people knew that, they'd probably just pity me even more so and think me a sad, pathetic little creature. Maybe that's what I am. Jett is going to love me regardless. She's going to want to see me, she's going to want to spend time with me and she's going to be upset when I leave. I don't like the last part but it's nice to know I'll be missed by someone or something.

It's kind of painful to think that most of the people I consider friends don't even think of me most of the time and yet, here I sit, spending all this time worrying and thinking about them and wishing that they were thinking of me too. Maybe some of them are, but I don't feel like anyone really is thinking about me. I don't feel like anyone would really miss me if I were to go. Some friends I considered good friends are nowhere to be found; nowhere to be seen; almost as though they were never in my life to begin with. You think if I went to a confessional (even though I am not catholic) I could get a few things off my chest? You are my confessional, to an extent, but I am so wary about divulging everything about myself and everything I do to you because I am so paranoid that someone else is going to read this after I'm finished writing it. The only way I wouldn't care about someone else reading this is if I was dead, because, really, what's going to be done about it then? And besides, some of the worst things are going to go to the grave with me anyway, but until then, I'll have to live with all those ghosts running through my mind and invading my dreams.

Life is all give and take anyway – you give a little, people take a little more. One of the problems I deal with is the fact I just can't let anything go. I carry every little thing with me; every hurt, every slight, every insecurity, every moment of fear – how can anyone live life that way? It's nearly impossible and most always intolerable. When people talk of forgiveness they often say that one must forgive themselves. I know that I've even said that, stating that it's the hardest thing to do, forgive oneself. Maybe that's why I am as I am. I can't forgive myself for not being perfect, for not being strong, for not being brave, for not being whom I think I should be. I can't forgive myself for not looking the way I want to look, not doing what I want to do, not living as I want to live. I punish myself because I believe I deserve punishment and unhappiness. Why I feel that way, I don't know. I've just never seemed to live up to what everyone's expectations are – least of all my own. But do I even truly know what other people's expectations of me are? Or are they all my own expectations? And I just make myself believe that's what everyone else expects of me as well. "You are your own worst critic," is what they say. My mind is totally screwed up and that is what it all basically boils down to. Unhappiness follows me like a shadow – it stretches out to the horizon and back.

Do you think I'm getting desperate? Speaking of desperation, my weight has been fluctuating like mad lately. I've become obsessed with maintaining a certain weight and it is beginning (ok, it has been for a long time) to be a very unhealthy habit of mine. I've been maintaining between 120 and 115. At the end of last week I was about 119. That's due to the manic work I was doing, mowing all the 'big' cemeteries in three days. Besides 119 isn't even as low as I've ever gotten. I'm not that thin anymore. What was it? When I got home from Indiana last year, I was kind of at a major danger point – anorexia was beginning to play in my every thought, but I put some weight back on, as it's very hard to refuse food in this family with everyone watching and gorging themselves and wondering why I'm not eating. I haven't even been able to work out lately, besides mowing, because I've been too damn tired. So tired and exhausted that I can't even sleep. I haven't been sleeping well at all for the past couple of weeks. Perhaps it's lack of exercise that causes the nighttime restlessness, but how can I exercise when I can barely bring myself to get out of bed in the morning. I don't know why I am so fatigued all the time. Sometimes I think it is chronic fatigue. Other times I blame it on the work and still other times I blame it on my nutritionally deprived diet which, in all fairness, is probably the real culprit. But even when I do eat, I can't do anything. I haven't had any real energy since being sick. I've only feigned energy and that is so very tiring to do.

I regret my fallibility. That one time where I drank nearly an entire bottle of Tequila before heading off to Augusta; crying as I knelt beside Katie's grave as if she could really help me.

Thing is; I never really liked drinking. I did it because when I did, I wasn't me anymore. I was fun and could laugh and could be crazy and do wild things without thinking things to death. I could speak, I could raise my voice; I wasn't so inhibited by anxiety. But I gave that up – I have had to give that lifestyle up many times over. I'm not supposed to be a weak, helpless little girl. I'm strong, independent, nothing gets to me. Such a façade.

My life as a captive inside my head. There's a girl in there just screaming to get out and my insecurity won't let her face the world, fear of judgment and dislike. And how is it that I expect other people to like me when I don't like myself? I really can't, can I? I'm sorry for letting people down. I'm sorry for the loss of my friendships with them. But how can I make things right when I don't understand what went wrong?

I have failed. It hurts deeply. I feel like I'm bleeding out and there is no way to close the wound and I wonder how long it will last.

So every now and then, like tonight, I sit myself right down and cry my sorrows out. All of this just eats me up inside and makes me wish that I had never been born. So many things I would take back; so many things in life. I wish I could have just a little bit of belief in myself, maybe I could get started then, maybe then I'd be on my way to something better, somewhere better. So much that I missed this past year. I can't expect to live my life in such complete and total regret though and I have to find a way around it somehow. It's like the Great Wall of China though; I don't know if I can get around the sucker. I'd have to travel many, many miles unless I could somehow shortcut the journey and leap across to the other side. I'm not that talented though. No, I'll have to make the long, arduous trek by foot, by hand, by crawling and dragging myself through the mud. Nothing comes easy, you know. And to expect it to is to set yourself up for disappointment again. Won't you please stop doing that?

OCTOBER 13, 2004

It's a gorgeous day outside today. I have set up shop outside today, am sitting here in a sports chair with this laptop plugged into the battery power of my car (which is literally falling apart now) and writing to you underneath the bluest sky, no clouds in sight, not a whisper of misfortune in the air. Today is by no means warm, it's not really Indian summer here, but it's not too cold. I could stand it to be a few degrees warmer but as long as the sun is shining in a clear blue sky, I'm going to be out here reveling in the sincere complexity of nature. The leaves are all turning, they are all falling about my head, landing crisply on the ever hardening ground. Nature is beginning its preparations of preservation for the upcoming winter months. Soon the trees will be naked and bare, left to stand alone in the harsh lashings of winter wind. That is the only thing about fall that I do not enjoy – the ever fading of glory and of life; it's a slow, hibernating death that envelops the earth during these months where everything is solidly alive yet firm in its undercurrent of stasis. It's all alive and yet it looks dead. Winter can be beautiful. When snow falls and accumulates enough to cover the brown leftovers of fall and summer. The scorched earth has time to regenerate during these loathsome winter months. I believe that just may be my favorite saying during this time of year: "loathsome winter months".

It feels good to be out here writing again. I'm not cooped up in some hole of a room nor am I enclosed in the confined structure of my home on wheels (my car). I'm outside in the fresh air with a wide open sky above me, trees swaying in the gentle breeze all around me, dirt crunching beneath the soles of my sneakers and the sun shining down all around me. Simple elemental nature brings such peace and tranquility if one is willing to accept it in their soul. I think I am ready to accept those things.

NOVEMBER 25, 2004

IT WOULD SEEM THAT lately I have been having bouts of insomnia again. Tonight, apparently, being one of them so what better way to bide my time than by writing to you. Sometimes I feel as though I cannot write because of the medication I'm on. I know how ridiculous that may sound but I feel like a lot of my motivation to write came from those moments when I couldn't find any other outlet and though I still don't have an 'outlet' per se, I feel like the medicine has just put a wall up against what I'm truly feeling, to guard from the inclination to despair. But don't you realize that I despair, also, because I cannot write. Or is it that somewhere contained within the over 1300 pages of my journals, I have already written all there is to me? I haven't written half as much of me as there is. I've yet to discover all of me. Maybe I need new experiences to bring me to life again; maybe I need new love; maybe that's why I was so hell bent on calling all my long lost friends the other week. Maybe I just need the connections. Maybe I'm realizing, for the first time, that I need….. Someone. Maybe I can't do this all alone, maybe I'm not strong enough to be alone for all time. All that is, is an early grave. You know I've dug part way down but I have never reached the six feet mark which means if I'm wounded than I'm still susceptible to the hungry jaws of beasts that roam around me, picking up my scent, seeking my blood. I am vulnerable in my position, but who isn't? Sure, I'm maimed and wounded, bleeding invisible pain, but I haven't been devoured yet and there is no reason to ever give up hope. Sometimes I just want to feel all the emotions again, all the pain, all the hurt; I got so much creativity and passion out of those emotions. Why can't I accomplish the same through happiness and excitement?

I relate so much easier to the dark side of things, the hurt and anguish. Why is that? It takes actual work on my part to be happy. I cannot wake up in the morning with a smile on my face. I still have to remind myself to get out of bed and try to make it through the day. Whether anything good or bad happens during the day, I don't dare speculate. I don't really start out the day with high hopes because I fear they will all just be dashed away just as quickly as a dream vanishes upon awakening.

And I am so tired right now, all I want to do is go to sleep, and I cannot. It is very aggravating. I had been doing so well with the whole sleeping thing, I had been doing so well with nearly everything (except my insecurities) but now I can't sleep, all those old demons are running a relay race to catch up with me. I can feel them peering around the corners of my mind, waiting for the right moment to spring on me and tear me to pieces.

I try not to think of the things which I should not be thinking but I can't help it. The thought of death looms near. The thought of peace is at my fingertips. But neither comes at this moment. At this moment the only thing that comes is the incessant click-clacking of the keyboard keys as I type this out to you. The only thing that surrounds me are the treasures of my youth, the treasures of my lifetime. I am comfortable within this realm of familiar confinement; trapped with all my innumerable memories of precious moments that I wouldn't trade for all the money in the world. I have been blessed in this life. I recognize that. I acknowledge that. I am thankful for it. So why do I want more?

NOVEMBER 28, 2004

I HAVEN'T BEEN DOING very much of anything lately except eating. I am putting on so much weight now I try not to think about it. I try to remind myself that I have to eat in order to be anything, do anything, stay anything, but I still don't want to put on any weight. It seems inevitable though. I've already put on about fifteen pounds from last June or July. If I'm not careful I'm going to be tipping the scales at 140 soon. I remember when I was afraid of being 130 or even 120 but I've surpassed that mark already and am ambling towards the dreaded 140. If that happens I'm going to fast for a week and try to lose ten pounds again. I'd like to lose ten pounds right now but I don't see it happening. There is nothing for me to do because it is winter and it is cold outside and it's quite intolerable once again. I shouldn't even be complaining about my weight. I know this. But I do complain about it because, well, I don't know why.

Why do I care so much about being thin? My friend sent me a few photos that he had taken at the Pen this past August and a couple of the photos were of me and 'my' Jeep and I was looking at those today and couldn't believe how skinny I was. And then I looked in the mirror and all I saw was fat. My mind is telling and whispering to me one thing while common sense is telling me another. I want to not care about it. I want to forget about being insecure and I want to learn how to not be so damn sensitive all the time. If people aren't going to like me because of the way I look, why would I even want to hang out with them? I realize I'm not a superstar, I'm not a glamour girl and I never will be no matter how badly I want to. Sure, I mean, if I looked like Naomi Watts, I'd probably be a lot more confident and sure of myself. If I couldn't look like Naomi Watts, Angelina Jolie of course.

7:37 PM

I'm eating… again. I guess when one goes for a year without eating a decent meal, it catches up to them eventually.

That's when, suddenly, someone balloons up to three hundred and eighty six pounds with seemingly no provocation. It may be a random number (386) but it's a fearsome reality. Ok, so I don't actually think I'm going to get that big but there are days when I feel like it. You know I have a very warped sense of self; even when I was thin (like 115) I still felt fat.

I need therapy, I'll be the first to admit it but that doesn't mean I'm going to do anything about it. I wish I could afford to have my own psychoanalyst like Natalie Wood did. Although, she had one and look how many problems she still had. I mean no disrespect to Natalie or anyone for that matter. The only person I can be unequivocally mean to, is me. It goes along with the self-depreciating humor and the self-destructive behavior that I so sadistically display. Of course, I have no one to blame but myself. This steady diet of M&Ms and Dove chocolate is not helping me out any. Every now and then I'll indulge with some chocolate; it's been a persistent craving of mine for the past two days though. I mainly eat salad and apples, still occasionally graham crackers and those stupid fruit rings cereal. I've been implementing more water into my diet though, at least four or five glasses a day, usually two glasses upon waking and then before going to bed and a few in between during the day.

Why I can still justify talking about this to you, I don't know. I guess because it weighs on my mind, no pun intended. I could blame society for making me so self-conscious but I won't because that's placing blame where I shouldn't be placing it. It doesn't help but it all comes down to me and only me; my perception of myself and my own sense of self-worth which you know I'm seriously lacking, right?

Remember when I was telling you, a long time ago, how

I sometimes just have the urge to drive straight through an intersection without stopping? I did that the other day. It was not on purpose; I was not in a suicidal, self-destructive mood, but rather I was enjoying the thoughts of something and was quite happy, blissfully unaware, you might call it. My heart surely got a work out after the incident but in an ironic way, I accomplished something that I've often dreamt about trying. Nothing like a brush with death to make you feel alive.

DECEMBER 22, 2004

I didn't feel good today, J. I'm not sick or anything like that but I just didn't feel good. You know how things have been going relatively good for me as of late, both in life and love, well today I felt like I used to. I didn't feel alive; didn't feel as though life were even worth living; didn't feel especially thankful for being alive at all. I really just wanted to run away and hide from the world again and I don't know why. Things began to irritate me today; things that I have not thought about for a long time; people began to ware on me, which has not happened, to this extent, in such a long time. It's been an interesting week.

Monday I was in an accident, perhaps that was the bad omen for this week. I was heading towards Readfield, coming from Augusta, and I was just passing J&S when a white car pulled out in front of me. I tried to swerve around the car, pulling into the left lane and eventually the middle lane, and I thought for sure the car had seen me but no, of course not. I was almost clear of the car when it collided into the side of my car by the rear tire. Pieces flew off my car as I skidded around in a slight 180 before coming to rest in the center lane. The good news is it wasn't my fault and we got free coffee from J&S because we'd been in an accident.

It would seem as though I am falling back into old habits. I am so desperate to break those chains and yet I am constantly held at bay by them. I have shackled myself with this faltering insecurity and I cannot seem to escape. It continues to eat away at my soul. I am feeling that desperation again, that insistent need for escape. My pulse still races with the same urgency. Why all of a sudden have you come back? I thought I was finally on the road to being well. I don't suppose there is such a road for me to travel down. It continues to be a dark, twisted path that I follow. Where's the light?

My mother, father, sister and I circa 1982

My sister Jen and I around 1982-83

Self-Portrait, 2008, 27 years old

2000, Fairmount, Indiana at the James Dean festival. This was 2 weeks after the death of my friend and the man who owns the car, a replica of James Dean's Porsche Spyder, allowed me to cross the velvet rope line and took photos of me in the car. A bittersweet moment but one I cherish.

As Maid of Honor at my sister's wedding, October 18, 2003. I had dropped 6 dress sizes in a couple of months, due to an eating disorder.

Waking up in Indiana and most likely working on a paper due that day for my Criminal Justice class at IUK. I admit, I'm a bit of a procrastinator.

Family portrait with me, my brother in law Ronnie, my father
Jeff, my sister Jen, my nephew, and my grandfather Fogg.

My first visit to Los Angeles found me at El Coyote Restaurant
honoring Sharon Tate. This restaurant is where Sharon
and her friends ate the night of their tragic deaths.

First visit to the grave of Sharon Tate. A pilgrimage many years in the making. February 9, 2007

A night on the town Indiana, most likely heading to Giant Bar and Grill in Fairmount.

My first trip to Los Angeles, 2007. I had to visit the
Griffith Observatory where scenes from *Rebel Without A
Cause* were filmed. I am standing next to the monument
that was erected in memoriam of James Dean, a bust
created by artist and sculptor, Kenneth Kendall.

A profound Deaner moment. I got to wear James Dean's
gloves. I did not want to take them off. I would probably still
be wearing them today if I had them in my possession. Thank
you to Marcus Winslow for the opportunity to wear them.

July 2012. I had just met Hannah a few months earlier.
Here we are celebrating the 4th of July in Industry, Maine.
As the famous quote from the movie *Casablanca* goes, "I
think this is the beginning of a beautiful friendship".

Paying homage to Jimmy. One of my many,
many visits to his grave in Fairmount, IN.

February 10, 2007. This was my first trip to Los Angeles. I ended up crashing a party at artist Kenneth Kendall's house in West Hollywood. Though he had passed away in 2006, a James Dean birthday celebration was still held at his house every year. By the end of the evening I had found myself here, in the back of a limousine, drinking Vodka and Sprite, listening to stories about Jimmy from Marlon Brando's former makeup artist. Spontaneity always seemed to serve me well.

With my friends Teresa and Liana at the Kennedy/ King memorial in Indianapolis.

My favorite photo I took at the inauguration of President Obama, January 20, 2009. Sitting outside in the freezing cold for hours upon hours, I thought my friends and I would all suffer from hypothermia.

My friend Joe and I being silly, practicing our "Breakfast Club" slide on the rooftop patio of the James Dean Gallery.

In my friend Mark's classic car. Photo
taken in Gas City, Indiana.

Getting ready to hit
the town while living
in Kokomo, Indiana.

Another proud Deaner moment. Here I am in the barn at the Winslow Farm in Fairmount, IN, where James Dean grew up. I have my hand in the cement print of Jimmy's hand.

Deaner's Hallowed ground. Standing near the spot where Jimmy had his photo taken in 1955 at the Winslow Farm, Fairmount, Indiana.

With my dear friend Mark at the James Dean Gallery.

Patrick and I at Barney's Beanery in West Hollywood.
This is where Janis Joplin spent her last night
before succumbing to a heroin overdose.

With my grandmother, Isobel, in 2013. Gram passed away
October 20, 2014. I was devastated. She was my best friend
and biggest supporter. The thing she wanted most was for
this book to be published before she died. Well, that and
a Jaguar car. I wish I could have made both happen.

Me at White Sands, New Mexico. This was a place I longed
to travel to for many years. When I moved to California,
I planned out a route that would take me there.

My mother and I on my 28th birthday.

In my element, at the billiards table. Pool is more than
a hobby, it's a passion! Photo taken by Joey Taylor.

June 2015. With my nearest and dearest, Katt. Meeting this girl saved me after my grandmother passed away. I couldn't ask for a better friend and roommate than this most wonderful person.

A picture taken right before heading to El Coyote with friends in Los Angeles.

A proud aunt with my nephew and my newborn niece. 2009.

In homage to Sharon
Tate, I donned the
hippie headband
for a photo op.

A photo op stop on Mulholland Drive in California.

My self-portrait entitled Three Faces of Eve,
referencing the movie of the same title.

June 2015, age 34. Most up to date photo of myself. Waiting
rather impatiently for this book to be published! But if
you're reading this then... Mission accomplished!

In NYC at the wax museum. Hanging out with the
Spice Girls. I always joked I got kicked out of the band
because I refused to wear a sequined halter top.

A dream is sometimes just a dream. At the wax museum
getting up close and personal with Brad Pitt.

One of my best friends, Patrick. Hanging out in Fairmount, IN.

Visiting Marilyn Monroe's final resting
place in Westwood, California.

My good friend Joey, an amazingly talented musician. We met in 2008 at Sawmania and have remained friends ever since.

My father and I in 2013 at my niece's birthday party.

Patrick and I doing our recreation of the iconic image of James Dean and Rolf Wutherich. We are on the original road, Highway 466 (now decomissioned). This is the last road James Dean would drive on before his tragic death on September 30, 1955.

Paying my respects at the crash site where James Dean died in Cholame, California.

A trip finally realized. Here I am at Joshua
Tree National Park in California.

With my sister, Jen, and niece, Katy, in 2013.

My little minions! My niece and nephew
and I celebrating my 33rd birthday.

Katt and I on a mini road trip, gearing up for a real road trip in fall of 2015. As my friend Joey said to me, "You two seem like the ultimate traveling duo". I think he's right!

With my dearest friend, Hannah, who has always supported and encouraged me.

My mother Penny, grandmother Isobel, sister
Jen and I, celebrating Christmas 2013.

A four generation family portrait. Christmas 2013.

Ruminations of Self

APRIL 4, 2005
2:02 AM

MY MIND IS RACING, just racing around and around in circles. I had this strange urge to dig out some of my photo albums so I have just spent the last twenty minutes or so looking through all of the photos that I had taken during my years in school. My friends, my classmates, strangers to me now. I am a stranger to myself. Maybe it's been the inactivity of the past couple of days that have worked me up so much right now.

Its past two in the morning on the fourth of April and I am more than wide awake. My heart seems to beat fast for no particular reason and yet my body feels so weak right now. My hands continue to tremble and shake and yet it seems to take every ounce of strength I have to type out these words. My eyes droop but can find no sleep. My mind is flooded with thoughts and can find no rest; images collect in my sight but everything remains dark. There is no place to go right now. Where does that leave me? I'm hoping that if I dispel enough words than I will eventually be able to render myself into a semi-sweet lullaby and fall asleep. Whether that will work or not, I don't know. I could lie back down on my bed and close my eyes but I am afraid of just lying there, indefinitely, with no consolation of sleep.

MAY 8, 2005
1:23 AM

MY FRIENDS: WHAT MAKES your time so much more precious and worthy than mine? You have a control over me that you know you can use to your own advantage. Try as I may, I cannot seem to refuse you. My time is spent thinking about how I can better your life. If I put the effort and time into thinking about my own life maybe I'd be able to get beyond this paralyzing moment. I don't know why I fear losing you. It's not as though I even have you and yet you seem to be omnipresent in my life.

I think I believe I love you. But I don't think I actually do. I think I like the idea of loving you and though I do love you I don't think I *can* love you; not in the way people are really meant to love one another. I don't think I can give you, nor anyone, all of me. Isn't that what one is supposed to want to do when they love? Maybe I still have an adolescent frame of mind when it comes to love. Then again, if I am feeling this conflicted it is probably not love, merely an infatuation is probably what I suffer from.

I am simply enamored with you; with the idea of you; with thoughts of protecting you from the big bad world. How can I protect you or anyone when I am the destructive force of my own life? How can I save someone else when I am destroying myself? Why won't you save me? I should think it would be pretty obvious that I am in need of saving. Maybe no one cares enough. Perhaps I'm just that good of an actor. My life is pretend. My life is an act. How can you be true to yourself when you have no real identity? My identity consists of extracurricular hobbies; my identity consists of perceptions.

My perceptions of Self: I don't think I can even answer that right now. Have I no perception of self? Have I no sense of my purpose? I used to think you were my purpose. I used to think he was my purpose. I used to think she was my purpose. I used to think I had a purpose; something meaningful; something that would make a real difference in the long run. Am I foolish to think I matter that much in the world? Do any of us? A handful of people, perhaps, but every day, common people? Do we matter to the world at large? No. Do we matter to the world that surrounds us; our own little atmospheres of friends and family? Yes.

So then why do I feel such worthlessness? Why do I retreat in such hopeless defeat when I do not get the recognition or the acknowledgement that I give to others? My life seems to revolve around everyone else's world. I guess I just haven't been intuitive enough to create my own world. I instead try to work my way through the outer shell of everyone else's.

Will they accept me as one of their own or keep me cast outside their inner sanctums only allowing me quick glimpses inside? Maybe I'm just happier and more content knowing that I inhabit my own planet; my own little world of solitary confinement. Give me a rose to take care of like the Little Prince and let me wander the worlds in search of friends. "Anything essential is invisible to the eye," the book by Antoine de Saint-Exupery says. You are essential because you are not here. My friends are essential because they are not here.

Is there no constant to be had? No consistency? The most obvious retort would be that the only thing that remains constant is the fact that everything changes. I love ironies, don't you? Life is an irony and death is even more of one. If I were to die, would you love me then? Would you miss me? Would you ever think about me? Have I not infected your mind as you have mine? My thoughts are often venomous to my well-being. Quite detrimental are my innermost yearnings and desires for knowledge: to know what no one can know; to understand the things that have no apparent reason; to gain the knowledge of why things happen the way they do, when they do.

Hurtful are the times of separation, but more hurtful is the time spent wondering if it could have been different. Many things should be different, but given the opportunity, would they be or even could they be?

It comes down to fate and destiny. Was it fate or destiny that led me to you? Or you to I? If things in the past had not happened exactly as they did, when they did, I would never have met you. Would I be better off for that or worse? I feel I would be dead. My heart would have stopped beating long ago because it would have given up on itself. The pain has become so subtle and dull when it was once so forceful and encompassing. I used to suffocate because of the pain but now I can breathe through the darkness that sometimes engulfs me with its passionate isolation. It is not as agonizing as it once was. But it is always there with every beat of my heart. Pain that stems from what, from who, from where and when. There are so many instances that are the cause of that ever-present pain. Am I even able to pinpoint just one?

I've been beat, I've been taken advantage of, I've been the victim of coercion and peer pressure; I've been unable to get a hold of my surroundings and stand on my own two feet.

The ground below me is constantly shifting. Tremors rumble below the surface disrupting the stability and causing me to stumble and fall so often I sometimes think it would be better if I were to never get up.

This isn't all because of you, of course. You hold power over me but not that much power. I don't suppose I live and die with your words and actions. I may feel that way in certain moments but they pass. As this too shall pass.

If I were able to sleep tonight, it would pass much more quickly. Perhaps I would wake up with an invigorated sense of worth and contentment. Or, more likely, I'd wake up with a headache and heart on the verge of combusting. It's not every morning this strikes me. Some mornings I rarely think of you. Some days pass when the thoughts of you are as few and far between as thoughts of the fall of the Roman dynasty. Those are the days when a smile seems to find me without my knowing it. Those are the days I look forward to without ever putting expectations upon them actually arriving. It's my addictive personality that is the bane of my existence. It's the obsessive-compulsiveness that distracts me from concentrating on anything for longer than a minute and a half; sidetracked, as always, by constantly changing thoughts all revolving in and out through an endlessly turning door. One second I am thinking of you, the next second I am thinking of him, the next of her. And yet it's you that I always come back to. It's you who I always seek out in times of distress or unease. I seek you out but I don't let you in so you never know just what is going on. It all goes back to the pretending bit I have become so good at. If I pretend everything is fine, then it will be. Of course I realize that this is very far from the truth but on my own little planet, it's the rule of thumb to live by. As I sit by and watch my rose wither and wilt away to nonexistence. Without my rose, I'll truly be alone.

But things are not as dire as I may have made them out to be. I'll lay the blame on the fact it's two o'clock in the morning; insomnia has stuck its claws into my eyelids again and I'm stuck here in an ongoing thought of you. Things could be worse, you know. By the time I go to sleep and wake up again I'll have forgotten about this transgression in my mind and I'll yet again be able to make it through another day.

Maybe it's time to get a start on that.

(2014: I had a friend during this time that I would have done anything for. This friend of mine gave no consistency in our friendship. I waited on him. I waited for him to acknowledge me in a way that left me feeling loved and wanted. At this point in my life I was yearning for nothing more than a meaningful relationship, friendship. Perhaps, for my entire life, I have wanted this. But during these years of such distress with my fluctuating emotions I wasn't able to give anyone all of myself. With no one I felt I could confide in, I felt truly and utterly alone. The one man I thought I may be able to love rejected me and I began to think I was not meant for love. In truth, even to this day (2014) I still have those feelings on occasion. But I have experienced friendship, relationships, that were, and are, meaningful. There is nothing as freeing as being able to be oneself with another).

MAY 25, 2005

THE MORE I READ of the book about Bulimia, the more convinced I am that it was actually I who wrote it. Ok, so I'm not crazy enough to believe that, but the symptoms, the feelings, everything they say in that book is describing me. And if it's describing me, that means I'm bulimic. Alright, that is not a news flash. It still takes a lot of honesty to admit it forthrightly. My mind is consumed by no other thoughts.

I found myself thinking about the situation and how dire it all seemed to be. No, not seemed to be, *seems* to be. Even after reading all these things, I still seem to be in the 'wrong' frame of mind. I suppose that's because my mind doesn't know how to work in any other way. I will have to train myself to think differently. I just read a chapter about that. Reading all this is fine and good, though I feel a bit more debilitated afterwards, but what good is it really going to do me if I don't do something with what I know? If I had asked myself that question when this all began, instead of naively assuming (as most bulimics do, that it was all a phase), maybe I wouldn't have gotten down this deep into the trench.

I now wonder whether or not Carole is going to tell Maggie about my own eating disorder.

It fluctuates. Sometimes I just decide that I won't eat and other times I eat and feel terrible so I purge. Right now I'm trying the not eating kick. Why? According to the book, in an effort to avoid the real, deep-seeded, emotional issues that are complicating and making my life into a living hell. They didn't exactly word it that way in the book, but perhaps they should have. I am the one who makes my life into a living hell even when I don't want to. I am the one who does these things when I know I don't want to be doing them and yet still I persist in the behavior because, for a few moments thereafter, I feel release. Then, of course, it seems to come back at me three-fold and the vicious cycle begins anew. For the past two evenings mother has prepared dinner and told me that the food was ready, and I have not ventured down to get any. I woke up this morning and went downstairs to find that my empty plate was still sitting on the counter. I will probably go down later tonight and find there is still a cheeseburger waiting for me and though I will probably want to eat it, I will not. And if I do, I'll probably feel guilty afterward and purge it out of my system.

Now the hard part is going to be: who am I going to talk to about this for real?

MAY 26, 2005

DON'T YOU THINK I'D be trying to get a handle on my situation instead of avoiding it, and food, entirely? I don't understand how my mind is working right now and I think reading about all of this has confused me even more. Reading through that book I bought kind of made me feel even more hopeless, like there's really no way I'm ever going to come through and get over this. There's not a chance that I'll recover. Then I have to take a look at all the other aspects of my life because, apparently, there lies the real root of the problem and when I do venture ahead and take a look at those other aspects of my life, I absolutely detest what I see and refuse to accept that it's me. Because this is not me is it? Aren't I more than this? Is it just who I have become?

I feel absolutely caged in right now. I feel I want my mind to just stop working altogether, stop thinking, stop obsessing, stop debating, stop this negative flow of thoughts that have me all wrapped up so tightly I can barely breathe. Reading that book and reading the paragraphs dealing with body image distortions, I can recognize, I honestly can, that I do the same thing. I look in the mirror as I have just done not two minutes ago, and I see myself as huge. And I try to tell myself that what I'm seeing is not really what other people see. Other people tell me I'm too thin (though I have gained a little since this time last year. Wait, this time last year I was nearly on my deathbed… unbeknownst to all, it really was a direct cause of my eating disorder. Had I not been bingeing and purging at the time, I would not have developed the abscess, and I would not have nearly died because of an ungodly infection that seeped its way like venom into my bloodstream). But I'm not too thin, I think to myself. In my head right now, at this moment, I can hear myself saying, "I'm not thin enough. If I could lose just ten more pounds then I'd be satisfied". And it never stops. It's constant. It's nagging. It's debilitating. It's an ultimate refusal of acceptance for myself. I cannot accept the things I do not like and I do not like myself. I don't see why I should. Here I go again – reading that goddamn book is going to split my personality until I'm a schizophrenic. Oh, and that brings me to another point: I probably have a personality disorder. Nothing is right about me whatsoever. My mind is so consumed right now that it's really no wonder I can't sleep. I can't stand talking or thinking about this anymore.

JUNE 18, 2005

I DON'T THINK I know how to give myself a break. I don't know if I've ever actually given myself a break, let myself calm down and relax. If I'm not all tensed up about something, then I'm afraid I'll get lulled into that false sense of security again, and when that cocoon wraps around me, it doesn't keep me safe, it suffocates me. It wraps that plastic bag of fear around my head so I cannot breathe. And then I begin to think, and then I can't stop thinking and then suddenly I find myself up and awake at two o'clock in the morning with no hope of getting to sleep anytime soon because of all the damn noises that infiltrate my ears and drives me to the brink again and again and again. I don't know how to stop this, J, or if it's even possible to stop it.

What is *it*?

It is that thing that keeps me up at night.

It is that thing that makes me wish I were dead or that I was never born to begin with.

It is that constant companion, that lingering shadow that lurks even in the dark, ready to trip me and watch me stumble over my own two feet as I try to regain my composure to try again.

It is that nagging little voice in my head that tells me I'm worthless and I have never done anything right in my life and that I have not bettered the world at all with my presence.

It is that persistent feeling that accompanies me whenever I try to do something new, it sets me up for failure before I even begin.

It leaves me no chance for success and barely any chance for survival. I survive merely because it's an automatic reflex to do so. I breathe not because I want to but merely because my body does not know how to stop and stay stopped.

It is that lifelong battle that I am faced with (for however long life may last)

I'm not suicidal, J, but sometimes I wish I didn't have to defend myself by saying it. There is a difference between being suicidal and simply wanting to die. Sometimes I wish that death would find me like it seems to find so many others. Others who, it would seem have (had) so much more to offer than I. What happened to me to make me believe that I don't have a chance in this world? Where did I go wrong? Was it I who took the wrong path or was I led astray by someone or something else? Is it all just an accumulative effort that makes me the way I am today? Too many questions, always too many questions and never enough answers. There are always answers, I guess, but they never seem to be right, they never seem to fit.

My body just wants to collapse into a heap sometimes because it feels as though I just cannot go on. There seems to be the question of: why go on? For what? For who?

JUNE 20, 2005

DO NOT BECOME CONSUMED.

Consumption is a nasty habit of mine. Consumption in the matter of obsessiveness. My compulsions overtake me for days, weeks, even months. Whatever it is becomes an all-consuming passion and I'm driven in the matter, whatever it may be. And when it wears itself out, I'm left openly exhausted, irritated, agitated, scornful even. Scornful because it has ended and, frankly, I get kind of pissed off about it. The fire eventually burns itself out. It has become a habit for me to tell myself, once another of my obsessions begins to just go with it because, sooner or later I reason, it's going to quiet down. The blaze will whittle itself down to a little flame. That flame will extinguish itself to a glowing ember. That ember will eventually cool down to reveal nothing but a charred remnant of what once lived there.

That kind of sums up how I feel inside right now. I'm a hollowed out, charred and burned building of something that once lived with passion and fervor and excitement. If only I could ignite that little glowing ember once again, maybe I'd find encouragement there. Maybe I'd find contentment. Maybe I'd find a future. How is it possible to hide in a burned out building? There are no walls so how is it that I'm still invisible? Shouldn't people be able to see me by now? Shouldn't they care? Were they the ones who unwittingly burned me down? Was it arson? Was it a pyromaniac gone awry? Did I torch myself to rid myself of the pain; to numb the emotional undercurrent away?

I don't think it worked. I wanted to be with someone today but when I get that way I seem to pull myself further away from everyone.

JULY 11, 2005

I'M IN OKLAHOMA CITY right now gearing up for the World Cup of Softball. I spent most of this afternoon looking for my hotel. After awhile, quite awhile, but I won't say just how long I spent doing it because it's embarrassing, I finally realized that I had spent all day looking for my hotel as I went south on I-35 when I should have been going North. When I finally realized that, I found my hotel no problem. Sometimes I'm just an idiot. Looking forward to the games!! All my favorite softball players!!! It will be amazing.

(2014: 2005 marked the first time I ventured to Oklahoma for the World Cup of Softball. I made friends there. I made friends that I had fun with. We went wild at the games. We cheered, we laughed, and we had an absolutely amazing time. It is in the moments of travel, still to this day (2014), when I feel free. The open road, me and my car, traveling to a destination I want to be. I often feel the need to be somewhere else. And though my disorders have never stopped me from travel they have inhibited me, to an extent, from interacting with strangers. I spent most of my time alone when I traveled. But there were times I opened myself up to the possibilities of making friends. And I made some incredible friends. Friends I still have to this day. It was through my years of travel that I experienced that feeling of peace that I so yearned for. The open road is still my favorite place to be).

SEPTEMBER 13, 2005

RESTLESSNESS, MY ONLY COMPANION, sits beside me tonight as I write to you. It needles my brain with its uneasiness and cradles me in a crushing embrace. My body doesn't obey my mind. I tell myself that I should be tired. I tell myself that I should be falling fast asleep but my body revolts against these assumptions and urges me to go outside and run, to jump, to do anything but try and rest. Do not relax, seems to be my body's motto. And though my body wants to keep going and going and going, physically, I'm drained. Emotionally, I'm destroyed.

This oppressive gray world is what I feel I belong to right now. I think it is what I was borne of. My little ol' demons seem to be popping up once again. I just had this image in my head of the 'whack-a-mole' game but instead of little mole heads, they're my demons and I get to just stand there and pummel them, one after another. But just like the game, you can't destroy them; they just keep popping back up, time and time again.

I have this incurable inability to believe in myself. Something that sounds so easy really shouldn't be so damn hard and yet whenever hopes do arise in me, I find myself being pulled down by an unseen anchor. This anchor harbors me to the ocean floor and only allows me so much reach. Wouldn't it be wonderful to break that chain someday? Wouldn't it be invigorating to be able to resurface in the world, swim ashore, dry off and walk through the white sands until I'm able to find a place among the rest of the world? But I continue to struggle. I flap my arms in useless circles and get nowhere. The undertow sucks me back under before I even get a chance to breathe. The anchor cuts and chafes at my skin where it's tied. One of these days the anchor may release me but then my body will be so bloated and lifeless that I'll continue to drift waywardly, deeper into the seas. I have to wonder if the tides hold any prosperity for me at all. Or will I continue this slow death of drowning.

A Solitary Existence

JANUARY 31, 2006

SOMETIMES I CANNOT FIND the depth of character to be pleasant. Wherever pleasantness derives from, whether it's the soul, the conscience, or simple learned manners, I seem to lack it on occasion.

I just quietly go about my business, which is none too exciting, and converse in mere chit-chat, small-talk, mindless questions and answers – the norm: 'how are you?' – 'I'm fine, and yourself' – 'good, thanks' – 'ok, have a nice day'. The conversations, as you can see, are none too stimulating. I find the fault to be my own though. I am still socially inept and though, I admit, at times I do crave conversation, I'm still a hard sell on tolerance. I keep trying to fight this solitude. I should be out there, mingling with the rest of common society. Sometimes I find myself out there doing just that but more often than not, I occupy my time doing something on my own. Maybe that's only because I haven't that one trustworthy friend that I so desire to have by my side. I have friends but not A FRIEND – do you know what I mean? Not one that I can count on, day or night, to rescue me from this banality. Not one for whom I can do the same. And like most other things, I find this lack of trustworthiness irritating. I would like to find a friend who would be as fiercely loyal as I, someone who will not betray me nor my heart; someone who will fight with me on certain points, not someone who will acquiesce constantly to my point of view (something of which I fear I do in hopes of sustaining the friendship)

I think that's one of the reasons that none of my relationships ever work out. The guys I date always surrender too easily. I find I can manipulate them so easily, even unintentionally. In essence, they are all too like me. I sometimes think I need someone who will grab me by the shoulders and literally shake some sense into me; someone who will not run away when I throw those piercing glances their way; someone who isn't afraid to step on my toes a bit and tell me that's just how it is. I may find I don't like it, actually I know I won't but it may be just what I need. I need someone strong – stronger than my stubbornness. I, for one, am not strong and I know this. I am weak, but my weaknesses are often mistaken for strengths; they guise themselves as confidence and fortitude, but all it really is, are my frayed nerves trembling so violently that there's complete stillness. There's a certain poise in being scared witless. There's a particular air of confidence that comes with being a nervous wreck. And that is me – all the time.

My inability to cope with stress in a reasonable manner is certainly going to do me in. My anxiety is reaching alarming heights yet again. My solitude is increasing as my social skills are going out the window. Never strong socially to begin with, I fear the only stableness I will ever find will come with a reclusively independent lifestyle.

Could I rise above? Or is it that I'm just so damn afraid of rejection and failure that I refuse to even try to accomplish anything?

APRIL 16, 2006

MY PRIORITIES NEED RESHAPING. I need to undergo a serious makeover: mind, body, and soul. Don't even get me going on the whole 'body image' thing right now. I have gained so much weight that I'm to the point where I feel it's useless for me to try and maintain a diet. I keep thinking about that day, how many years ago is it now? When I was house-sitting for the Perry's and mother had brought me over a pizza and as I sat there eating it, I suddenly felt as though I were 600 pounds and I vowed right then and there that I was going to put a stop to it. And I did. From that moment on, I began to eat only one meal a day. Soon, that one meal a day, turned to barely a meal a day. Then 2003 came. I got a job coaching JV softball. I began to be even more self-conscious and would only eat when someone mentioned that she never sees me eat anything – then she would practically force feed me a cookie or something. I remember when she made me sit with her on the bus to an away game one afternoon and she called me anorexic – which is funny to me still considering that I was by no means underweight at that point in time. That would come later – almost a year later. But then things went from tolerable to intolerable. I received some bad news, I mentally crashed, and then occasional eating took a downward spiral and became an obsession with losing weight. An eating disorder developed; a combination of bulimia and anorexia. By the time 2004 came around, the only things I was eating were bananas and chocolate milk. I was riding my bike forty or fifty miles a day. Anything less and I would feel as though I would gain weight simply by existing. And then, April of '04, I stopped eating all together. The fast only lasted for a month or so but my quality of life slipped even further downhill. I had no energy and yet I was still riding my bike, playing tennis, playing basketball, and doing Tae Bo every day. And when I started to eat again, I would get sick. Then I really got sick. Then I nearly died because of an infection.

I managed to eat while I was on my deathbed but after I got better, and after the 'recovery' meal at the Olive Garden, I stepped right back onto the path of old habits and it began again. Summer of '04 found me at my thinnest and frailest. When I saw photos of myself I would gasp because my arms were nothing but skin and bone. I decided to get healthier. Then I would revert back to the obsessions. Then I would say I was sick of being that way and I would try to get better. Then I would again slip back into those old comfy slippers of self-denial and waste way. Up and down, up and down. That was my life, my battle, my instability. I vowed to get better. And then this winter came and I was unable to resist food for the first time in three years. I haven't been able to go a day without eating like I so often used to. My perspectives on food and health haven't really changed but my body has demanded that I fuel it with energy and I haven't had enough energy to fight the urge. I have no real resistance anymore. And I am by no means saying that is a bad thing. My views about food and nutrition are still warped but deep down I do know the right and wrongs and am trying to correct it. I am trying to come to terms with the fact that my idea of perfection is unattainable; that perfection in and of itself is unattainable and I shouldn't have to try to be a certain way in order to please others out there. I try to tell myself that I need to get healthy, but I have been struggling with this for so long that I've forgotten just what it feels like to be healthy.... to wake up in the morning energized and ready to set out for the day. I am hoping that one day I will find out what it feels like to be healthy again. I'm not giving up. You've at least got to give me some credit for that.

JUNE 11, 2006

I SEEM TO LOSE people just as soon as I think I have them by my side. I find myself suddenly drifting away from them, as though they are standing still somewhere and I am being pulled away by the tug of an unfeeling wind. I feel as though I am screaming at them for help. Pleading with them to hold me close, but the wind drowns my cries and they can't hear me. They think I am drifting off towards independence, but I know that I am being forcibly dragged away towards my dungeon again: towards the dark abyss that awaits me as though I was born of it. Maybe I was. Maybe I was born of this dark isolation that suffocates me – a plastic bag over my head that kills me with my own breath. I am being pulled away without my consent and I am reaching out to my friends who are standing firm and still. They are right there and they seem to only be an arms' length away – and yet I can't reach them. My fingertips lightly brush against their skin but the touch is so faint and insignificant that they don't notice the urgency contained therein. My pain and despair cannot transcend the touch and I continue forth, falling blindly into the current of air that transports me farther and farther away from those I wish to be near. And there is still that nagging little voice in my head: a voice I recognize as a variation of my own, but it is deeper and resonates more darkly inside my mind. It is a voice that continues to tell me of the worthlessness of my existence. It seems to delight in brandishing me with incompetence and reaffirming me with an almost lethal dose of self-doubt. It urges me to pull the trigger of decision. But the decision it wishes me to make is not a decision I am going to entertain. The thoughts rumble through my head but I try to cast them aside. I use every little ember of hope that still exists within me to fight the onslaught. Embers can only burn for so long before they are extinguished though. What will happen then? What can reignite that hopeful fight within? I wish I possessed a brilliant conflagration of Hope, but I must continue to sift through these coals, scrambling around on my hands and knees trying to find any sign of orange glow, a burning coal that I can softly breathe upon and give life to. With the winds that threaten to carry me farther away, you'd think hope would be burning brightly, but too much wind, too much air, too much breath upon the coals and they die out. That which is supposed to give life can also cause death. There is a fine line between too little and too much. We must search for the balance, the happy medium, so to speak. But I do not know if there is such a thing. My emotions teeter so violently on the edge that one simple word may be enough to break me. My emotions feel so volatile inside my head. There is this tumultuous yearning I have; a yearning to feel accepted, a yearning to belong somewhere, to feel as though I belong somewhere.

I am living but I barely feel alive.

These dreams of mine seem to slide through my fingers like sand. I feel that if I could just pick up one tiny granule of sand and keep it locked tightly inside my palm, then that one dream may come true. Out of all the dreams I have, out of all the things I want, all those little granules of sand that contain one dream, if I could just hold onto one of them, I may begin to believe in the possibilities of attaining more. But those little granules of dreams fall through my fingers and scatter on the ground, landing among everyone else's lost desires. My hands are too big and my fingers too clumsy to ever be able to hold onto something so delicate. And my dreams, like the sand, shatter beneath the weight of trampling feet. They get scuffed out and kicked around by unfeeling and unknowing people. And that one tiny granule that I long to feel tickling the skin of my hand falls aimlessly and silently to the ground. There are no discernible cries of despair as it dies and there are no pangs of guilt it feels as it leaves me because it doesn't know that it's just broken my heart. It figures that I have more hopes and dreams to hold onto and I won't miss it. It feels it can be replaced but it can't. And I become frantic in my search to regain it. But it gets lost among the ruins and time doesn't comply.

Time doesn't know of the pain it causes. Time doesn't know how I measure it into interludes of happiness, anticipation, excitement, disappointment, and fear. Time doesn't know when it's being wasted or when it's being relished. At times I wish I were that naïve. I wish I wasn't so aware of all these little undercurrents of emotion. I wish I could exist without hinging my happiness on things I have no real control over. But it is not so easy to change. Not after twenty-five years. But on the other hand, twenty-five years is a long time to have never been able to change. And it all comes back to that vicious little voice in my head that tells me everything is my fault. I am guilt-ridden for things that don't even pertain to me. But that is how I am, who I am. How do I become someone else?

SEPTEMBER 24, 2006

I DON'T KNOW WHY I seem to insist upon putting my life on the slow burner when, really, it seems more like a pressure cooker. At any moment I feel I am about to burst; I am about to lose all control.

Simple joys, like writing, have become things I fear. I turned the tables on myself until I was terrified of turning on the computer and writing to you. I feared you. I don't know why. It seems to be a pattern though. Every time I seem to find something that I so thoroughly enjoy I find some way to sabotage it. I find reason, as irrational as they may be, to turn the things I love into things I fear, despise, hate, even loathe. I don't know if it stems from that innate guilt I seem to carry around that tells me I should be punished or if it's because I'm afraid of allowing myself happiness and joy for fear that it will all suddenly be ripped away from me and I'll become so desolate because of its absence that I would chastise myself for ever having loved to begin with. So maybe, subconsciously, I have decided to forsake the things I most love and cherish so I won't be desolated when something inevitably happens and takes it away from me. I don't know why I do the things I do. Then again, there is no real logic in madness is there? Isn't that why it's referred to as madness? It is chaos imbued with fear. I start projects full of hope but soon find myself at a crossroads – one that is so familiar and yet I've never ventured forth, I've only retreated, cowardly, back into the womb of my own false sense of security.

My whole life seems to implode upon itself day after day after day. I am waiting for the moment when I will find the correct keypad sequence to change the trajectory of this silent attacker so I may be the victor for once and not the victim. Don't get me wrong, J, I'm not labeling myself a victim or anything because that's ridiculous. My problems don't deserve such glorification. I'm no martyr.

There is too much to sit and contemplate all of the time that I find myself once again in a paralyzing stasis. In moments such as this one, I find myself often going back and poring through my old journal entries. And when I do this I realize just how long this has been going on. And it makes me wonder why nothing has been able to correct it thus far. And I get angry because nothing has changed. Even when I think something has changed or something will change, I usually end up right back here. It's not even the starting point that I end up back at. I haven't even been able to reach the starting point yet. I'm nowhere near the blocks, nowhere near the point of launch when I can propel myself into action. I'm still wandering through the players tunnel, lost in the dark, unsure of which way to go, which way to travel, which way will bring me out into the open light of the arena. I'm afraid the race is going to be long over once I do find my way out and the new arena is going to be as old as the Roman Coliseum. And then what could I possibly do to catch up with the rest of society or civilization for that matter?? Why do these players tunnels have to be so confusing? A labyrinth of perplexing portions and I haven't a guide to lead me! No, the guides have all be reserved for the players with money and I haven't any. I can't afford a guide so I'm left to wander around the tunnels of this bleak underground for as long as it takes me to find my own way out. It really shouldn't be so hard should it? One of these days, I swear, I'm going to stop walking altogether and I am going to sit down on the cold hard floor with my back leaning against the wall and I'm going to stop. The darkness will become icy. Frost will bite at me with its gnashing teeth, feeding off the warmth of my body. But my muscles will stiffen; they will atrophy from this forlorn paralysis and will forget the basic elements of movement. The darkness will only become darker. It will engulf me with its own solitude, enveloping me within its own inhuman structure and it will devour my eyes, plucking them out of my head like gumballs from a machine. The walls will seem to constrict, to fold in upon themselves until the tunnel's passageways seem no bigger than a tomb. My warm breath will collide with the cold air and the floor and walls will become slick with condensation. Bugs and worms will find their way in through the cracks and crevices and burrow themselves underneath my skin, consuming whatever is left of my ravaged body. Centuries may pass before they ever find me. Some advantageous archaeologist will unearth this quiet tomb that buried me and I'll become the find of the century – the "Lucy" of Gen Y!

2007

A Change of View, but nothing really changes

(2014: I MOVED TO Indiana in December of 2006, to begin classes at IUK. Criminal Justice was my major. I lived in Kokomo, IN. Kokomo was roughly 30 miles from my second home, Fairmount, where I had friends. But the isolation ensued. While I attended classes, I made no real friends. I spent nearly all my time alone in my apartment with my two cats. It was a solitary existence, living in Indiana, away from my family but I felt it was something I needed to do. I wanted to see if I could survive on my own. But I soon found that I was nearly incapable of maintaining a healthy way of life. I dealt with the loneliness by self-destructing and reverting back to old habits).

JANUARY 4, 2007

I'VE BEEN AT IUK for the past few days, dealing with people. I do not deal with people well and I don't know why. It's becoming more of an issue. I know the Prozac did not help. Trazedone was like taking a horse tranquilizer. I do not put much stock into any medicine as it is. I should go to the doctor but I detest such interaction as what takes place in the doctor's office. I cannot calmly sit in that little cubicle of an exam room and wait for endless minutes. It leaves me with too much time to think, too much time to change my mind, too much time to think of lies and ways to escape scrutiny. But it leaves me time to criticize myself, to deliberate on my decisions. It simply leaves me with too much time to think. And when I have too much time to think, I analyze, I criticize, and I imagine scenarios that really have no likelihood of happening but become more and more plausible with each passing minute. And when the doctor's assistant finally comes in to ask me what the problem is and why I scheduled a visit for that day, I smile as though nothing is really wrong and say, 'anxiety' or whatever the problem is. Then they ask the initial questions as though they are warming me up for an interrogation. But then the doctor comes in, flips open the folder that bears my name, briefly scans the page and says, in his or her best impression of a Freudian disciple, 'what seems to be the problem". I always feel like saying, 'well, doesn't it say right there in the folder why I'm here? Why should I have to repeat myself? First I told them over the phone why I wanted to schedule an appointment, then I had to confirm with the receptionist upon check in as to why I'm here, then you sent your little stooge in here beforehand for a prelim of questions and now you're here asking me the same thing! Do you think my story is going to change or are you unable to read what the paper in my folder says?" But I never say that. I only sigh, a slightly longer-winded exhale as though in minor irritation or exasperation, and repeat myself once again, "anxiety". Then they ask me to diagnose myself, he or she says, "Why do you think you have anxiety?" and it leaves me wondering why do these doctors get paid so much when all they seem to do is ask the patients to self-analyze their own problems? The only thing we as patients are unable to do is write our own prescriptions... probably because when we would self-medicate we would find ourselves in the emergency room getting our stomachs pumped. When someone has severe anxiety and is prone to panic attacks at the drop of a dime, the last thing they need is to be essentially interrogated by someone they deem a threat. And let the record show that

Katherine L. Fogg

most people within close proximity of someone with severe anxiety is more than likely considered a threat.

There are so few that we let in, that we let get close, that we allow to see the vulnerable side of us. And we may not even let those closest to us see the vulnerable side... but we let them know there is one. They may not see it, but they know of its existence. And just the fact that someone out there knows that we are vulnerable, knows that we are susceptible to such things, calms us in a way that would surprise most. Most often we are afraid of letting people get that close or know that much about us. Most times we do not want to admit to ourselves, let alone anyone else, that we are so vulnerable. But when that outer shell is cracked open enough to let someone see us in such a way, know us in such a way, it does bring a feeling of peace and a certain sense of calm. Be we are very, very picky about who gets to see us that way, about who we let in. It doesn't happen very often and most often it happens only with someone similar. It happens with someone to whom we feel instantly comfortable. We follow our instincts more often than most.

JANUARY 7, 2007

I SEE MYSELF AS a spool of thread... once packaged and wound so tightly together, I was brand new, unflawed.....
But a few scissor snips later and I have come unspooled. I'm no longer a fine point that can be threaded through the hole in a needle, but I am frayed – and when trying to thread me through the slight opening, the only opening that leads to the

open air on the other side, I cannot find my way through. I unintentionally put up a resistance to that opening because I've come undone. The frayed ends disperse in such an erratic manner that there is no hope for recovery except to snip off another piece of the line and hope that the thread stays together long enough to see itself through another opening. But it inevitably happens again. The thread becomes frayed so another piece is snipped from the end until nothing is left but a bare spool. I am not only fraying at the ends but there are knots and a multitude of flaws to deal with. I suppose that is how I see myself sometimes. I am desperately trying to fit through that small opening, but after repeatedly banging into the sides of it, I become frayed at the ends. I suppose the term 'frayed nerves' can be derived from similar reasoning??

APRIL 16, 2007

THE TOPIC OF THE day here in English class is to write a paper about what you are passionate about. Of course, I am exempt from writing this particular paper simply because I was one of the chosen ones. That is, I was picked to write a short story in lieu of regular class assignments during the second half of this semester. I chose to 'write' about my (previously written) short story, "Buried Alive." I wrote that story nearly five years ago, I believe. My instructor seems absolutely intrigued by it. I chose to re-write that story because I have not had it in me to create any new stories of my own. I have not had much creativity in me in any capacity whatsoever.

I was reading through some of my journal entries last night (my 2007 journal edition is paltry) reading up on my 'all-consuming' thoughts. I am having more of those. Albeit, these thoughts are of a different light than my all-consuming, passionate thoughts about: I MUST GO TO L.A. (although, I am having more of those same thoughts recently…they are not as intense as two months ago, only because I have satiated the need to explore L.A. already….but I am more than ready to go back.) Lately, my thoughts have centered on my appliances. Namely, the shower drain and why it is clogged. As you can probably tell, nothing exciting has been happening here in Indiana. Kokomo is not an exciting place. Indiana is not an exciting place. Then again, nothing is as exciting and lively as L.A. and Hollywood. I was spoiled by my experiences there. I was spoiled by the incessant activity that envelops the city. I do adore Indiana, but only because of James Dean. I have come to realize that, contrary to what I have always believed and thought, I may need to be someplace like L.A. or Hollywood. I may need to be somewhere where something is always happening and there is always somewhere to go, something to see, people to meet and talk to. L.A. has a culture of its very own, steeped in rich Hollywood history, and you know that I am attracted to that. Perhaps the biggest attraction I have is that of the Hollywood scene. I would never move to L.A. or Hollywood with the sole intent of becoming a paparazzi stalker, but to be in the vicinity where so many productions take place, well, that would be fascinating.

(2014: My trip to Los Angeles was incredible. It was a whim. I woke up one morning and said, "I must go to L.A." I booked a plane ticket that night and reserved a rental car. My first stop in L.A. was when I got pulled over by an officer for, apparently, nearly running over a pedestrian in the sidewalk! When it was brought to my attention I merely thought to myself, "Welcome to L.A.". Despite that ominous beginning, I fell in love with L.A. My first stop was to Sharon Tate's gravesite at Holy Cross Cemetery in Culver City. A pilgrimage I thought I must go on, much like paying homage to James Dean. While I was there I had it on good authority there would be a James Dean birthday party at famous artist Kenneth Kendall's house in West Hollywood. He had passed away but there was still to be a gathering at his house. I crashed it. I didn't know a soul there but I found the house and walked in to find many other Deaner's there. This is where I met my very good friend Patrick for the first time. The party was amazing. Being lucky enough to go through the house of Kenneth Kendall and see all of his magnificent works, paintings, sculptures, I felt blessed. And the night concluded with me in a limousine drinking vodka and sprite while conversing with Marlon Brando's makeup artist and his wife. I came away from that, and still think that, it was one of the most amazing experiences of my life).

APRIL 23, 2007
10:08PM

TONIGHT I TRIED TO think of what I wanted to do, of what I could accomplish if I tried. I had wild ideas for a novel. I had an intense urge to write, write, write. I still would like to write. I have been on the cusp of writing a book for such a long time now and I don't know what is holding me back. Besides myself, that is. I am the only thing in my way. My fear, my insecurities, my impending sense of failure and doom persist in holding me back. I don't know how to get over that hurdle. I do not know how to move beyond that obstacle or even around it. I'd sidestep it if I could – but to circumvent such a thing would be like trying to walk around the Grand Canyon; I would give up or die before I ever finished the trek. My mind feels like a ditch, where all these murky, muddy ideas are collectively discarded and left to ruminate in their own solitude. I give them no life and I do not nurture them into existence. My ideas remain on the side of the road, hidden beneath the trash and litter that accumulates in the ditch alongside them. They slowly and silently drown in the water, slowly fading away to non-existence. I would like to be able to breathe life into them again. I would like to be able to breathe a little bit of life into myself as well. I hope that day is soon; the day when I will find the courage and the strength to believe in myself and at least try to make my ideal destiny a reality.

APRIL 24, 2007
8:58AM

YOU KNOW THAT I do not know how to sit still, to be in one place and one time. Whenever I go somewhere, whether it is to class, to a movie, or even sitting here at home, I am never just 'here.' I am always away, somewhere in my mind drifting along the shallow tides of my imagination, hoping to be carried out to sea. Part of me longs to be lost, floating absent-mindedly on the waves of my own creativity, rolling on top of the sea of dreams and wild imaginings. But as soon as my mind drifts off in one direction, there is a black hole waiting to suck me up and unceremoniously transport me back to the reality of life. Not all of reality is a bad thing.

Not all of reality is a barren land of red dust, rattle-snakes, and vacant yearnings. Maybe I do have the potential to become what I want to be. Maybe I do possess some sort of talent. I must somehow find it within myself to realize that potential, that talent, and utilize its strengths in order to go somewhere, do something, be someone. I just do not know how to reign it in. I do not understand that I am capable of many great things because I have no sense of self – I have no confidence nor would I know what to do if I had any. Part of me longs for the simplicities of life, while yet another longs for the recognition that comes with accomplishment. Most times I feel like hiding away (and I do) in my own, safe little world, but there is yet another part of me that wants to break free and step out into the light and be seen, be heard. I am at constant odds with these two selves – they are a disproportionate pairing; they do not compliment the other at all; they simply fight a game of tug-of-war at all hours of the day. Maybe it really all comes down to what I mentioned before: that feeling of having no sense of self. When it comes to me, I realize that I do not know myself. I always say that there is no one in the world, not friend nor family, who really, truly knows me. But I am beginning to realize just how much of a mystery I am to even myself. I am an enigma that seems too complex to unravel because, simply put, I am a contradiction of every sort. I am 'wishy-washy' on my best days. I cannot seem to utter a declarative statement to save my life. I seem to focus only on the negative aspects of myself. I can see no positives. There must be something about myself that I find endearing? Isn't there? Nothing comes to mind. Maybe I should go get some coffee now. It has been a long morning so far.

2008

Restlessness and Indecision

(2014: I MOVED TO California in October 2007 to attend Brooks Institute of Photography in Santa Barbara. I moved in with a roommate in Oxnard, CA. The funny thing is, when I left Indiana for my final destination, California, I had no apartment waiting for me. I had nowhere to stay. It was when I was in Albuquerque, NM watching a Women's USA National soccer team game that I got the call informing me I had a place to stay! I'm not sure what I'd have done if that call had not come through but I imagine it would have involved me living in my car for awhile. Simple little miracles can save! However, my time at Brooke's Institute of Photography was not well spent. I decided that I knew how to take photographs and anything else I may learn, I could learn on my own and not spend $30,000 a year in tuition. I decided to enroll for online classes. I did this knowing that I'd be able to travel and attend classes. I wouldn't be buckled down in one place, one time, essentially shackled to a learning institution that kept me grounded in place. My urge to travel dominated my desire to attend classes in a classroom and the solution seemed so simple: attend online classes).

JANUARY 1, 2008
9:15 PM

I HAVE TO DO something meaningful with my life. I need to feel as though I am making a difference. That being said, I know that you are probably none too surprised to be hearing it.

Christmas was interesting, spending it alone here in California.

JANUARY 6, 2008

IT IS DONE. I am no longer a student at Brooks Institute of Photography. I have disembarked from that fleeting aspiration and have taken a seat aboard a new Line with a new destination. The same morning that I withdrew from Brooks, I was enrolled @ Kaplan University, an online regionally accredited school. I now find myself in pursuit of a degree in Criminal Justice. My lifelong vigilantism gene may finally get the satisfaction it has so long been awaiting. That is, if I can follow through this time. You know I have never been good at following through with things. I am not good at keeping in touch with those briefly encountered acquaintances when promises of lifelong friendships seem so attainable. I have never been one to seek out the long-term relationship of any kind: friendship, romance, career..... Everything in my life seems to be an opportunistic foray: from the people I meet to the places I go. It really is as though I have no purposeful destination in mind when I set out to do things. I may think I do, but sooner or later I find myself reorganizing my thoughts and ideas and suddenly I am thrust into a different direction. Every route I seek out seems to end, not abruptly, but in a rotary... around and around I go before choosing a different exit, an alternate route that may or may not lead me to the beginning of the end, so to speak.

JANUARY 14, 2008

IT IS ALWAYS A bit difficult to change even when you are running from that which you never did enjoy. I have hardly had a chance to really settle in here in California and I am disrupting the flow of things already. I don't think it is possible for me to be still, even though outside appearances would have one believe that all I am doing in life is idling along with no real ambition or purpose. Sometimes I begin to believe that too. I simply cannot seem to make up my mind. Life is so short, opportunities brief, and indecisions flourish with every breath.

JANUARY 15, 2008

MY SKIN (IN FACT, my entire body) has softened with the perils of inactivity. Perhaps it is not 'too little, too late,' and perhaps it is. I do have a tendency to throw the white towel in long before it is necessary. I have to get back into shape. I will feel better. I will have more energy. I may even boost those serotonin levels and give myself a boost of confidence along the way. They say it takes 7-14 days for the body to learn a new behavioral pattern, such as exercising. I have completed three full days so far so I can't give in now. I keep remembering the days last spring and summer when I would go out and run six miles at five thirty in the morning. I don't know what or who possessed me except maybe Prefontaine's spirit but even so, those days have long since passed as well. I went out and ran a couple times here a few weeks ago but that soon lost its luster. The cyst on my left foot swells with each determined step on the pavement and at the end of a two and a half mile run, my foot and my knees are throbbing in sync with my heartbeat. (Obviously.) I once entertained the idea of getting into swimming because it is so low impact, but that would involve the whole sordid affair of bathing suits and going to a public place, like the Y, to swim in a pool. There is the ocean, but c'mon, it's January for starters and I hate the feeling of being a shivering, salted peanut upon emerging from the ocean.

Lately I have been fighting that temptation to run away. I wrote to Sharon earlier this morning and told her how that wanderlust has been trying to seize me lately. The temptation is so strong sometimes that I find it so hard to resist. I keep planning, plotting and scheming in my mind on ways to take an adventure. Maybe that temptation wasn't abated by reading the book, "Into the Wild." I do not want to go tramping around the Alaskan Bush with nothing but five pounds of rice and a book on edible plants, but I would like to venture far away from this little nest. Perhaps another reason why that wanderlust has not been abated has been because of my enrollment @ Kaplan University, an online school. Now that I have no real educational purpose of staying put, the urge to move is upon me like mountain lion on a deer's carcass. (A vivid description, no?) The temptation to run is a ravaging assault you know. Unless you have been at the mercy of such a thing, you cannot understand how it feels. My heart pumps and with every dull beat I can hear a whispering encouragement to run. My mind is tackled by thoughts of adventure and my entire body reacts to such enticing stories with that primal survival of the fittest tactic. There is a vibration deep within my soul that begins at the center and spreads out like a ripple on a staid pond surface until my entire being is hit with the ramifications of that one simple thought: RUN. And until an action is manifested, the ripple becomes larger and more prominent until I am quite literally drowning in my own ignorant refusal of compliance. When I do not cave into such intuitive urges, my body and soul deflate and crash. It is loud and jarring, this crash. The impact sends me spiraling down into that all too familiar void of defeat and failure. It feels like the end of the world, Doomsday is upon me when I relinquish and resign to idle wonder instead of taking part in an active pursuit of adventure. But the world is bigger than you and I. These problems are trite and of little consequence in the grand scheme of things.

JANUARY 28, 2008
12:27 PM

I AM HAVING SUCH a terrible time lately. It is my own fault. I have tried to correct this problem for years and years and it just never seems to go away. I cannot figure it out nor can I seem to maintain control over it. Lately it is has been getting a little too out of control. I suppose that is what it all comes down to in the end anyway: control, or lack thereof. We all strive for control and when we realize control is just an illusion we feel powerless, helpless and, oftentimes, hopeless. There are too many questions that I keep asking myself; too many questions that I keep expecting to find an answer to that have no answers because it is all hypothetical nonsense. I have been feeling sick lately anyway. I have been feeling Sylvia Plath sick; trying so hard to reach the highest summit but slipping and ultimately falling down, far below the beginning line. It is exhaustive to try and regain that sense of purpose once you've fallen to the ground again.

There are reminders everywhere I turn; there are memories; moments; there is honesty when I don't want to hear it and won't acknowledge it even when it is bashing against the side of my head. Too much honesty makes a soul weary. When one it truly honest with themselves, that honesty seems to be a discouraging antagonist. That truthfulness is a mocking tribute to inadequacy and failure. I have failed and there is no denying myself of that truth; it is a glaring reminder, there every time I dare to open my eyes wide enough to see. I immerse myself in the meaningless trivialities in order to sustain some semblance of normality when all it accomplishes is to remind me of the attributed flaws that possess me in these moments of self-loathing. I am of the type who try to convince themselves that if we do not see something, it does not exist; if we have the instructions before us but choose not to touch the paper or read it or acknowledge it then it will not be our fault for screwing up; we can rightfully claim ignorance without letting others know that we had the opportunity to read the correct procedures. It is a silly little game to play yet it is another strategy for keeping myself safely locked in my cage; concealed behind imposing steel bars that can only be penetrated with my acceptance and willingness; both of which I keep vested inside, afraid of the consequences of allowing people in. Don't think I haven't tried. I have tried. I have succeeded and failed. Such is life, I suppose.

FEBRUARY 13, 2008
5:33 PM
BARNES & NOBLE: VENTURA, CA

JUST THREE DAYS AFTER writing the above entry I was on a plane headed for Maine. Friday morning, February 1ˢᵗ, I awoke with only one thought on my mind: "I have to get out of here at any cost." Without even getting out of bed, I reached over to my desk and grabbed my laptop computer, got online, found a reasonably affordable flight, booked it, and began packing. My flight was to leave the next morning, Saturday, February 2ⁿᵈ, at 11:15 in the morning. I didn't bother to mention it to anyone and it was only by happenstance that my roommate found out I had a trip on the horizon when he walked into the apartment and, with my bedroom door ajar, noticed the suitcase on the floor. "What's with the suitcases?" he asked me. I said, "Going on a little trip." He inquired as to where and for how long but I sidestepped with vague answers knowing full well that it was pointless to circumvent around the truth when it would be blatantly obvious thanks to Facebook and Myspace. Before parting he did mention that he hoped I wasn't planning on moving away indefinitely because I was the best roommate he has ever had thus far. That little comment tweaked a nerve-ending of guilt in my brain for a split-second before I pushed the thought from my mind and focused on my own mental well-being. (Of which, may I add, is in dire need of medical assistance if this path continues on the same trajectory.)

I arrived at LAX thanks to the shuttle that runs from parking lot B to the terminals. I had no idea how I suddenly came to be at LAX, one carry-on suitcase with me and no real plan. I had to call my mother and tell her that I needed her to do me a favor and pick me up at the Portland Jetport Saturday night around ten thirty. So she and Antonio were the only people who knew what I was doing. No one else had any idea. I didn't really even have the time to realize what I was doing either before I found myself sitting at the gate waiting for my flight to board. I happened to be walking through the terminal and was about to turn a corner when I came face to face with Martin Sheen. It was very odd. I said, "Oh, hi. Excuse me," in that flustered way one talks to a stranger they inadvertently bump into on the street. He smiled and replied with a greeting of hello and that was that. I walked away thinking to myself, "Hmmmm….. That was Martin Sheen." As you can see, not a real poignant moment of excitement

I have lost my train of thought, as so frequently happens when I find myself going on a tangent on an unrelated topic. I was telling you how I had impulsively purchased a ticket to Maine. Yes, I ran into Martin Sheen at LAX and that was a moment to remember, I suppose. I boarded my flight and we took off. I had to change planes in Philadelphia but that was the only connecting flight I had to catch.

And I suppose I don't have to tell you how wonderful it was to walk through the doors of the house and find Mackie and Chance there! My two little fur balls of joy who are always happy to see me.

Sunday was an ice-fishing excursion on Flying Pond. It was to be my nephew's first ice-fishing experience and I wanted to capture the moment with my camera, which I succeeded in doing even though I detest ice-fishing. I got soaked to the bone and was shivering cold for much of the day thanks to not having the proper attire and staying longer than I had anticipated out on the frozen lake. When we first arrived at the ice-shack, everyone dismounted the snowmobiles and began organizing their things. As they were busy talking and sorting things out, I looked out across the lake and noticed three very large deer. I alerted everyone else to the sight and they just couldn't believe it. They had never seen deer out on the lake with such deep snow before. And they were large deer, very large. It was a beautiful little sight, reminding me of a Winter Wonderland scene.

Of course, lest I forget to mention, Sunday, February 3rd, was the Super bowl showdown between the Patriots and the Giants. I didn't really want to mention it because it was disastrous. I don't know who was out on the field in Patriots uniforms but it wasn't our team. What a horrible showing. That's all I really care to say about it. Except that my nephew was dressed in a little Patriots uniform and looked adorable. He was the best part of the night, save for the reactions of Gram, Grandpa, Patty, Marvin and Tabitha when they all walked through the door and saw me. Luckily Gram did not have a heart attack at the sight of me but, boy oh boy was she ever surprised. Grandpa couldn't manage to get his words out, except to say hello a few times, like a broken record.

It wasn't very long before I had to head back to the airport to board a plane back to L.A. My ten day stay in Maine went very fast and it snowed nearly every day. It was nice to be able to be there with Mackie and Chance though. They did remember me. And I felt even worse when I had to leave them behind again. I did not want to come back to my apartment here in Oxnard.

I boarded my flight to L.A., with a connection in Chicago, around five thirty in the evening on Monday, February 11th. There was an hour delay in Chicago due to weather. The flight from Portland to Chicago was interesting only for the fact that the woman who sat next to me tried very hard to find things to say and even though I replied with courtesy and cordialness, I didn't want conversation. I felt a little guilty at that because she was a very nice woman. She was of middle-eastern descent, small, petite, about a foot shorter than I. She reminded me of Malika Oufkir. I never got her name but she was from Laredo, TX and said she didn't think she could stand another winter in Maine. I concurred and she had my sympathies for that. We chatted more as we neared Chicago, but for most of the flight I tried to keep my nose in the book I was reading: "In The Dark of Night," by John Saul. I read the biography of Clara Bow on the flight from L.A. to Portland and wanted to go a different literary route for the flight back to L.A.: something mindlessly entertaining and I remembered how much I used to love John Saul books for he is still my favorite horror story author, even though I don't often read those kinds of books anymore.

The flight from Chicago to L.A was much nicer because I had the three seat row all to myself so I could stretch out, which was rather difficult considering I still had to be seat-belted in. It was a very long flight, filled with a mixture of tension and anticipation. I wanted to get back to L.A. so badly but I didn't want to go home to the apartment in Oxnard. The plane landed around midnight, or a little thereafter, I can't quite recall, and then I had a hell of a time getting onto the shuttle that would take me to parking lot B, where my trusty little Leganza was, hopefully, still waiting for me.

When I did flag down the appropriate shuttle and, miracle upon miracle, it actually stopped to pick me up, I was on my way. I found my car no problem, paid my 80 dollar parking fee, and headed out onto the streets of L.A.

FEBRUARY 15, 2008
6:19PM

BACK IN THE OLD familiar Ventura Starbucks after a long day on the road and I am exhausted. I did not expect to be on the road for about seven hours today. I woke up this morning and decided to try my luck again and head up North towards Cholame. Last time I tried that little venture I got pulled over for speeding. This trip, however, saw no run-ins with the law. I did not realize when I set out this morning to visit the site of James Dean's death that it was so very far away. I looked up the directions on MapQuest and that really should have been my first clue that this was not going to be a simple little jaunt down the 101 to route 46. When I finally did arrive in Cholame and saw the Jack Ranch Café where the chrome tribute to James Dean sits wrapped around the Heaven tree, it was very strange. Further down the road when I actually came upon the James Dean Memorial Junction, it was even more strange. In fact, after nearly three hours of driving to get there, I was uncertain that I wanted to be there. There was an unsettling feeling in the air. I didn't really want to stay very long so I took a few pictures and was on my way back nearly as soon as I arrived. I spent probably thirty minutes or so there, which was plenty considering there is nothing to see given the fact that Jimmy pretty much died in the middle of Nowhere, California. Still, it was something I had to do. I have directions to 10066 Cielo drive. I've been debating about it for a long time. And by the way, 10066 Cielo drive is the new address. Sharon and Roman's house address was 10050 Cielo drive and after the house was razed in 1994, the new house was given a different address. Anyway, I don't know how I feel about going there. Actually, it's quite obvious how I feel about going there: it will be more than emotional and I don't think I'm really going to be able to handle it.

FEBRUARY 19, 2008
7:38PM

SUNDAY NIGHT FOUND ME at El Coyote, my favorite restaurant, enjoying a pleasant conversation with Caleb, one of my favorite people! It turned out that only Caleb and I decided to celebrate Jimmy's birthday... belated as it was. I arrived at El Coyote quite early, nearly an hour before we were to meet, only because I wanted to get out of the apartment (no real surprise there, right.) It was my first encounter with Valet parking as well and I can honestly tell you that I would prefer to drive and park my own car only because I hate paying. That being said, I did enjoy having the car door opened for me. Too bad I have to pay for such chivalry. I did not know who was going to show up at El Coyote so I did not put my name in for a table. I instead waited patiently inside the entrance for nearly an hour before Caleb showed up. During that time I ran into Robert Osbourne. When this older gentleman walked through the doors I felt a twinge of recognition but couldn't quite put my finger on what his name was. So after he sat down, I kept stealing glances over at him, and noticed that he kept stealing glances at me which was rather odd, but then it hit me, TCM Robert Osbourne! When the rest of his party arrived and he stood to greet them and spoke a few words I knew for certain that it was him because of his voice. How many introductions have I heard that man give? So he walked up to the counter to tell them his name and, just to confirm what I already knew, he said, "Osbourne." That was the only real 'celebrity' encounter of the evening. Caleb texted me and wanted to know if I had gotten Sharon's booth but I did not ask for it because I didn't know how many people were going to come, even though I had a feeling that it was going to only be Caleb and I. (which was for the best really.) I also told him that I didn't know which booth was Sharon's even though I had a feeling I knew but I had never asked them because part of me didn't really want to know. But I remember the feeling I got when Sophie, Brooke and I went to the El for lunch one day and they sat us in this booth in the back and as I sat down I got this feeling that it was Sharon's booth, where she and her friends sat that fateful evening in '69. All throughout lunch that day I couldn't concentrate and I kept looking around at the surroundings of the booth and I just had this feeling. Well, at dinner Sunday night, Caleb and I were led to our table and he asked if I wanted to know which table was Sharon's or not. I told him that I did and didn't but that my curiosity would get the better of me so he asked one of our waiters. Sure enough the man pointed to the table where Brooke, Sophie and I had sat that day at lunch and though I wasn't surprised by the revelation because I had that feeling that day, I was still overcome with such profound sadness that I nearly started crying right then and there. The only thing that saved me from making a fool out of myself and crying in the restaurant that evening was being in the company of Caleb. We had such a lovely evening. At least I did. We had a couple drinks, he the house margarita and me the Tequila sunrise. I had my chicken taco salad and he enjoyed a beef burrito. We talked for a couple hours while we sat in El Coyote reminiscing about Jimmy and he indulged me in my love of Sharon and listened ardently as I spoke about her. There are not many people with whom I can talk about Sharon with that know anything about her as I do. We spoke of politics, the government, the upcoming election, traveling, the Black Dahlia, criminal justice, crime investigation, photography, my grievances at living with a roommate, his previous marriage, my reluctance to get involved, cars, racing. I don't know what we didn't mention in our conversation. After we finished our respective meals we drove over to Melrose Ave. and walked the street taking photos. He had his Lomo camera and I, of course, my Nikon D80. All in all we spent nearly four hours together. It was so great to be able to go out with a real friend and just enjoy the evening. I do not have many real friends out here. As I grow older and older it becomes more difficult to find someone with similar interests, humor, and demeanor. I am truly amazed and awed at the way things seem to come together.

NOVEMBER 2008

THIS IS MY THIRD attempt at writing a blog about my NYC experience.

I once read a quote from someone who said, "One

should never meet their idols because they will ultimately be disappointed".

Let me just say that I think this is complete bullshit. There is always a possibility that someone will disappoint you but never a certainty. Rest assured that I was not disappointed in the slightest upon meeting one of my idols: someone that I have admired from the time I was ten years old. (And for the sake of my own sanity, let's not tabulate just how long ago that actually was, okay).

I used to be adamant that there was nothing on or in this great big blue and green earth of ours that could get me to go to NYC by myself. I travel everywhere else alone; I drive across the country by myself all the time, since I was eighteen and first struck out to the Midwest with nothing but youthful exuberance and diet coke stockpiled in the cooler in the backseat of my car. But NYC? Hell no. Not alone.

Well that was before I saw these little words all strung together: "Sawmania"; "November 14-16"; "Shawnee Smith"; "NYC".

Apparently my fastidious determination to never go solo to NYC had been called into question. I had an easy answer though. Ten minutes after finding out about Sawmania, I had already called and coerced two people into lending me money and/or buying me a 'gift' for my (then) upcoming birthday, November 17th. Fifteen minutes after finding out about it, I had called and ordered tickets. Twenty minutes later I found myself staring at my computer screen mapping out my route. Four days later, I was on the road to NYC for the first time. Alone.

I left my house at 9:30 PM Friday night. I had already been up since 5:30 that morning so I don't think it's necessary to tell you how insanely exhausted I already was. I was banking on adrenalin and excitement to keep my eyes open through the long, dark, rain soaked night. Well, that and my Janis Joplin tunes blaring from the CD player. Janis and I made quite a duet for eight hours. My favorite song to sing is Mercedes Benz and though I felt as though I was rockin' the tunes, looking back I am now considering the possibility that it was sleep deprivation and a little bit of tone-deafness that made me think I was hittin' the notes Joplin style (this is also another perk of traveling alone...no one has to be verbally assaulted by my rockstar impressions).

Mercifully, I landed in NYC at 6:30 AM Saturday without having fallen asleep behind the wheel. But now what? I had to wait until 9 AM for the doors to open and I was in Chinatown without a clue as to where to go. I parked my car, not in a garage, but in one of those parking places that puts cars on lifts...so I couldn't hang out in my car to wait. I had to walk around. After an eight hour drive, it's always nice to get out and walk around but I was in NYC alone, it was raining, I was severely sleep-deprived and a little bit overwhelmed by what was going on. Never have I felt like such a little girl, small and vulnerable in the big city. I don't like admitting that but it's true....especially as I walked the Manhattan bridge.... seeing every shadow out of the corner of my eye and sensing danger in every hidden crevice of the darkened subway tunnel. Overactive imagination is never more rampant that when I've been awake for twenty-six hours straight and in a city I've never been to before, especially NYC. When I went to Los Angeles for the first time (again I was alone... and no one even knew I'd gone). Anyway, when I went to L.A. the only thing I felt like was that I was home. In NYC, completely different.

But let's get back to what's really important here: Sawmania, Shawnee Smith, Tobin Bell, Costas Mandylor, Beverley Mitchell, Mike Butters, Mark Rolston, and Betsy Russell. All these fine actors in one setting, for one weekend, to meet 'n greet the diverse "SawManiacs" who traveled from far and wide to be there. When I walked into the "inner-sanctum" of Sawmania, the first person I see was Costas Mandylor (not a bad first sight to behold!) the first room was privy to Mark Rolston, Costas, and Mike Butters: all had separate tables cordoned off with little ropes in an effort to corral the fans and maintain some semblance of order. I had picked up my tickets at the will-call beforehand and only had an autograph ticket for Tobin Bell and Shawnee Smith. I wasn't sure how much money I was going to have going into this venture so I obviously ordered those two tickets beforehand (and ended up purchasing quite a few more as the day wore on!) Tobin Bell's autograph table was downstairs in "Crash Mansion", owing to the inevitability of long lines of autograph seekers for the legend himself. Beverley Mitchell was in a room with Betsy Russel who eventually did show up – having to take a red-eye from Los Angeles (where she's starring in a play). Shawnee's room, separate from the rest on a split-level, and became a haven for a diverse array of Shawnee Smith groupies, myself included of course.

Given the task of ascribing one word to each of these individuals, I came up with these, based on my own brief encounters with each:

Costas Mandylor = delectable (what else can I say! He's just awesome)

Mike Butters = amusing (see Sat night pictures for proof)

Mark Rolston = pleasant (didn't get to talk much to Mark but he was always very kind and patient with everyone there...and I just saw him on an episode of The Mentalist last week!)

Betsy Russel = dedicated (I say this because she took a red-eye to be there for part of the day...other than that, I didn't really interact all that much with her)

Beverley Mitchell = delightful (she's a charming young woman...her role in Saw II was so atypical for how 'we' are accustomed to seeing her...but she's so personable and lovely! And so damn adorable!)

Tobin Bell = supercool (yes, it's one word and yes it's true. The man just has that 'quality' about him; intangible and indescribable, he just exudes coolness)

Shawnee Smith = divine (this list could really go on and on ...for the reason that I don't think there's just one word I can use to describe Shawnee Smith because, let's face it, she's been one of my favorite actresses since I was ten. How can that possibly be equated to one word? It's like trying to sum up my feelings for James Dean or Sharon Tate – and we all know that's an impossible task. Regardless, Shawnee is absolutely wonderful. She's fabulous and beautiful!)

Shawnee and her pal, who, by the way, sets the standard against which all other 'light monitors' are measured, well, they were the most awesome people around. The words that come to mind when I think of them are words like: awesome, totally cool, sweet, wonderful, beautiful, and genuine. It was my birthday in a couple days and somehow, some way, it happened that Shawnee and Jane gave me the Smith & Pyle CD for my birthday – Shawnee signed it for me and I thought to myself, 'this is the coolest birthday present I have ever gotten!' and it was. It is.

We, as in the Smith groupies, spent hours in that little room hanging out, talking to one another, and, at one point, engaging in an impromptu jam session with Shawnee (thanks to Joey who had his guitar with him) of course I, at this point, was taking pictures...pictures, pictures, and pictures, like I always do. If you've ever been on the other end of my camera lens (and chances are you have) then you know what I'm talking about....and the only thing I can say to both Jane and Shawnee is THANK YOU for putting up with it! But of course, as I always do, I edited and took the best pics to give back to those ladies...the memories belong to us all. I did manage to get us all (Claire, Pat, Joey, Shawnee, and me) into a group shot to 'commemorate' the jam session, plaintively adding, "hey, I kinda want to get in this picture here!" to which Shawnee replied "you're like Jane, always behind the camera and never in the pictures!" this is not the first time someone has said that to me and I often make that same remark...hazard of the trade I guess.

I managed to get some really cool shots during this time and also during the Q&A sessions.

Anyway, the jam session was beyond awesome simply because it was so unexpected and so spur of the moment. (Special thanks to Joey for helping me to remember the list of songs performed!)

Joey began things by playing one of his original songs, "Breathless." I think Pat may have taken over next, playing "Under the Bridge" by Red hot Chilli Peppers, followed again by Joey playing "Plush" by STP. Then it was Shawnee who graced us with a couple songs, both playing guitar and singing for us. First playing a cover of what we (as in Joey and I) are tentatively calling a G. Brooks song, but we can't be certain because we don't really remember. But next up she performed one of her songs, "Flower", which just happens to be my favorite. It's such a beautiful song. Really, nothing could top having Shawnee perform that song right then and there but our little group had one more song in mind and we had a little group chorus going as we 'performed' "Killer Inside" by Hydrovibe. Of course ;-)

Much of the day was spent right there in that room. I met the most amazing people. I made some great new friends. It really was more than I could have ever expected. I could go on and on about every little detail but I won't. Suffice to say, the word "Amazing" doesn't even begin to describe all the little moments that made up that day.

And the Saturday night party – man o man – what a time! Really, the only thing you need to do is look at my pictures from Saturday night and you can get the whole story, or at least make up your own story to go with the pictures.... and you probably wouldn't be far from the truth!

Towards the end of the evening Saturday night, when Jane and Shawnee were making the rounds and preparing to leave, I was talking with them and John Raybin when Jane pulled me aside and suggested I tell John how great the weekend was and how much fun I was having. "Okay", I said, "I can do that". So I tapped him on the shoulder and exuberantly told him how great Sawmania was and how much fun I was having. Then I remember Jane pulling me aside again and telling me I should get a picture of Shawnee and John together. "Okay," I said, "I can do that". So I tapped him on the shoulder again and asked if I could get a picture of Shawnee and him together. No problem. Then I remember Jane pulling me aside again and saying, "Okay, now tell John that before you found out that Shawnee was going to be here you were on the fence about coming down and weren't sure but once you found out that he had her signed on for it, then that settled it for you." "Okay," I said, then added, "that was a lot to take in, I'm not sure….." but she said I should say that to him and so I did. I'd had so much to drink by that point in the evening I would have said most anything. I tapped John on the shoulder again and said, "You know, John, I just want to tell you that I wasn't sure I was going to come down here or not because it's such a long drive for me and I really had no money to spend but once I found out that you got Shawnee to come here, well…" (And here I paused for dramatic effect and added more enthusiasm and maybe even some hand gestures to really sell my point) "I moved heaven and earth to get here! I called in favors from ten years ago and coerced people into lending me money so I could come down here to meet her!" Then I quieted down for a minute before adding, "I just wanted you to know that. Thanks again for an incredible weekend". Now, I can't be certain, but I think as I was saying this to John, Jane was telling Shawnee what she had put me up to – though coercion at that point in the evening was not hard to come by. Had she asked me to get on the countertop and perform an Irish Jig I just may have…because I was feeling that good.

Before it was time to say goodbye to all my new friends, Jane and Shawnee gave a couple of my new friends and I each a Smith & Pyle t-shirt (which I proudly wear every chance I get). The reason behind this awesome gift, I'm not sure, they are just two of the nicest people and I know we all felt so privileged to have been able to spend so much time with them. It is probably the most memorable weekend I have ever had. I feel so blessed. Blessed to have met someone I've admired for eighteen years, blessed to have met so many cool, great new friends; blessed to have survived my first solo trip to NYC.

So I used to think that I would never go to NYC alone. Sawmania and Shawnee Smith changed that. I had no expectations of coming away from Sawmania with any new friends but my fellow Smith Groupies, not to mention Shawnee, changed all that.

The entire trip to NYC, to Sawmania, just furthers my belief about how some of the best things in life arise from the most unexpected circumstances.

DECEMBER 1, 2008
9:07 PM

DRIVING TO WORK THIS morning I found myself sliding haphazardly into the ditch. You have got to love Mondays. Six fifteen in the morning, dark outside, sleet, unplowed roads, and Blake Hill all made for an impossible task of driving to work. And work, mind you, is not a place that I am ever eager to go. I haven't quite made up my mind yet about whether or not I actually like it. Actually, I know that I don't like it - in fact today I was about two seconds from walking out the door and running away forever. If I had any money I may just have done that. But I have no money therefore I really have no choice. Classes start again for me on Wednesday and I'm feeling so completely detached from school that I'm questioning why I'm still taking classes. Is it really going to pay off or am I chasing a dream that is no longer a dream? Or maybe I'm just questioning everything right now because I'm tired, have a headache, and am waiting for December 20th to roll around when Trevor and I will be heading back to New York City to see Missi Pyle in Boeing, Boeing on Broadway. I'm beyond excited about it but am wondering about the money situation...... because I have no money. Trevor already bought the tickets and he says they are "Dead Center" - I'm assuming orchestra seating - which means I'm going to be set back at least a hundred and fifty bucks.

I feel I left my creativity a long time ago - I've been trying to infuse myself with imagination and creative ambitions again and Shawnee helped inspire me when she looked at my Little Rebel drawings and encouraged me. Having Shawnee Smith call me talented was amazing.

DECEMBER 2, 2008
7:33 AM

HERE I AM, STUCK at work, pretending like I give a damn. Okay, so maybe that's a little harsh but I am in no mood to be here, least of all to be around people today... especially little children with whom I have to be courteous and delightful with. Maybe not delightful inasmuch as amiable. The children, actually, aren't so bad. The adults really aren't so bad either.... I think maybe I'm the bad variable in this equation. It never fails.... you're up so high at one point and then you come crashing down so hard ... and it's so jarring that your soul becomes lost and confused, scrambling around inside of you, suddenly fearful of its limitations, it's trapped existence - when it realizes that the only thing it really wants, it really needs, is to be free... or at least to feel free. But it's this trapped existence that causes such discontent. It's almost as though I can feel my skin stretch and bend as my soul tests its barriers for weaknesses - trying to find that one thin point where it will be able to break through and fly away.

Friends. Yes, I miss my friends. I miss my Sawmania buds. I miss my Deaner pals. I know I could have gone out last Friday evening to catch up with Amanda, Keegan and Roger but that was the last place I wanted to go. For one thing, I did not want to drive all the way in there only to spend money that I don't have on drinks that I don't need. I know I haven't seen Amanda in a couple years and I haven't seen Roger or Keegan in nearly ten years and even though I did want to see them, and do eventually, it didn't seem like a life and death sort of thing.... I didn't feel as though I would regret not going. And I don't. I don't feel I missed anything. Sure, they're friends, but they're no longer close friends. High School was ten years ago. I love our memories and the times we spent together, but we're all so far removed from that. I don't want to sound like I'm making excuses or justifications for bailing out of the little reunion last Friday but it became apparent that it just wasn't all that important to me. You know it's true... obviously... that friendships come and go... and though there will always be a tenuous hold on the friendship.... it's just not as significant as it used to be. It's just what happens.... we all grow up and grow apart. It's nice to reminisce about the good ol' days but sometimes that's all there is to do. Regardless, I do miss those times. We had so much fun together back then. But you can't live in the past right? I have new memories to make.

Pain, Loss, Hope, Promise

JANUARY 17, 2009

I GOT A CALL the other morning. A call I never wanted to receive. My dear friend, Jesse, has passed away. She lost her battle with Lupus. How to deal with this? How to come to terms with the fact I shall never see her smiling face again, never laugh mischievously again, never concoct crazy ideas like dressing up as Amy Winehouse on a bender and hittin' the town. She was one of the first real friends I made in Fairmount. She will forever be a friend but now I will no longer be able to see her, but in my dreams and memories. The loss of a friend is so difficult to come to terms with. She was so young too. I'm flooded with emotions. Flooded with despair. I am going to miss her so much. Rest easy, Jesse. Know you tamed me, like the Little Prince and the fox. I will love you forever.

(2014: The Little Prince, a book beloved by all Deaner's, serves as a reminder to us all of the friends we seek. The chapter where the Little Prince meets and tames the fox is a favorite passage. It tells how friendships are forged. So whenever I feel lost, I pick up the book and read that chapter and am reminded of all the friends I have tamed and all the friends who have tamed me. Jesse will forever be one of those friends).

JANUARY 2009

WASHINGTON D.C. Recap
THE 2009 PRESIDENTIAL INAUGURATION
OF BARACK OBAMA

IS IT POSSIBLE TO sum up in words this momentous occasion? I've struggled with this question since January 20ᵗʰ simply because I cannot seem to fully grasp the magnitude of what my friends and I were on hand to witness: the 56ᵗʰ Presidential Inauguration. I don't think it's necessary to delve into the significance of this particular inauguration since we are all aware of its historic merit. So I'll just begin with the basics of our Inauguration Adventure!

About a week before January 20ᵗʰ is when we decided we would go. ("We" includes Trevor and me.) It took just slightly longer than the blink of an eye to talk Emily into flying to D.C. from Indianapolis for the 19ᵗʰ and 20ᵗʰ. Trevor made a call to his friend who lives in VA to see if the offer for room & board still applied. It did. We said, "Let's go then!" All very simple.

Long-term ruminations (or real planning of any kind) are not really our style. We get an idea: we say, "what is it going to take to make this happen?" we figure it out: we go.

This 'planning strategy' is really like *Basic Planning Skills 101 For People with Spontaneous Wanderlust in conjunction with East Coast Blues"* - the prerequisites include: Innate desire to wander, run-away, travel, explore, and drink good wine. (For no trip can truly begin without uncorking a bottle of sweet **Pink SPARKLING Wine!** And no trip can end without a nightcap of Riesling or an Iguana Margarita.... or two).

Katherine L. Fogg

SATURDAY, JANUARY 17, 2009

I MAKE MY WAY down to Amherst, MA, to spend some quality time with Trevor before we have to drive down to D.C. on the 18th. As evidenced from picture number one of the weekend - Robot had the upper-hand (as usual) when it comes to monitoring our intake of **Pink SPARKLING wine**, Riesling, Sake, Maraschino cherries, and M&M's. Ah, the Sake... my first taste of such smooth Asian liquor. I survived four or five shots before realizing it actually **was** having an effect on my motor skills. So, of course, I switched to the Riesling. Big mistake. That 6.99 bottle was not all it was cracked up to be (go figure!) The best thing about it was the pretty label. So the **Pink SPARKLING wine** was uncorked and saved the day.

SUNDAY, JANUARY 18, 2009

WE SPENT SUNDAY ON the road...a seemingly endless drive to Briana's house in Alexandria, VA. When we eventually made it to Trevor's friends place. The first thing we did was go out to eat at a great little Mexican restaurant which serves some of the best margaritas around! (And though it seems that all we really do is drink wine, sake, and margaritas..... it's really not ALL we do... it's just that the wine is so good it's worth mentioning!)

MONDAY MORNING, JANUARY 19, 2009

TREVOR AND I WAKE up too damn early in order to pick up Emily at the Dulles Airport. Her flight was scheduled to land at 7:32 (so randomly specific, I know) in the morning and being the bright, cheery, morning people that we are... Trevor and I had NO PROBLEM waking up and driving 35 minutes to the airport... no problem at all. So, of course, her flight had a temporary setback, had to move to a different terminal, she had to be shuttled back, etcetera, etcetera. After twice being shooed away by the security officers in the passenger pick-up zone, we drove around and around, each time improving our lap time until I was sure a running in this year's Daytona 500 was in our future (unfortunately, going 20 mph around an airport terminal oval track can't really compare to going 200 mph around the Daytona track! of which I would looooove to do!)

Anyway, after about 237 laps, Emily calls and says she's waiting on the sidewalk! This is the first time she and I have seen each other somewhere other than on that sacred Indiana soil where **James Dean** lived and was lain to rest.

We made our way back to Trevor's friends place and once we got there Trevor and I promptly stated we were going to take a nap. Of course, this didn't happen..... and we didn't really get any sleep until Tuesday night.... but so much happened in those hours between picking up Emily at the airport and falling down in sheer exhaustion Tuesday night after dropping her off at the airport. A whirlwind trip doesn't begin to describe it really. But it's a start.

Monday morning began and it doesn't seem like it ended until Wednesday morning. It seemed like we were on the go from the moment we picked up Emily from the airport. Trevor's friend gave the 3 of us a ride to the Metro station (my first Metro experience!) which was about 2 to 2 1/2 miles from her place (foreshadowing here... keep in mind)....

FINALLY: we get to the city. My first time in D.C. The skies were gray, the air was cold but not frigid (like Tuesday turned out to be....oy... more on that little bit o' misery later).... We walk from the Metro station on the streets and I'm actually a little star-struck.... if it's possible to be star-struck with a city and/or the monuments therein. I suppose it is possible if you take time to consider that the city itself is a character, depicted in movies, television shows, the media.... the city is always an on-set location. But there was a different feeling in the air that day..... The feeling of unadulterated anticipation. It was the day before the inauguration and already the atmosphere buzzed with the electricity of two million people united for a common goal ... a celebration of change.... a moment of hope.

Walking. Walking. Walking. This is what Monday entailed. WE WALKED EVERYWHERE. After stopping in a little Pizzeria and chowing down on some pizza and calzones, we thought we had carbo-loaded enough for the day. I don't think we knew that we were going to be walking non-stop for the next 10 hours or so.

The sights of D.C., the history, the monuments, the grandness..... All within "walking distance" of one another. What's unfortunate is that "walking distance" is a relative term.... dependent upon the individual.... and after the first 20 miles or so had been tucked away beneath the soles of our shoes, "walking distance" became a real pain in the ass (quite literally, actually). BUT - the adrenalin, the excitement, the epic-ness of the moment is what kept us going..... And it wasn't even Tuesday yet! Monday was purely a sightseeing extravaganza! Unfortunately, the one monument I most wanted to see: The Lincoln Memorial: was the only one we couldn't get close to. Used as the stage for numerous celebratory concerts, the Lincoln Memorial was closed off to public access. Next time, I guess.

What struck me the most, besides the grandiosity of the architecture & the history of D.C., was going to Arlington Cemetery. Obviously, it was a somber & humbling experience. To see the Eternal Flame where John F. Kennedy is laid to rest was at once very moving and very hard to comprehend simply because it was like a tourist trap there - it was a spectacle. There was no time to stand and ruminate, to pay respect, or to have a simple moment by yourself to experience the gravity of the situation, the moment. Instead of standing quietly and reflecting upon what it all means, people were treating the scene as though it was something inconsequential. I wonder, is it too much to ask for, that when a large group is assembled in such a place, around the grave of one of our Nation's most prominent Presidents, that they act with a certain sense of decorum and respect? I think it was just aggravating to not be able to have a real moment there, but to instead be herded through the line like cattle. On the other hand, when we went to the Tomb of The Unknown Soldier, no one spoke. No one made a sound. It felt wrong to even take pictures there (though that didn't stop me completely...nor did it prevent anyone else from doing so.)

The bitter cold didn't really come into play on Monday

until the latter part of the day. The wind began to pick up as my knees began to give out thanks to all the walking. For the last five miles I relied on my ability to compartmentalize my emotions. Despite the physical pain of walking, of which I knew a bottle of Ibuprofen was in my future, I kept reminding myself of the situation and that pain is only momentary (even though it seems to LAST FOREVER). Somehow I managed to limp my way through the remainder of the day.... thinking I'd rest up Monday night, enjoy some pizza, wine, and good company, and be ready and good to go Tuesday morning. I was a little off in my assessment of what "rest up" would actually be and by the time Tuesday morning actually arrived (getting up at 3 o'clock in the morning isn't conducive with getting enough rest to be physically mended for the next day's activities) I knew it was going to be a GLORIOUS day for our Nation..... But an exhaustive and physically painful day for myself.

TUESDAY, JANUARY 20, 2009: INAUGURATION DAY

3 AM. ALARM GOES off. Eyes open. Body rejects first 10 initial attempts to get up. Wearily, exhaustively, one by one, we all get up and get ready. We had called the cab company the night before to request a cab at 4 AM to pick us up at Briana's and take us the 2 ½ miles to the Metro Station.

4 AM comes and goes. We call the cab company. "A little backed up," they say, but the cab will "be there in the next 10 minutes or so". 15 minutes pass. Another call to the cab company. "Just a little busy today, running a little behind schedule still," they say. We say we are going to begin to walk and please have the cab look out for us. Yeah. You can pretty much guess how that went.

Our cab never came. WE HAD TO WALK 2 1/2 miles, at 4:25 AM, to the Metro Station. The previous day of walking and taken its toll on me. SEVERELY. Both of my knees threatened to give out on me. My hip flexor was stressed to the max and each step felt like someone jabbed me with a knife. Not pleasant. It was cold. Far colder than the previous day. But the discomfort was (temporarily) overshadowed by the moment at hand. When we got to the Metro station we were greeted by an armed SWAT member standing guard. We got our fare cards, waited for train, and then the ride truly began.

The people we met on the Metro train that morning gave us our first glimpse into how incredible the day was going to be. People were excited. People were joyous. People were generous and obliging. The first ten minutes on the train proved (if one hadn't already known) that this was no ordinary day. This was an *extraordinary* day.

When we disembarked the train, we faced our first "mob scene" @ the Metro Station. Jam-packed doesn't even do justice to the number of people squeezed into that station. Shoulder to shoulder, we walked in small little steps. It made me think of a march of penguins & how their little bodies sway back and forth as they waddle to their destination.

When we finally made it to the street, I didn't see how we were ever going to maneuver our way through the crowds and make it to the National Mall. Trevor, his friend, Emily, and I grabbed the hand or sleeve of the person in front of us and held on, forming our own little human chain so none of us got lost in the crowd. It was not easy, weaving our little human chain through the crowd of a million other human chains. (Somewhere in the fray I lost my brand new sunglasses! grrrrrr!!! I hate when that happens... you know how I am with my sunglasses). We knew we were making real progress when we bailed through an open chain-link fence door (left agape by the police officers who had just walked through).

And then..... There it was.

The National Mall.

The Capitol.

We briefly hesitated when we first set foot on the National Mall ground and stood looking at the Capitol, brilliantly lit and illuminated against the dark morning sky. Still holding hands, Trevor, Emily, Briana and I looked at one another with utter amazement and we started running. It really was a moment that seems straight out of the movies! Holding hands and running through the grounds at the National Mall towards the Capitol, laughing, yelling, "I can't believe we're here!" We ran until we couldn't run anymore, when we caught up with the crowd that had already amassed on the grounds.

It was about 5:30 in the morning now. We had 6 hours before the start of the Inauguration. The excitement fueled our adrenalin which fueled our endorphins which numbed the initial pain of the bitter cold. After the first 40 minutes of pure bliss.... the adrenalin slightly ebbed..... But the cold did not. I'm not here to complain about the cold... BUT...suffice to say... *HOLY SHIT!! I DIDN'T THINK I WAS GOING TO SURVIVE!!! THE PAIN WAS NEARLY INTOLERABLE!! I HAD TEARS IN MY EYES IT HURT SO MUCH AND*

WOULD HAVE CRIED BUT IT WAS TOO COLD!! 11 HOURS IN THOSE FREEZING TEMPERATURES WAS ENOUGH FOR A LIFETIME!!! MY KNEES AND HIP FLEXOR MUSCLES REVOLTED WITH EVERY STEP AND TREVOR ACTUALLY HAD TO HOLD ME UP AS WE EXITED THE NATIONAL MALL AT THE END OF THE INAUGURATION!!! BUT THE COLD... THE COLD... COLD ... COLD!!! OMG - it was horrible.

THAT BEING SAID.....

2 Million Strong

Being there at the Inauguration, I can honestly say, is probably the most significant moment I've ever been privileged to be a part of. I have never before experienced such camaraderie. I have never been surrounded by millions of people all gathered in a unifying celebration. We were hugging each other, we were hugging strangers, people were crying, we were shaking hands, smiling, laughing, and loving every moment, every person. When you smiled at someone walking by, they smiled at you. Two million people and no dissension, no ill-will, no complaints *(except the cold!)*. Two million strangers: two million friends.

Two million people radiating hope.

The historic merit of this day, the first African American President of the United States being sworn in, is too monumental to fully comprehend. Listening to President Obama's inauguration speech, I was overwhelmed with a sense of hope, inspiration, and patriotism. I felt like I was witnessing a cross between John F. Kennedy's 1961 Inaugural address and Martin Luther King Jr's, August 28, 1963 "I have a dream speech". President Obama's speech was, and is, that momentous, that historic, and that important.

Being at the inauguration was such an extraordinary moment. I still struggle to find the words to fully express my emotions. It still hasn't completely 'sunk in' yet, that Trevor, Briana, Emily, and I were there on that historic day. It will probably take some time before the full gravity of the moment takes hold, if it ever does. I have my pictures and I have my memories of that day and, most of all, I still have that sense of extraordinary wonder, of being so awe-inspired that I can't even articulate the words to describe it.

MASS EXODUS

LEAVING THE NATIONAL MALL was like a nightmare.

I actually would not have minded the confusing, jumbled, streets of D.C. as two million people tried to leave all at once, but I was in such devastating physical pain that I could hardly walk. I have to say, if Trevor hadn't been there to hold me up, I probably would've crumpled to the ground and never gotten up again! It was absolutely ridiculous, the pain, the cold.

After President Obama's speech, we began the journey back to the Metro Station. But the Metro station was pretty much inaccessible. We tried another one. Same problem. So we decided to walk I don't know how many blocks to a (rather) far away station in hopes of gaining entry as well as access to a train. But it was like a maze. The police had cordoned off streets, streets that no one knew were going to be closed. We had to circumvent the easy access routes and take a ten block detour... just more walking... more and more and more.... and I wanted to cut my own legs off near the end. The crowds packed into the streets were so condensed that we were actually at a standstill for quite some time. There was nowhere to go. People would try to move, end up pushing someone in front of them, and that one push would reverberate throughout the entire crowd, like ripples in a pond, cascading outward. But like I said previously, I would not have minded this minor (okay, major) setback had I not been in such pain. But I was. So the whole time we were trying to leave was like a nightmare. Obviously, we made it. By the time we got to the far-away Metro station, which was relatively (and mercifully) calm and empty, we got on the train, were lucky enough to grab seats, and all four of us, without saying it, were so relieved to be somewhere 'warm', and sitting down that, I think, we could have stayed on that train for five hours straight. When we got off the train we all agreed that there was absolutely no way we were going to WALK back to Briana's place and we got a cab.

We got home to Briana's in time to watch the parade on television.

We all pretty much crumpled onto the floor, hid under layers of blankets, and tried to comprehend the experience we had just had. It wasn't possible.

A little while later, Trevor and Briana left to go get food (Chinese). Emily and I stayed right where we were and didn't move until it was absolutely necessary to do so.... when we had to bring her back to the Dulles airport so she could catch her flight back to Indianapolis. After Trevor and I returned to Briana's, we pretty much fell asleep and didn't wake up for 12 hours. The next day we got up late, helped Briana move her stuff into her boyfriend's apartment, had lunch at an Ethiopian Restaurant, and drove back to Massachusetts....

where we slept for another 16 hours I think... then I had to drive back to Maine.

Then our trip was officially over.

And the United States has a new President as well as a renewed sense of HOPE.

MARCH 7, 2009

I NEARLY DIED A couple days ago. I should have died a couple days ago. I got into a snowmobile accident. To be accurate, I got into two snowmobile accidents in the span of five minutes. I was cruising down the lake at 55 mph when I hit a large patch of glare ice. I lost control of the machine and when it hit the snow again the machine was sideways and it flipped four or five times throwing me about twenty feet where I landed on my right shoulder breaking my clavicle, tearing ligaments in my shoulder. I got back on the machine and started it. As I began to drive away I look down and see all these little fissures in the ice. I thought, "Well, this can't be good." And then SPLASH! Right down under did we go. I remember being under water and looking at the sled as it sank to the bottom. I somehow managed to pull myself up and out of the water. No one knows how I was able to do that. Even the divers who went down to get my sled said they couldn't understand how I'd gotten myself out of the water. In all likelihood I should have drowned then and there. But I got out of the cold water, all my snowmobile gear wet and weighing me down. I was alone so I had to walk to the nearest house which was about a mile and a half. While I was in the water, this may sound strange, but while I was bobbing there like a buoy, I thought of Jesse. I thought of Katie. I thought of Kate. And I thought, "I'm not going to die here in Maranacook Lake." And by the grace of God, I got out, relatively unscathed. The funny part was when I got home and my mom looked at me and said, "I can't even get you to go into the pool in summer."

MARCH 2, 2009
8:31 PM

WELL, I CAN SAY with certainty that this past weekend did not go as planned, not for me and most definitely not for Trevor. I am in no mood to be around anyone lately. The fact of the matter is: I have not had any real time to myself since my impromptu trip to NYC to see Boeing, Boeing for the second time. Ever since that night (which ended with a terrible migraine... which was worth it because I got to meet Missi Pyle and the rest of the cast) I have had to endure a constant barrage of people. Family is always around. And when I am not around them, I am in Massachusetts with Trevor. Now, don't get me wrong, I do enjoy (usually) spending time with Trevor but it takes so much energy out of me because I feel I am still showing a false veneer of myself. Well, let me clarify that: I do not feel I am showing a false veneer as much as I KNOW I am showing one. Because that is what I do: I pretend. I am a pretender. I placate. I am basically whomever I think someone wants me to be. That is really not the way to live. It's exhausting. And it makes me a liar. A liar to everyone I know because I am someone different with every person.

MARCH 18, 2009

IT'S HARD TO GET a handle on things, especially when you find yourself succumbing to the foibles of everyday life. It's hard to justify feelings of sadness when nothing about your life is really going to change because of said situation. It's hard to find rationality once you've lost it. I don't know the date of when I lost mine but I am sure that I have. I am feeling uneasy and sick right now.... due to circumstances ultimately out of my control. And really.... everything is out of my control.... right now, at this very moment, if it so chose ("it" being fate, God, some other all-powerful entity or deity.. whatever you want to label it is fine by me)... If "it" so chose... 'It' could push the breath right out of my lungs leaving me gasping for life and finding none. Fatalism has always been part of my personality, even more so lately thanks to my little rendezvous with near death... of which I still feel somewhat eerily detached from. I'm not sure what it is... or why it is.... but it's there. I feel as though I am making no sense right now. All I know is that I am desperate to begin writing again... and I am really going to have to try and make the effort to do so on a semi-consistent basis.

We'll see, I guess. (That's how the story goes anyway.)

*April 2010.... I still have not had a 'normal' reaction to the snowmobile incident... I think I pushed it out of my mind... or at the very least, to the back of my mind... the dark recess where all near tragedies are kept in storage and therefore effectively blocked from my mind so my emotional being has nothing to digest and ponder over... or... I just analyzed the situation so rationally that there was no need for an emotional reaction. I like the latter explanation... that sounds more on par with how I deal with "me" situations of the like.... just wanted to update the findings.)

APRIL 21, 2009

I'M NEVER SURE OF how to begin nowadays. Do I delve right into the drama without any segue or do I pilfer through what remaining memories I have and try to sort them out chronologically? Can I just sit and moan and bitch and complain because I have nothing better to do and then realize that even if I did have something better to do I would probably not do it because then I'd have less time to sit around, moan, bitch and complain. Do I really get that much enjoyment and productivity out of it? No, of course I don't. I'm just so damn good at it that it has become the one and only thing that I can find to salvage my sanity and remind myself that, for all intents and purposes, I'm still alive. I know I seem to say this a lot... but let's face it... nowadays when I turn to your solace, J, it's because I've reached the end of my rope... which is really no longer than a shoelace at this point... and no stronger than a wet noodle at that... but as I was saying... I seem to say this a lot but things are just rapidly moving downhill, straight into the abyss of Hell. I wonder sometimes at how I became so lost.... lost to myself... lost to the world around me? What pivotal moment in time was it that catapulted me into such a directionless fall? Pratfall is really more like it because my life is not tragic. My life is not something to be remembered..... I've not persevered and triumphed... I've not overcome staggering odds to find success.... I've not even contributed the best of myself to the people around me: my friends, my family. They see a shadow of me... an abject silhouette consisting of unspoken desires and long-lost dreams. A simplified projection of SELF that accomplishes nothing more than a purveyance of oblique tediousness. And it's down, down, down, further, faster, longer the trail becomes. I am more than partly convinced that this is Purgatory for I must certainly be in one of Dante's circles of Hell. The self-realizations I try so desperately to discard are the only ones that really matter. I try so valiantly to toss them aside as if they were nothing more than a passing fancy, a slight hobby that only serves to distract, not produce effective outcomes. My life has been routed to serving as nothing more than an obligatory existence. I have got to find a way to change that. How can I though? Is it possible to change something that is innate? An inherent characteristic that I perceive as a tragic flaw need only be a flaw if I treat it as such.... if I instead embrace that which I so desperately loathe about myself and 'make the most of it' (as they like to say) won't I be the better for it? To take a proactive stance and fight instead of wallow and die a thousand times a day. Being dramatic is positively essential in getting my point across, you know. I never show such emotion in "real life", only to you Dear J do I go so far off the deep end. Maybe that's part of the problem... maybe if I emoted more in life, I'd be able to let go of things sooner, more effectively. Then again, maybe not. They say you can teach an old dog new tricks... but make no mention of whether or not that dog is fully optimistic in his newfound role. That's a tired cliché and if I'm putting forth an effort to make myself feel better or trying to invigorate a sense of self-worth into myself... I'm not sure comparing myself to a dog is the way to go.

APRIL 22, 2009
9:30 AM

MY HEAD FEELS FULL of clouds ... thunderous clouds.

SEPTEMBER 2009

HOW TO EXPLAIN TO everyone how much I loathe where I am right now! Frustration mounts as the days pass.

How can one say they are 'home' when the place they reside feels no more like home than a foreign country? But, alas, given that analogy I'd have to say that I'm the foreigner here because everyone else fits right in.

Looking for answers in all the wrong places. Other people aren't going to give me anything; no answers, no guidance, nothing. If I want to move, I have to be the one to do it.

Still - motivation and confidence seem to rely on each other and when one is running on empty the other is close to stalling.

Maybe after complaining I'll be able to gain perspective.

I'm desperate to get out of here. So why can't I seem to take that first step?!?!?

I told you... frustration mounts.... days pass... nothing changes.

I'm far too restless for my own good.

Searching and looking.... for what??

I don't even know anymore.

Now... deep breaths...

Venting always helps in the short race...

It's the long run that tends to worry me....

OCTOBER 10, 2009
2:41 PM

To sit down and begin to write, something of which I have wanted to do and thought about doing every day since arriving back here in Maine in August, well... sitting down to actually do it has proven troublesome. Why? I'm not really sure. Sometimes I think that I have so much to say and I'm just afraid to say it... to bring it out into the light of day for the world to see. Not that the world is going to see this anytime soon.... not while I'm alive anyway... after I'm dead and gone I'm sure someone is going to read through these pitiful little journal entries of mine and still they will get the wrong impression of me. How can someone be "real" when all you know of them amount to nothing more than ink stains on a piece of paper? I say this and yet I recognize the hypocrisy of the statement already. Sylvia Plath? You're right, I don't know her because I never met her... but if I had met her, would that have made a difference? I think of the people I have met, who have met me, and I think to myself, "The only things they truly know about me are the things I let them know... which is not a whole hell of a lot." I am someone different with every person in my life. When am I ever "real"? Not to say that personalities are (or should be) one-dimensional because that would be far too boring, but does my outward personality, that I project for others to see, does that truly represent my 'real' personality? Absolutely not. I count on my hand the people with whom I have ever been totally 'real' with.... but I can't really say because I've never been totally 'real' with myself - I've never been honest with myself because who I am... is not someone I am comfortable with. Or maybe who I am is in conflict with the person I am trying to be, maybe that's where the problem lies. And it creates more problems than simple identity-crisis. Lately things have been dire. I'm still in Maine. I still loathe and despise it here. I still am reliant on others. I still hate myself for it. I still can't seem to get up, get motivated, and get out. My motivation for all things (except sleep) has eroded away into a pathetic little sputter. I think about this past summer, my epic road trip... of which I wish I had written to you about but I opted to write blogs instead... in the vain hopes that someone out there cared enough to read them. I have since re-read them and they are all tinged with subtle despair. I can read between the lines of what I write (obviously) and I am much surprised that no one else seems able to. Or if they do, it doesn't seem to affect them in any discernible way. A long time ago I began writing about Sylvia Plath... I meant to continue that discussion by furthering my own explanation about how people really only know other people in a one-dimensional way. Of course there are people out there who wear their heart on their sleeve on almost all occasions (annoying) but even they, I'm betting, have their secrets. I never met Sylvia in life and yet I do feel that I know her.... why? By reading her poems? By reading her journal? Yes and yes. Her journal is insightful... but it is insightful in the sense that it offers only a small glimpse into her psyche, her momentary feelings from a transitory time. And that, really, is all that any of us can convey.

Time chugs along oblivious of the affect is has on us while we are sometimes caught unaware by its sudden passing or its lingering presence. But all in all, time is the one thing that we can count on to not stop, to not stall, to not deviate from its current path... time is a constant evolution of life.... even when we die... time surreptitiously marches on. And so I only know moments of Sylvia Plath. People only know moments of me. People only know moments of one another. We can do our best to make those moments worthwhile and meaningful but it seems that more often than not (with me especially) those moments are marked with regrets. And regret lingers. It rots. It destroys peace of mind with an infection of doubt. It can overwhelm and it can cause one to lie awake at night and wonder why, time after time, it seems to plunge its infectious needle deep into their soul. The Worriers have it worst of all. They are the ones who can find no rest - they are the ones that insomnia seeks out and the mind never shuts down. The Worriers carry unnecessary burdens on their shoulders... it is not something one can carry with pride... it is something one carries with despair, sorrow, unwavering guilt. It is something intangible and most often it revolves around an imaginary transgression. Perspective is a funny thing. When I say something and I know instinctively that it 'came out wrong'... or not at all how I intended... I have no way of knowing if the other person found the same to be true. Another person's perspective is unique and totally inherent to them... so I have no way of knowing if what I said hit its intended mark or not. From someone else's perspective the sarcasm of my comment could have done a fly by, could have been lost in translation, or could have been disregarded. I am a Worrier. To the point where the things I say almost have to be read from a script because I am so wary of saying the wrong things. And when one worries that much, it can pretty much be guaranteed that I will say the wrong thing or say the right thing the wrong way. Perspective and perception....

both devious in nature. The perception that some people have of me is so far off the mark from what I perceive and know myself to be that I am literally taken aback at times when I hear someone describe how they see me or when they make a comment about my free-spirit, my easy-going nature. My spirit is not free.... it yearns to be free... but I have it locked up in a cage so small and tight that it's a wonder it hasn't completely died yet. My easy-going nature is a facade... a thin veneer of protection I shield myself with so people won't notice what a wreck I am. I can pull off the illusion as long as I'm not forced to talk too much... when I begin to talk... (To certain people)... I can hear the quiver in my voice... it's the uncertainty, the anxiety making its way through my veins and infiltrating every thought I have and every word I speak with Worry... and Doubt... and Fear. That is how it always is. I imagine that is how it will remain. Some days are better than others but lately I feel as though I have been thrown from the ledge.... and I'm plummeting down further and further into this great abyss, this hopelessness. The fury of my mind is attacking my soul.

2010

Acknowledgment

MARCH 4, 2010

I CAN BE SUCH a hypocrite sometimes.... talking in class about the importance of trying to achieve a level where you can be comfortable with yourself... where you can accept yourself for who you are... no matter if it flies in the face of what other people or society at large deems 'conventional'..... When am I going to step up to that proverbial plate and come to terms with it all? How can I spout off these little diatribes while not recognizing my own inability to come to terms with facets of myself, my personality, my lifestyle that don't adhere to "convention"? When? Perhaps never.

MARCH 30, 2010

ENGAGING IN SELF-DESTRUCTIVE BEHAVIOR is a willful act of defiance.

I understand Sylvia Plath.

But I understand her on a superficial level where depression and anxiety meet depression and anxiety - a mirror image - felt, expressed through words more-so than by actions. Aspects of individuals inherently reflect in another but similarities do not represent matching identities.

But I understand Sylvia.

With a slight manic desperation, with red-hot, iron-glow jealousy, with ambition, desire - which rejection in the slightest form could waylay - and diminish.

But no one can truly understand her joy and pain - no one can understand the true motivation behind another person's decision or actions - That is what makes us unique - individual - independent thinkers - And while we may very well be inspired or influenced by another - by their life, their words, their death - the influence is slight in retrospect - no one can be relegated to action unless a small seed of such desire already has taken root in their mind.

It is impossible for me to be underscored by someone else's supposed authority and to have to play out, in a spectacle nonetheless, my ineptness (brought about by insecurity) for unsuspecting patrons to be subjected to. All in all.... I don't think I will ever be able to work with other people, on any level, because the risk seems too great - too powerful - or perhaps I am merely too weak and have an irrational fear of succumbing to such superficial judgment. I think maybe now would be a good time to get up and walk away... if even briefly... people swarm and gather ... the real locusts invade as the plague.

APRIL 3, 2010
12:15 AM

OFTENTIMES, IT TAKES A monumental effort to make only a slight difference.

I've been inspired to crack-open the classics again.

Am reading Voltaire's "Candide" once again - I think the satirical brilliance was lost on me the first time I read it, nearly a decade ago. It is savagely funny with its hypocrisy and dark humor. And to think it was written in 1759. This is why literature is the greatest invention humankind EVER created. What would I do, who would I be, without my books? Without my eyes, I could not see the beauty of the written word nor relish the sight of how emotions flow from mind, to fingertips, to page. The most astounding work of art is language, letters, words. The best form of communication, articulate and imaginative. My most cherished ability.

APRIL 26, 2010
1:10 AM

WHEN I GET AN idea in my head, when I get a thought or a task.... I cannot do anything else until I quench whatever thirst of an idea it may be.

MAY 4, 2010
9:44 AM

WHY IS IT THAT the only place I find even remotely comfortable to be is in a cemetery. Perhaps because there are never many people here, if any, and it is quiet, offering to me silence (of a sort) and ample time to sit and pontificate. Not that pontificating for a significant amount of time has EVER served me well, it is still something of which I enjoy doing. Anything to get out and away for a little bit. Maybe part of my problem stems from thinking TOO much. That is possible you know. I mean, I know some people who seem to hardly think at all... it is as if I am picking up their slack. I'm sitting here in the cemetery near my ancestor's gravesites. Bet they never even entertained the thought that 150 years after their lives, a great-great-great granddaughter would be sitting in her car with a laptop and typing out useless drivel for no reason other than for posterity. Not that any of what I am saying right now is even worth remembering for posterity's sake, because it's not.

Half-moon in the sky right now, surrounded by robin's egg blue and no clouds. All these steadfast signifiers of the past stand askew in their defiance of time. Stone-washed, mildewed, bleached, slate-grey stone slabs, sunken relics of decayed history. What is the purpose, I wonder. Who visits these long-forgotten sons, mothers, daughters, fathers, and friends? No one can say what they were like when they were alive - died in 1890, aged 21, it says, and I wonder, were you kind? Did you love? Were you loved? Did you anticipate the coming of a certain suitor, did you long to hear your name called out by the boy down the road? Abigail. Were you enthusiastic, brash, quiet, and outgoing? Were you a pioneer, an advocate? Did you get along with your family? Your sister, your brother? Did your imagination take you to places you never saw before? I wonder what you looked like. Was there untold pressure to fit a certain mold, a certain look, to carry yourself a certain way? Were you bred into a life of society or hard-work? Did your hands know the feel of coarse earth or gentle fabric? Were you a literary sort? I wonder, did you ever read Alcott's "Little Women"? Were you like Jo? Or Beth? Or Amy? Dying young, you'd be like Beth. What about Anna Karenina? Did you love like Kitty and Levin, or have a doomed love affair like Anna and Vronsky? Was there a boy who held your hand, who kissed you and told you he loved you? I'm left to wonder... With no trace of recorded posterity, I don't know who you were, what you were like, and I imagine there is not a soul left on this earth who does know. Do you know what it's like to be forgotten? Forsaken? Taken for granted? To prove non-existent despite a once predominant relevance in life. If the little stone statue was to be taken away, no one would even know you were here any longer - until an excavation unearthed the silent reminder that, yes, you did in fact live and, once, you were real. Once you breathed air. Once you touched, laughed, loved, and cried. Once you died. Who is there to remember you now?

MAY 22, 2010

THE SEARCH FOR A place to call "home" is a natural and easy process for many people. For people like myself, it's almost certainly a never-ending process filled with disappointment, desire, and an insatiable need to continue the journey, to find a little niche in this world to call one's own, to feel safe, peaceful, relaxed. Is home a place? Is it a state of mind? Is it out there at all? I wonder.

JUNE 6, 2010

DO NOT WISH TO be there, do not wish to be here. Wish to be in a perpetual state of motion.

JULY 25, 2010

EVERYTHING FEELS AS THOUGH it is slipping from my grasp. I'm going to chalk all these pestering feelings up to lack of sleep. My mind has been racing for the past week – thoughts are often erratic and inconsequential but regardless of their level of importance, they are there – feasting away at the little banquet table in my mind – as they devour the logical and rational aspects of normal, everyday thought, they replace the portions with negativity, insecurity, and doubt. It is very feast or famine. I am still weary. I feel as though I have gone 18 rounds every day for the past few weeks.

AUGUST 2010

IT's TIME. I MUST admit to myself that I can no longer live the way I have been living. It has been how many years now? How many years spent dwelling in the darkness? How many years digging my own grave? I am the one that puts myself there, nearly six feet down. Life is not supposed to be this way is it? Life is not meant to be lived in the ever-present glare of doom and despair. I don't know what I'm going to do. I only know that something must be done before I go so far over the edge there's no turning back. I need guidance and yet I'm too afraid to ask for it. I suppose it's all in my hands. The choice is mine. Will I make the right one?

2011

Rise from the Ashes

FEBRUARY 10, 2011
11:07 PM

I HAVE FELT JADED recently. More than that, I have felt angry, bitter, resentful, and I have felt hatred. It is not a pleasant feeling and it is one that I wish would fade away soon. Like most things in my life, it will fade away. Nothing about my life and nothing in my life is immune from that slow evaporation – whether it be friendships, emotions, relationships, or simple interest – it all eventually fades. The fever pitch I feel when something just begins, the intensity, the obsessive compulsion – it eventually recedes until the urgency is no longer present. And once it is gone, instead of relaxing I find that I tense even more. My thoughts and emotions are violently unstable and erratic and I cannot function on any kind of systematic levels. But I have felt angry lately. And I've felt angry at all the wrong people, I'm afraid. Though I do have every right to feel resentful, to a point, and I do feel justified in directing my anger at a certain someone who blatantly took advantage of me – still, I find my hatred to be misdirected. And misdirection seems second nature for someone like me.

FEBRUARY 14, 2011
12:34 AM

VALENTINE'S DAY: I THINK you know my sentiments concerning this holiday already so there is no need to rehash it. They say the best time to write in a journal is upon first waking in the morning. When one never really goes to sleep, what options does that leave them? I am on my fifth day with hardly a wink of sleep. I got an angry text this morning from him. After all the bullshit he put me through… I get so riled up inside… and so angry… and so resentful…. He has the nerve to tell me that everything's my fault. He's an egocentric son of a bitch, is what he is. I will never change my opinion on that. I pretended. We both know I am good at pretending. And I was quite convincing on a multitude of levels but inside I was screaming – all the time I was screaming. I am still screaming. And suddenly I'm thinking of Hannibal Lecter…. "Do you hear the lambs, Clarice?" Oh yes, the lambs are screaming inside my head at a breakneck pace.

I have another counseling appointment tomorrow at eleven. I've been diagnosed as bipolar, severe anxiety, and social phobia. She says I'm on the cusp of bipolar 1 and 2. I guess it could go either way. I know I've had bouts of mania before, just as I know, and probably everyone knows, that I've had bouts of manic depressiveness, more so than anything else. I think I'll try to write some more tomorrow. But of course there are no guarantees. I would very much like to get some sleep but I'm not hopeful. Night.

FEBRUARY 15, 2011
12:30 AM

THERE IS A RUSH of wind I feel, slithering through the cracks and crevices. I am frozen in place, in a moment in time, a statue of frost and bitterness, solitary and confined.

Crying Virgin Mary tears of blood, crimson pain, droplets of fire fall from my weathered eyes;

Sadness lingers in this vast empty space, foreigners tread upon my little space, this little plot of land.

I do not run anymore. I cannot leave. This little plot of land has taken hold of me.

You do not see. You do not listen. I am here with frozen lips, with granite words – that fall flat – dead upon your ears.

And here I thought granite was a conductor – a great sound wave, a cacophony of screams – and yet you do not listen – you cannot hear me.

There is a rush of wind I feel, frostbitten to the core. I am frozen. I am solitaire. You are gone.

<u>12:12 AM</u>

I "talked" with my friend online today. It seems the only way we talk is in some clandestine form. I do not think we are going to be as close as either of us initially hoped. Too much has happened. I cannot pretend any longer. I pretended for six months. I gave into every whim and every fantasy and it got me nowhere. But now I must live with the memories. Now I must live with the regrets I've made. Now I must live with the remembrances of a lifestyle I engaged in that was not my own. I feel as though that part of my life, or that person I was, is far removed from me now. I look back upon those recollections and think to myself, "that could not have been me. I would never have done something like that". And yet it was me. It was I who engaged in that loathsome time of exploitation. I do not think I will go back there again. However, if I again enter into that hypomanic state, I probably will end up there again. Of course, on the other hand you have me, and what

I was exposed to. I never expected my life to be on such a crash course. I never expected the turn of events that took place. I do recall the dates, you know. I may never really know what the present date is, but for significant 'events', I can usually summon up the correct ones. January 14th was the easy one. It was the night I took myself to the ER. Angry that I had a bottle of champagne opened and had two glasses of champagne. My friend came down and said, "What's goin' on?" I replied, "Nothing", and walked downstairs. Then he blew up. "I'm done! I am all set with this!" and he went off on a tangent. I was downstairs meanwhile, listening to his rant and his yelling. Then I interjected finally and said, calmly and in monotone, "Why don't you come down here and actually talk to me". He came down but he didn't talk to me, he talked at me. I told him he was very condescending. After listening to his condemnations of me for ten minutes, I blew up. I yelled. He threatened to call the cops on me if I left trying to scare me into submission, trying to scare me by telling me how terrible the ER is when you're there and they think you're crazy or suicidal or whatever. I didn't say a thing. So then I left. I loaded my car and left

It's always a painful recognition to make, that the one person you put your trust into, the one person you want to always be there for can't seem to reciprocate equivalent feelings. But I take myself to the ER one night because I am scared and fearful of the thoughts rushing through my head, thoughts of suicide. And though those thoughts are nothing new for me the urgency of the thought was. It was not a normal thought process for me and I recognized it and it truly scared me. I really wanted to die that night. But I took myself to the ER, sans best friend, sans any kind of support whatsoever. All the while I'm fighting my emotions and fighting all those thoughts in my head that are telling me, "See, you are worthless. Your best friend doesn't even want to be around you anymore." But that's on the inside... on the outside, everything is roses and sunshine.... It's on the inside where the real me lives – in the dark, cold, abscess of my soul.

FEBRUARY 20, 2011
11:49 PM

MY CLASSES ARE TERRIBLE. Well, only one class is terrible because I must change my entire writing style to accommodate the unyielding structure and sedentary standards of the class. And besides, I just don't like the subject matter. It is a research class, ergo, no persuasive essays (which I excel at) but rather fact based ramblings that are such a bore I have an even harder time sustaining my concentration than usual. And that, dear J, is a rather ominous sign. I am running out of things and time and sanity I think. Being diagnosed as Bipolar, I at least feel a little justified in my craziness. However, being diagnosed as bipolar does nothing for my already diminished self-esteem. Not to mention my already debilitated sense of Self. I have suffered another blow. I am reaching that point where I feel almost as if it is of no use whatsoever to continue on. But I've been there before, haven't I? I do so want to change but I do feel it's impossible.

FEBRUARY 23, 2011
7:40 AM

I'M LISTENING TO BETH Hart's "My California" right now –
it's beautiful. I think Beth Hart is my kindred soul. She writes,
sings, and expresses things in a way I could never do but that
express my own thoughts and feelings so well. I suppose that
is why I admire her so much. We have a tendency to admire
those who exhibit the same feelings and common threads of
consciousness as we do. She surely does.

I have another appointment with the doctor today. I don't
think I've even mentioned that to you before, J. I'm not sure if
I have anyway. This will be round two with the head shrinker.
I don't know what's in store for me today but it promises to
be a long day anyway. I've been diagnosed as bipolar. Come
to think of it, I know I've mentioned this before because I
remember speaking of how I disliked or was unsure of how
I felt about labeled Bipolar. I do feel a little like I'm going
crazy. I suppose that is nothing new. Maybe, if and when, I
am prescribed some medication, things will improve. I have
my doubts, as always, but there is a slight glimmer of hope
bound within the idea of medication.

FEBRUARY 28, 2011
8:12 AM

I SUPPOSEDLY HAVE A counseling appointment in Farmington
today. It is snowing. I half expect to get a call telling me not
to come in. And the other half expects that I will go all

the way to Farmington only to turn around and come back because no one's there and no one bothered to call and tell me. I've only done that once or twice. Such a waste of time. I'm beginning to think counseling is a waste of time. I'm beginning to think a lot of things are a waste of time.

Although I do feel it, I do feel I am constantly being pulled in two opposing directions. There is a battle waging within that has been going on for years and years, my entire life perhaps. I don't know how I've been able to stand upright all this time and not give in to the temptation of self-annihilation. The temptation is always there in the back of my mind. It whispers incessantly, never ceasing its melodic and tremulous voice. It is a sing-song little mantra inside my head that invites varied irrational responses from me in order to drown it out. Imagine living with such a voice, twenty-four hours a day, for thirty years. I have been in the company of friends and family and still those voices are chattering away in the back of my mind. How to pretend they are not there has become a bit of an obstacle. Now that crazy has been established as my affliction, the voices seem to be getting louder, more insistent, and edgier. There is no fine-tuning of melodies anymore – there is no care taken in the sing-song mantra – it just bellows out now. It's like a bad open mic night inside my head – the karaoke tunes carry the weight of amateur and sub-par singers who think they can carry a tune. All it really is, is screeching; it's nails on a chalkboard, it is furies screaming out their pain, and it's a banshee wailing that someone will die. Since I am the only one who hears, I suppose that someone will probably be me. There is no one else here. Unless it decided to kill my other Self; you know her. There are always two; there is always a dichotomy of personality. And in my case especially, of course there are two. The very definition of Bipolar resides in the land of TWO. One is going to die. That is the only way to get any real relief from this I think. I've kept everything so cloistered for so long that the time to uncork the bottle is nearly here. And when I am at the counselor's or the doctor's office, I can feel myself trivializing what is there and I can hear Self #1 inside of me screaming and trying to get me to tell of the horror in its basest and most vile form. And I won't. I don't want them to know the full extent. I mix my words; I have a good enough vocabulary to sound as though I'm being completely forthright and honest; I have enough skills to pretend and say and act the 'right' way. But inside is turmoil – constant. A raw nerve is what I am – and this exposure to the open air is making everything hurt that much more.

I'm sitting here listening to the Black Swan soundtrack. When I saw that movie (twice) I could relate to the character of Nina Sayers and her ultimate tragedy – her descent into madness and her subsequent loss on the scope of reality around her. I don't hallucinate as she does but other symptoms of similarity do exist. Nina Sayers, portrayed brilliantly by Natalie Portman, of course, was tragically flawed by her meek disposition, her inability to stand up for herself, her submissiveness, her perfectionist drive, and her lack of belief. The other Nina Sayers, Self #2, was head-strong, willful, determined, violent, hedonistic, and an ultimate detriment to herself and those around her. These two opposing sides, the White Swan and her evil twin, the Black Swan (this is why I loved the movie so much – the parallel between the ballet and Nina's personal life), were each struggling to get out. One would show itself every now and then and just as suddenly would disappear and Nina would be left confused and shaken. I can relate to this. I am left confused, shaken, and quite often as broken as Nina Sayers because of these two polarizing aspects of Self that are each struggling to take hold of me. I have fought, if not valiantly, then at least doggedly, in order to ascertain some semblance of normality. The aggressive nature of this disease is so persistent it leaves me in a ceaseless, paralyzing state of flux, always in fear of when the trap door is going to spring open again, sending me plummeting down into the empty spaces of the abysmal chasm of despair that encircles my Being like a moat around a castle. What is lurking beneath the dark waters is a mystery. Whatever is there always makes a play at taking me under and drowning me with its unnatural method of abduction. And still I try to swim across. I always try to swim across even when I know what awaits me. Is it foolishness or determined zealousness that keeps me going back for more? Do I not know any better or do I know too well that all things must crumble at some point – perhaps I am testing for weaknesses in the systematic preservation of Self #2, in order to annihilate her myself.

<u>10:42 PM</u>

The night closes in yet again. Cloistered in the darkness, I feel at home.

I need for something to happen. I could get a job but you know as well as I that my mental instability does not support a full-time (or part-time) occupation. The only occupation I have is dealing with my mental health issues. This bipolar disorder is a real pain in the ass, you know.

I have my appointment tomorrow morning in regards to

my knee. I wish it were the surgery. My knee is getting even worse. I hope the surgery is scheduled soon though because I don't know how much longer I want to wait. Do you suppose, J, there will come a day when I'll actually be able to function somewhat normally and rationally and be able to maintain some semblance of a productive life? I hope so.

MARCH 1, 2011
7:34 AM

WE ARE NEARING THAT time of March which will mark the two year anniversary of my near death. The snowmobile accident will have occurred two years ago come March sixth (I think). My counselor still believes that had a huge impact on me even though I keep insisting that is hasn't. She can't believe it didn't bother me. I can't believe it bothered everyone else so much. I told her that, yes, while most people probably would have panicked and drowned, I found it relatively easy to get out of the water. I still believe I had a little help from Jesse, if not others. It felt like someone was pushing me up to the ice and that it wasn't just me there in the water. Do you suppose...... Oh, I can't go down that road now. All that spiritual conjecture will drive me mad if I try to find a real answer. Just believe.

My counselor also told me that while she has been doing this job for thirty-five years, it's pretty difficult for someone to pull the wool over her eyes – but with me, she's seen me ten or eleven times and it took nearly as long for her to notice that I did present some signs of bipolar instead of just anxiety. She said she is "baffled" by me. What does it say when both your counselor and your doctor find you complicated enough to be baffled? I guess I'm still doing a good job of keeping people guessing.

11:22 PM

April first will be my surgery. I would be lying if I said I was not totally, one hundred percent thrilled about it. I can't wait. I wish it were tomorrow.

Other than that.... My professor called me an "impressive writer" ... and then gave me a 71 on my paper. I just cannot win in that class. I have to say though, since last week I have managed to get my grade from an 82 to a 91, so I can't be completely useless when it comes to that class. I feel as if I am. But my feelings of inadequacy stem from something far more rooted than academic failure. Failure in all things is my fear. Which is ironic, in a sense, all things considered, J – you know what I mean. My inadequacy and fear of failure are exactly why I fail things. I may not fail classes, and I may not fail at all things in life, but I feel as though I do. A 91 in a class, to me, is like failing. If I can't be perfect, absolutely perfect with no flaws, then it just doesn't seem good enough. How can one live with such expectation of Self? How can one possibly manage to muddle through every day when the bar is set so obscenely high? I don't think it's possible. I am not a demigod of any sort and cannot demand such abstract perfection from myself. And yet that is precisely what I do. I feel I am a failure when I perceive others as being disappointed in me (which is often); I feel I am a failure when I cannot concentrate on a simple task long enough to see it through (which is more often); I feel I am a failure when I can't resist the second or third Oreo cookie (ridiculous);

I feel I am a failure when I eat a candy bar, when I drink alcohol, when I sit and watch a movie instead of going out running, when I sequester myself in my room because I'm too reluctant to face anyone. Yes, I feel I am a failure. I cannot escape that damning self-assertion and it wreaks havoc on an already fragile state of mind. This fear, this paranoia, it throws me either into a paralyzing stasis where the inertia of my emotional balance is thrown so far off kilter I am either depressed and suicidal or manic and suicidal. And the fact that I am not suicidal at all just confuses matters more. I am not suicidal. There is a difference between being suicidal and having suicidal ideations. There is a huge difference. I have ideations, yes, they are thoughts that I cannot control no matter how happy or sad I may be at any given moment. The thoughts are there constantly. But I do not wish to kill myself. I may wish to die more often than most but I do not wish to kill myself. If I truly did, I would have done it long ago. Instead, I trudge along this lifeline of mine despite the fact that I have been rendered nearly useless in all things because of my polarizing personality.

I'm not entirely sure where all this is going, where I am going, if I'm going anywhere at all. Failure. Failure to move, failure to initiate, failure to communicate; it is all-pervading.

MARCH 2, 2011
8:54 AM

I COULD WRITE ABOUT how I'm feeling this morning. I'm feeling lost and slightly panicked. I'm feeling a complete loss of identity at the same time as I feel I'm back to my old Self.

303

This old Self is the one who was there before August through January ever happened. This old Self was the one who was there before the dangerous debauchery and drinking into oblivion. This old Self was a bit more subdued and calm. I know I just said I felt lost AND panicked – but the calmness I'm referring to is always tinged with a bit of panic and the level is nowhere near as high as it was every single day that I was living up there with them. Talk about trying to find out what your triggers are.

I believe there is something after all of this mess but I can't say that our Fate is truly predestined. How intricate would that be? Then again, everything that seems to be in such chaos has a certain pattern to it. Chaos itself is never truly madness – it can be perceived as madness but there is always a cause for it and always a consequence and true chaos would have it as no cause and no ultimate consequence. Chaos is structured to look like madness but really there is an underlining of patterns that evolve and change and it happens at such a rapid pace our minds are not noticing the design and therefore we refer to it as chaos. There is madness though. There is madness and pain and brutality. These are all structured as a form of chaos. Something that our minds cannot rightly comprehend, such as the brutality of murder, the depravity of man, the sicknesses that take hold of the Mind and wrap it up in a tightly confined plethora of psychosis – with nowhere to go, the thoughts then manifest themselves into actions and the aftermath leaves a stain of crimson on the walls and floors.

Yes, there is madness and chaos in the world but it is structured in its own dizzying way. I don't think we are meant to understand it. If we were meant to, we would. As it is, I know I cannot figure out why things happen as they do. I only know that whatever happens, it will have to be dealt with. These mistakes we make, I think we think we have to believe we make them for a reason in order to try and correct them. It is a fallback mechanism for the chaos we don't understand, this sentiment of 'things happen for a reason'. But is it a fallback instinct of thought or does it derive from truth? It's hard to say.

MARCH 4, 2011
8:24 AM

SOMETHING FEELS VERY OFF and it doesn't feel as though it's an alignment issue (I sound like an automobile). It feels off with my Soul, or at least the physical aspect of my Soul. I know that doesn't seem possible. Souls do not have physical components; but don't they? Aren't we the physical embodiment of a Soul? Yes, I think so. Something feels very wrong. I don't know if it's the medication I'm on or what but the sensations have begun since I've been taking those meds. What the connection is, what the ailment is, I'm not entirely sure but it is affecting everything I do, especially my sleeping patterns. I cannot get comfortable.

<u>11:08 PM</u>

I used to write all the time about how I thought that, just once, people need to be completely honest with themselves. Just once they need to lay open the baggage of their lives and let people take a look. It's going to be like a rummage sale of my mind, pieces to buy and sell. I don't know what I have that is really of any worth to anyone but I'm hoping someone out there may deem it worthy enough to at least read, and I'm hoping someone out there will find a bit of comfort in what I write, to have the sensation of finally not feeling like they are alone with whatever it is they are feeling and where it derives from. Whether it's from something like Bipolar or some other circumstance. I have a story that can probably relate to a lot of people, if only they'd read it.

MARCH 9, 2011
8:26 PM

MY BLOOD PRESSURE WAS elevated today. My biggest problem is that I'm too good an actress when it comes to covering up my emotions. This is what my counselor tells me. She can't figure me out. She actually used the word "baffled" when describing it. My doctor told me today that I 'use fun words'. She had asked me how I was feeling this week compared to last week and I told her I felt complacent. She laughed a little and said, "You use such fun words". I guess she is not accustomed to her other clients using good vocabulary.

I am supposed to be writing notes about my 'feelings' (sounds so therapeutic) so I can give my counselor a better idea of what I do and what I feel during the week when I don't see or talk to her.

MARCH 10, 2011
1:37 PM

In accordance with my counselor's wishes that I write
down and keep track of my moods so she may have a better
understanding of what I feel throughout the week, I'll try to
comply. I awoke this morning most reluctantly. This morning,
like most mornings, found me wanting nothing more than to
fall back into a deep sleep and forget the world. Forget about
mornings, that is how I feel throughout every hour of the day
and night. To sleep is to forget. To sleep is to avoid. To sleep is
to dream. Being awake is the hard part, which is perhaps why
I find it so difficult to stay asleep, because of some twisted
need for self-destruction.

I feel like I'm bursting at the seams with things to say
and yet I can't articulate, in any capacity, what I need to say.
It's not just the things I want to say, it's the things I *need* to
say and my tongue is stilled, my voice wavers and disappears
and my will is diminished. Leaving me a deaf mute; leaving
me alone with thoughts that linger and destroy everything
in their path. Words spoken aloud can cause hurt and pain,
but words that remain silent can be just as destructive.

I fear my own storm is too powerful to be washed away
so easily. My storm rages. It wails and bellows. There is no
quiet in my storm. There is no lull or respite. My storm is
constant – irreversible. My storm is growing, becoming a
force all its own; a force I will soon be unable to handle on
my own. Not that I have ever been able to handle this on
my own – but there comes a time when even trying to do so

becomes so wearisome that one falters in faith – one resigns themselves to the obvious and unavoidable consequence. Failure. What will failure to subdue this storm mean for me? My end? The end of all things. My world will continue to grow – but without me – as it has done in years past. So it really will be no different. People don't understand now – and they will continue on, not understanding. That is my world. Welcome.

MARCH 11, 2011
3:15 PM

THERE HAS BEEN MASSIVE destruction in Japan after an 8.9 earthquake, epicenter offshore, created a 23 foot tsunami that ravaged the northeastern coastline of Japan. Naomi lives in Osaka and as of a few hours ago has said she is alright. There was just another earthquake, 6.6, in central Japan and I am waiting to hear something from Naomi again and perhaps to keep hearing something from her until this disaster subsides and Japan is stilled and blessed with solid, firm ground again; no more quakes, no more tsunamis, just stillness. The devastation looks horrific. I am so thankful Naomi wasn't in the midst of it, but my heart goes out to all those who were.

Thoughts and prayers are with Naomi, her friends and family, right now. So devastating.

(2014: Naomi is a friend whom I met in Fairmount, IN. She is from Japan and travels all the way to Fairmount in remembrance of James Dean. It still amazes me that all these people, from all over the world, come to this little town to remember and honor the life of a man most of us never knew.

As I've mentioned before, Fairmount, and James Dean, has afforded me the greatest of gifts; unyielding friendships).

<u>9:55 PM</u>
If there is any good that can come from such devastation, it is the fact that the world unites. Why does it always take such a tragedy to remind us all that we can help one another? That we can be there for one another, not only in a time of need, but in times of good, in times of prosperity? Why is it always the tragedies that bring us together, that remind us that there truly are more important things in the world than our differences. The fact that we are all so alike when it comes down to the core of our souls. It's the superficial differences that work to separate us. I will never understand this world, or the people in it.

MARCH 12, 2011
9:33 AM

I THINK BACK ON those inebriated six months I lived through and I can't even recognize myself. The things I did are not things I would normally do. The things I said and agreed to were not things I would normally do. I could blame it all on the influence of alcohol but I have to take some of the responsibility upon myself because I was still slightly aware of what I was doing and the fact that I did not really want to be doing it. That thought was always with me and yet I went ahead with it all anyway? Why? To not disappoint? How sick and twisted is that? But true nonetheless. I twisted my insides all around in order to fit in with the crowd. The crowd which offered no consistency in friendship, only a manipulative desire which held me at bay. It is my own fault. I caved to peer pressure.

MARCH 15, 2011
10:06 AM

I WOULD LIKE A nice quiet place to sit and write until I can write no more. I cannot find such a place. Even the Quiet seems to scream. It bleeds of tension and the smallest spark ignites a panic from the well within me that drowns me as I sleep and slumber through the day. I walk in a daze – in an abashed sense of forlornness. I seek Quiet and yet I know if I ever found it, I would be subdued by the Silence rather than released. There is no Place for me – no Place where I may unleash this torrent of emotion and words that sit in the deep pit of my soul waiting for release. It is like I hold them captive – depriving them of the nourishment they need to survive. I torment these words - these words that want nothing more than to be heard – to be given Voice. I torment them by inhibiting them in all their capacities. I silence them before they even have the opportunity to Speak. Cloistered in their dark space as I am cloistered in mine. I long for a moment without fear, without worry, without panic. Why am I so afraid to be heard when all I want is some understanding? Why am I so afraid to be heard when I know I speak the truth, when honesty is the only key to the Soul – why be afraid to turn the key? To be heard is to be known. Maybe I do not wish to have that – no recognition – to be Mist upon the world instead of something concrete and tangible – to be ethereal – a corporal specter. To walk through this world as such is the only way I know how to survive. Why so keen on survival, I sometimes wonder to myself. What is it that keeps me holding on to this Life when all around me I see the grieved faces of loss, frustration, anger, and a frailty of heart so magnificent it's a wonder the heart still plods on. The heart doesn't know of loss, it doesn't know of love, hate, anger, or joy. The heart is nothing. It encompasses nothing but four chambers. Four chambers devoid of sentiment, of any emotional carrion; the heart is nothing but a muscle – one that, in time, may atrophy of its own accord. The heart is nothing. The Soul is the lively spark that initiates all bodily function – without the soul, the body is nothing more than an empty vessel and the heart may as well stop its fervent beating. The Soul carries emotion, carries what we deem 'heartbreak'; the Soul is Self. The body means nothing. The body is a transport, a corporal physical vessel that's only real purpose is to carry the Soul around until it learns what it needs to learn, until it accomplishes its intended goals, until it's time to move on. The body will die but the Soul will continue to soar. Survival of Life is guaranteed – death or no. The Soul will continue to live even as the body dies – so why so keen on the survival of this vessel that is nothing more than a housing project? My Soul is encased within this body – and as the body ages, withers, and eventually dies – the Soul is set free – never forgetting what it has learned, never forgetting the other Souls it connected with, and never regretting the Life it led. Soul regret is the hardest to overcome. The very basis of our existence rests in our Soul and when regret burrows so deeply as that, the Soul is tormented. An anguished Soul can never be at rest. An anguished Soul can never find Quiet. Perhaps that is why the Quiet eludes me so. My Soul is anguished, it is guilt-ridden over something I cannot even identify; it just is. The Quiet is all I yearn for. A place to concentrate, to set my sights on my goal and attempt to achieve it – I cannot even attempt to achieve what I long for when all around me (inside of me) is chaos and confusion. Quiet sought and never found creates such a disagreeable state of mind. I know my suffering is because of my beleaguered Soul. It is wrenching itself into two – and the process is like self-persecution. You've seen the game 'tug-of-war' – imagine a grief-stricken Soul incorporating that game into a battle of wills of its own – playing tug of war with one thing – one Soul. What good can possibly come from that? Being ripped in two will only create more confusion. To mend itself together is what my Soul should aspire. But mending the Soul together requires Faith – an abundance of Faith which I do not possess. I think to find the Quiet would be the first step of mending – a Quiet solitude where my Soul can sit in repose; can contemplate without interruption the causes which prompted the cessation of peace and tranquility; which terminated the incentives to learning, to Living, to being aware. Who longs to be ignorant? Who wishes to not know, not be informed, and not be aware of what is going on? Only a Soul in search of Quiet wishes for those things. I wish I did not know, had not heard, and was not aware of the world's troubles, of my troubles, of my people's troubles. I wish I were ignorant of the ways in which things work. But I am not. I am very much aware. I am aware enough to know that my survival is not based on Will alone; it is based on every one of those instances that I wish I was not aware of. Perhaps that is why I wish I were unaware in the first place. Without knowing those things I would not know that my survival so heavily depends upon them. It just so happens that is the way it is. Life is a series of codependent relationships and when the Soul refuses to participate, when the Soul rebuffs such intimacies, the Soul is dying. The Quiet is all I yearn for right now. The Quiet is the one thing I cannot find.

MARCH 15, 2011

WRITING HAS TAKEN ON an aura of hesitancy that stymies me. Inaction of the written thought subdues all thoughts. All thoughts then get lost in the myriad of my mind. It can be quite a desolate place to be – rife with isolation, fear, and sadness. It is sadness with no bearing, it is directionless in the way it has no relevant purpose for being. It exists merely as an appendage of my Soul. I believe I may have been born discontented and am merely trying to adjust to the fate that long ago adhered itself to my Being. My thoughts are dizzying in their array. Illogical and tempestuous. Thoughts rise within me, testing the barriers of my mind and trying to evoke some probative form of escapism and yet my hand is staid. My fingers rest lightly upon the keyboard, anxious to speak but reluctant to begin. To begin would signify there is an End. I am not ready to end so I never begin. I have been thinking a lot about past transgressions. I know regret is a damaging frame of mind to reside in, but from time to time I think it can be beneficial as well. My regrets loom large in the retrospect of my Eye

APRIL 9, 2011 10:31 PM

I CANNOT COME AWAY from watching a movie such as Splendor in the Grass (as I have just finished watching) without feeling a kinship with the characters. Movies like Girl, Interrupted; books like Prozac Nation, or all of Sylvia Plath's works, there is a soulful connection that takes place. Perhaps it is because I can understand the madness behind a breakdown. I can understand feeling as though I want to die. I can understand the hopelessness that consumes and the darkness that spreads. I know that fictional characters are created but they are created through someone, by someone, because of someone. It can be a bit terrifying to realize that when I truly want to feel connected to someone or something, I have to search for a connection with one of these people, either portrayed fictionally or real like Sylvia P. or Susanna K. or Elizabeth W. There is a deep-seeded affinity that I have for characters in emotional pain, in an emotional struggle to keep their heads above the water. There is a yearning to be there to say, "I understand", and to hold them the way I wish to be held; by arms that will not betray nor judge; by arms that will love and gently sway to the rhythm of my heart. My longing to be understood and accepted. Accepted in spite of my madness, accepted in spite of my longing to fade away. To be understood for once in this lifetime. I cannot come away from watching a movie such as this without a resurgence of feelings and emotions that leave me teetering on the edge; there is a ledge I come to every now and then, a ledge which tempts me and beckons me; just beyond this ledge, though I cannot see, I can feel an infinite release impending; I can feel eternity as it attempts to close its fists on my life, sealing my fate. I sometimes feel that it is my fate, or it is my destiny, to succumb to these whims I so often talk of. I feel I am intended to close in upon my life in such a manner as to render me a lost cause. I can say a prayer to St. Jude, but it is still all that I am. I feel time tick-tocking away as I founder in the depths of my mind; these thoughts tumble and fall as though it is they who have taken the leap. To dangle one foot over the ledge, wagging it to and fro as if enticing a gust of wind or a stray bird to swoop down and knock me off balance so I fall. It would not be my fault then, it would be an act of God; accidental and yet natural.

My little world is distinguished by its defense. The wall of self-protection is so high and carved with such delicate and intricate warnings that no one dares trespass – my wraith can be devastating. Still I wonder what the day will be like when my wall crumbles and my world is flooded by a stampede of well-intentioned hearts. The day will be dark though the sun will shine. The day will come to a restless night that knows no end. The day will dwell on hours spent never recognizing the hours passed. The day will see me as a ghost upon their world, finally free from mine

APRIL 11, 2011
12:30 AM

THERE IS THIS FEELING deep within the well of my soul that whispers to me, "I do not care". I am beginning to wonder if that is true. There are so many things that I would like NOT to care about and yet I find myself in agony over them nonetheless. There are so many instances which should not warrant a second glance and yet I look upon them with worn eyes three or four more times. I am beginning to not care about the fact that I still care. I don't want to care. I don't want to feel. I don't want to do anything but be comfortably numb to this great big world; this big ol' world that does nothing for me – as I do nothing for it. This big world is a different creature from my own little world. The big bad world inhabits my little world by force. My little world is my Poland. The big bad world crushes in on me, throwing its formidable weight around and causing me to lose balance, to lose hope, to lose….. This feeling gnaws at me and all my good intentions are counter-acted by a shroud of ensuing hopelessness. I thought I was supposed to be getting better. And yet here I am. Perhaps I need more time to adjust to the medication.

I would drift away if I could allow myself to do so. But I can't. I am still anchored down; a captive; a hostage in this Life. It tricks me into believing in tomorrow when all tomorrow really promises are more lies and broken dreams. My disappointment is not borne of pessimism… my pessimism is borne of disappointment. But what am I disappointed in? Myself? Easy answer; my life, my friends, my instability, my disorder, my existence; I am disappointed in all of these; I am disappointed in me.

APRIL 27, 2011
10:32

AT TIMES I FEEL like a conquering soul who can do anything and two minutes later I believe I'm the most desolate soul on the earth. Back and forth, back and forth do these emotions ricochet within. I would rather sleep my time away than be awake.

<u>10:53 PM</u>

So all the chocolate, candy, and breadsticks I ate today totally negate the workouts I've done in the past few days. I rode the bike a couple of miles again but this time went up the big hill by the house. I made it but my legs were burning almost the entire way. I keep having these thoughts about losing weight – the same thoughts that got me into trouble before with the eating disorder. I don't think I'm capable of returning to an eating disorder because I haven't got the dedication to achieve it. I'm not saying this is a bad thing in any way because I don't want to go through what I did from '03 on. I still struggle with abstaining from that behavior but I know how damaging it is. Not that I should at all be concerned with potential damage from an eating disorder, it's a matter of will to desist. I think of those times and realize that it was not just an eating disorder that I was afflicted with, it was also a manic phase because I was able to not eat a thing and I was on the go all the time; riding my bike fifty or sixty miles a day, kayaking, playing tennis and basketball, and running. All of these things I would do daily on hardly any sleep and no food. I remember sustaining myself by Oakhurst Low-fat Chocolate Milk and bananas. That is all I would eat except for the time I went 18 days without eating at all. I honestly don't know how I survived. I told my counselor about my past bike rides and not eating and she was amazed that I hadn't keeled over and died with the amount of exercise I was getting. I don't know why I survived. I also don't know how I survived going through the ice with the snowmobile. I should have been dead when that happened but I have to say, when that happened, I felt I was not alone in the water. My thoughts immediately turned to Jesse who had just passed away nearly two months before. I do think I had some divine help that day; Jesse, Katie, etc. So many times I have cheated death and all times that natural instinct for survival kicked in. It's amazing what the body will do on instinct rather than thought. I didn't panic when I was in the water but I also don't remember thinking clearly. I was thinking how cold the water was and how ignorant I was to do what I did. It was completely my fault and I own up to that but how I made it through that ordeal, I still am not certain how.

MAY 3, 2011
11:59 AM

RESPONSIBILITY BECKONS WITH ITS mighty hand and yet this Self is too preoccupied with the vision rather than the discernible implications. Responsibility is easy to ignore. Responsibility to Self is the easiest of all to ignore. Self sits in wait and in want and often goes neglected for months at a time while this other part resumes control over mind, body, and soul, leaving Self to wither and decay in the abscess of Mind. The pattern of behavior is too easy to assume and the passage of time does nothing but perpetuate the needling attempts of self-correction into the background with the thought, "I'll get to that later." Later. Is there such a thing? Is there a moment in time that truly encompasses the term 'later' – or is it all now, now, now! Every moment is now because all we have are these moments we are in. Tomorrow's moments may not present themselves. This evening's moments may not be ready to reveal themselves. My moments may end as soon, or before, I shut this computer down. Moments are now – now are moments. And when will the moments cease? At times I wish they would cease abruptly and irrevocably NOW. I am in the *motions* and yet feel no obligations towards them. They, like me, simply are. But neither is fulfilling the Great Promise; A foolhardy notion to believe in, if you ask me. The Great Promise of life, of the future, even of these moments, a ridiculous sentiment to believe in. Life is nothing more, nothing less, than the *motions* we go through. A means to the end is all this life is going to provide. Moments of joy never last, moments of sorrow never heal, moments of contentment fade away like the horizon at dusk, and moments of liberty are merely confined moments of a structured familiarity we all adhere to. Liberty is not freedom nor is freedom liberty. Neither truly exists except in the ethereal sense of the word. My Liberty is hinged to the foundations of a country I was borne into. I could exile myself but still would find no liberty. I could throw propaganda around, as per my 'rights', but my 'rights' do not exemplify liberty. True liberty only comes with death. Life is structured and formed around the concept of liberty but it does not intone the word in all its derivative diatribes. Liberty is a sanctioned freedom that is ruled by confining expectations and measured doctrines. Liberty precludes our freedom.

<u>9:03 PM</u>

Why I continue to blindly believe in tomorrow is a mystery. I suppose that is all hope really is – a mystery. Why have hope when nothing ever seems to change and every night finds you where every other night has always found you: alone and feeling completely disregarded by the world entire. I don't expect the world to recognize me, but I would at least expect recognition from myself. But it is I who chooses to disregard myself. How is that possible, you wonder, but it really is not so difficult. My existence is merely a precursor to the existence which awaits. It awaits my arrival as I await its. A formidable codependence we seem to have formed without anyone else knowing.

7:44 PM

It was truly a day to reminisce. I posted those photos from high school and I think it made a lot of people's day to look through those. It makes my day to know that maybe, just maybe, the fact I posted those made someone smile. But it brings about a bittersweet feeling – almost a remorse on my part – for the past and all its promise. But what I remember most about that time was not an upbeat, looking-ahead, enthusiastic outlook of the future. It was a devastating realization that life was going to change and I knew I was not ready to run the race of trying to catch up with the future as it unfolded. I knew I would always be at least two steps behind. These thoughts that are with me now are thoughts that have been with me my entire life. I cherish my memories from that time but I regret a lot of them as well because they are all tinged with the familiar downcast pessimism that permeated, and continues to permeate, my existence as it was, as it is, as it will presumably remain. The past is something to revere not regret. And while I do not regret my time spent with my friends, I do regret the forlornness that held me captive during those moments. I was never free. I was always trapped within my mind. I longed for that one person to know me in a way that even I didn't know myself. I longed for someone to understand my plight and my hesitations without my having to utter a single word. I longed for a friend I didn't have to explain away my neuroses to but that understood me and my inhibitions in a sympathetic way. But I would never allow anyone to get that close to me. Who I was then is who I am now. I am taking the steps to allow people in but I have to wonder if it is too little too late. I have a sense of remorse about the future. It doesn't seem possible to have remorse for something that has not yet happened but the questions that will linger after the fact, the memories that will be tainted and questioned ceaselessly and doggedly, I have remorse for that. For all that will be left behind, there is remorse and a bittersweet sense of joy in the moments that made life worthwhile. It was a day to reminisce about the people and the moments that shaped me. The people in my life who made me a better person; the people who made me smile, laugh; the people who brought joy and gratitude in my life and made me realize the real purpose of being here: Friendship. Life is about the people in it; it is not what we do or what we perceive we should have done; life is about friendship; it is about bonds forged and moments shared. And I feel my moments with friends have run dry. I have been usurped by tragedy rather than promise. And this remorse I feel, even while relishing the joy I brought to others today with those silly photographs, the remorse makes me smile sentimentally. It is a conflicting response to have but in its own way, it makes perfect sense. In my mind, it is often the conflicting reactions that make the most sense to me.

At times, I can see things so clearly. At other times, things are so cloudy that I don't think a clear view will ever be seen again. Those moments I see clearly, those are moments marked with an almost surreal sense of recognition. Things I see are not only clearer, they are significantly more *real*. Colors are more vibrant, texture is denser; it is as if my eyesight is peeling back the layers of everything I see and truly seeing them for what they are; contours are more marked while silver shines in almost a luminescence. Watching the world through these eyes, I see more, I feel more, I am more; my thoughts are clear, my mind is focused, and my senses are content. But then in a flash, imperceptible to see, my vision clouds again and my mind jumps into an erratic motion of thoughts that tumble and ricochet in a tumultuous cavalcade. The moments of clarity never seem to last as the moments of confusion do.

I am my own future.

You may not wish to be here, but you are. You may not wish to breathe, but you do. You are not going to get anywhere if you do not move. SO MOVE. Get out and find something that you know you can do. If you stay where you are, you will cease to be. Find them again. You need to find them again even if it's the last thing that you do.

MARCH 11, 2011

I FEEL THE NEED to get out there and reconnect with the world. I've been in my own little world for so long now that the prospect of 'getting out there' feels quite foreign to me.

Self-realization can be devastating. It can be awakening. It can be revolutionary in terms of identity. Self-realization can make you want to hide yourself away to shield yourself from the world and its hypocritical standards or it can make you want to reach the highest peak and scream your truth, the rest of the world be damned. Self-realization can be all encompassing in the way of future ideals. It can be scary. It can be confusing. It can be soul searching or soul destructive. Soul destruction carries a heavy burden – the soul carries a heavy burden when self-realization is never truly realized – it just sits at the bottom of your soul, atrophying from inactivity, dying from stale air, petrifying from the cold, frigid atmosphere. Being honest with oneself can be a hard thing to do. Being honest with others can be impossible if one is not first honest with themselves. Am I honest? No.

MAY 20, 2011
11:08 PM

THE WORLD DOES NOT seem as dire as it usually does for me. I have finally dragged myself out of the house and socially interacted with someone today. I know, it's a big step from the lonesome, solitary figure I have cut myself out to be. Now, if only I could make a habit of this I may be able to get somewhere in my life. I know I have to make a concerted effort in order to achieve this somewhat lofty goal (lofty for me) but I see no reason, no logical reason, why it cannot be so.

MAY 23, 2011
8:47 PM

I AM DISTRACTED. My distraction stems from worry and loneliness. There is no one around here and there is nothing for me to do. I cannot go out and get a job, as is evident by my failed attempts, not to mention I don't feel as though I'm capable of doing anything with fervor and without having a panic induced anxiety attack. I am not ready to face this big World. I am not ready to face myself yet.

I feel damned.

I feel thrown into purgatory and forsaken.

JUNE 8, 2011
9:36 PM

ONLY TIME WILL TELL all. The story of my Life will be a testament to the Time spent dwelling on the unimportant and the time spent relishing the sweet victories that friendships bring to a beleaguered and weary soul.

JUNE 11, 2011
9:50 PM

LIFE IS BEGINNING TO feel more real. I'm not sure I enjoy the sensation.

JUNE 12, 2011
7:34 PM

I ALIENATE PEOPLE WITH my awkwardness.

JUNE 13, 2011

MY SILENCE IS ANYTHING but Golden. My silence is borne of fear and desperation.

JUNE 16, 2011

AS LIFE BEGINS TO feel more and more real, I find myself taking a step back and surveying my surroundings; what I find, I don't like. What I wish to find, I will never see. My eyes will close upon the world tonight and delve into the dreams I do not dare to see. Perhaps the medication is allowing me to see more clearly the effect my disposition has on others. I am beginning to feel the need to come clean. I am beginning to feel the need to open the closet of my soul and spill forth the real me for the world to see. To be understood is what I crave. To have others realize what has been going on with me, giving them the answers they seek as to why I am the way I am, why I have been the person I have been. I am just realizing for myself that I've wasted a lot of time by ignoring the emotions that rumble through my mind. I am beginning to understand it is not my fault. It is no one's fault. I am the way I am because of something ultimately out of my control.

All the years I sought control, I delved into dangerous and self-destructive behavior. I am tired of that life. I am tired of trying to maintain alone. I needed help. I sought help. I am reaping the rewards of finally making the decision to get help.

10:44 PM

Went out to dinner with some friends Tuesday evening. It was such a pleasant time. It was the best two hours I've had in a long time. Mary looks wonderful, she's doing incredibly well, and she seems to have her life streamlined in order with goals and ambition. It's incredibly nice to see her doing so well. I always knew she'd find her way, find her niche in this world and be extraordinary. Jane is Jane. It's impossible not to adore her; so energetic and lively with such a pleasant and sincere demeanor. It was wonderful to see them both and to spend two hours with them.

JULY 19, 2011
9:05 AM
B&N

TIME CAN BE AN elusive creature. It doesn't seem possible, but it's true. How often time gets away from me and how often I willingly let it. Time cannot get away from me unless I provoke it to do so and that seems to be exactly what I have been doing. I have neglected many things, most of all myself, but I have been adamant about resisting the end of time as I know it.

So you wonder, what has been happening with me, to me, around me.

I am currently reading Portia de Rossi's memoir about her anorexia and bulimia problems. The book hits home on so many levels and at times I feel as though it could have been me who was writing the words. It is such a personal look into the life of a public figure who, in many ways, is much like me. While I cannot relate to fame and fortune, I can relate to the Voice that resides in one's head that berates and mocks, insults and demeans. The Voice can be heard at any time, day or night, and it is almost an omnipresent life-force all its own. I have been hearing the Voice again in my own way lately. It is most usually present when things begin to look promising; it is then the Voice rushes in, bulldozing its way into my mind with a force so powerful it cannot be ignored. Portia's book is her personal recollection and yet it strikes a chord within me and makes my soul vibrate with recognition.

As for myself, I have compiled my book into 485 pages. My journals are deeply personal and yet I want nothing more than for others to read the words, to relate to the words, to say to themselves, 'I'm not alone, there is another like me'. When life seems hopeless, I write in a frenzy. When life seems uplifting, I do not write at all.

For the longest time life was something of a burden and an obligation; living seemed necessary but not desired. Life had a way of pulling away from me and the distance proved troublesome as I sought solace and found none within my disquieted mind. And disquiet is precisely the word to describe my mind; itself is a frenzied adversary at times. How funny it seems to face off against myself, fighting an internal foe that is really only a shadow of my better half, living in the darkness whilst trying to envelop the remaining light. It has dimmed, this light, but it has not been extinguished. I fear there may come a day when the light burns out, stifling its last breath with uncertainty and languishing in its last moments with a purveyance of sustenance that does nothing more than feast upon itself. It devours itself as it devours peace of mind. There is a moment, marked well within the future, when the light will eventually fade away. And here we go back to Time. Time marked with interludes of transitory emotions that take flight, circle back, and make the rounds again.

I am stymied by insecurity when it comes to talking with those who I am supposed to be most comfortable talking to. I find myself most awkward around those who are closest to me. And yet, to those I do not know, I feel an affinity with our respective anonymity. I like the feeling of being anonymous in this great big world. Yet at the same time, I yearn to be seen. I yearn to be heard. The only way I am going to be heard is if I find it within myself to speak. I am not adept at that little attribute. Speaking has never been my forte.

As life seems to tumble on, I find myself wanting to catch up to it. It seems all of life is serenely just out of reach. My fingertips brush along the side of Life but cannot get a firm grasp.

AUGUST 1, 2010
3:07 PM

WITH NO DISTRACTIONS, IT is easy to be swept away by idealism.

Distractions, at least, counteract the thoughts of perfection that drive one to the brink.

It is coming back that is the most difficult obstacle.

How to live in a world where idealism is the peak of the mountain, the unattainable, unfeasible, rung on the ladder of perfection?

My survival hinges on this ambitious and often self-defeating train of thought that sees me unraveling within my mind the hesitations which stop me in my tracks. It is my ambition to overcome those hesitations that stop me. But my ambition falters, often and unerringly, it falters. This ideal I set before myself is no longer attainable. Perhaps it never was attainable, not sustaining in any way. Perhaps it was a once in a lifetime achievement that can no longer be achieved and should no longer be sought. And yet I do seek it. I seek it and long for it and wish I had the fortitude to endeavor on the cycle again but I do not. I do not possess the strength I once did. I am tired of the fight and wish for nothing more than for it to be over. I fear it will never be over, not so long as I breathe in this fleshly world. There is a tug-of-war within me that rages throughout the day, throughout the night, and no one guesses at its urgency. No one knows of its lingering and malignant presence. It maligns my being with the thoughts of perfection. But what is perfection? Who can measure perfection with any real accuracy? Perfection is an afterthought that echoes within the mind. It resides in the back corner, it has found a comfortable niche within my psyche and it beckons with promises of fulfillment and contentment. Perfection is the apple so high in the tree that it sways with every breath of wind and it remains just out of reach from our fingertips. We brush alongside the idea of perfection but never do we achieve the lofty goal. There is always someone else, somewhere, something else, somewhere, which sets new sights on perfection; which defines perfection in a new and bolder way than ever before and so the cycle begins anew. And the downtrodden and weary tire from the fight, the struggle to reach the goal, and they succumb to the lowliness of perceived defeat.

And I wonder, have I been defeated? My defeat seems all but sealed, stamped, and notarized by a higher authority than myself. But defeat resides only in my mind. The thoughts that scream at me, defeat! echo only in my mind. My mind can be a desolate adversary. It can destroy any peace, any contentment, any compliment, and any accomplishment I may yield. My mind is my own black hole; it is an abyss of thought that I find myself resigned to. My mind is my judgment, my sentence, and my foe. It is within the mind where I struggle most. And it is a wearying battle but one I will not easily succumb to.

AUGUST 3, 2011
6:57 PM

THE MEEK OF HEART always sacrifice their will.

AUGUST 11, 2011
4:24PM

DRINKING WINE AND LISTENING to Brandi Carlile; at this moment, life is good. Life is great. Life is suddenly worth living. Why, why, why do I feel these feelings now, when so many moments have passed me by, why suddenly do I find myself here, reveling in these newfound emotions and this newfound arena to play the game of Life in. Why do I suddenly find myself becoming surrounded by a new and different group of people who not only define themselves singularly and independently, but in turn define me as well? Me; someone who has always been searching for the right identity and here I am, being shown an identity that I recognize as a mirror image of my own. Why do I suddenly find myself smiling at a mere memory, a lingering thought; smiling at possibility when ever before I just found myself wishing for the thoughts to stop. But the thoughts have changed in perception and view. I feel my world has been somewhat toppled upside down and I am liking the view better than ever before. There is so much left to discover but for once I am looking forward to the journey. Of course, it is not without hesitation or second-guessing. I have not suddenly become invincible in an armor of happy gratitude but I have a bit more of a shield now than ever before. All you need is Love. But what I have now is encouragement for the next day, and the next, and the next.

<u>11:00 PM</u>
And the night rolls on, the darkness spreads, the time for

sleep slumbers near, and my mind races with thoughts that leave a deliriously delicious aftertaste of desire. Never before have I felt this intense. I keep writing and writing and writing but there is no course of action I can take to alleviate it. Nor do I want to alleviate it. I want to revel in it. I want to swim in it and burrow within the firmament of it. I want to lap up the flame and have it burn within me to fan the fire of this desire. I want the desire to be satiated but at the same time the anticipation of it is what makes the ride so thrilling.

Things progress in their own time and, like I mentioned before, the anticipation of the ongoing progress keeps me on the tip of my toes trying to peer over to catch a glimpse of what the future may hold.

AUGUST 12, 2011
10:40PM

I WONDER HOW I managed to end up where I am; all of the little things that had to be set in place in order to get me here. It's the connection with someone, more than anything else, it's the connection that keeps us all wanting more. To have that connection with another human being, regardless of race or gender, to connect with another on this great big earth, just one person, it's an amazing thing to ponder. It's amazing to think of the world and the people in it and the people who end up in your life. Every moment is marked by something extraordinary if we just stop to look at the moments, to breathe in the moments, to revel in them and take them for what they are and for what they potentially could be.

AUGUST 27, 2011

I HAVE NOT SUFFERED a severe anxiety attack in weeks. I think the medication is working small little miracles for me. My body, once so tense and rigid has become almost languid in repose. My heart which used to beat so erratically and so fervently has steadied itself to a somewhat dull and common pace, fueled not by anxiety but by simple Life. Life has become a treasure rather than a burden. I have been going out with friends and I have been restful rather than restless. The ease with which I now find myself in social situations is such a relief to me. To be unburdened in social situations rather than carrying around the proverbial weight of the world has lessened my overall anxiety to a dull beating rhythmic occurrence. Relief does not actually do justice to the feeling of tranquility that has catapulted me back into the World once more. I have never felt so free. My body can rest instead of being held in restraint. My body can relax instead of being alert and focused on the anxiety that once used to paralyze me.

My depression, as well, has become a relic to me. No longer do I have suicidal ideations. No longer do I wish to die. No longer do I cloister myself in my room, talking to no one, seeing no one, avoiding everyone. My depression has taken a nosedive into obscurity and I couldn't be more relieved. To live every day with an insatiable desire to live is a new experience, one which helps ease the anxiety within my mind.

My mind, as well, has become more concentrated and focused. It is not where it could be when it comes to concentration and focus but it is slowly making its mark on my psyche and working to alleviate the once constant and unbearable frenzy of thought and despair. My depression no longer defines me and no longer accompanies me wherever I go. I have not felt depressed in weeks and I've never before experienced such a stretch of time, of calmness, of contentment. My body no longer longs for the peaceful retreat of solitude, it longs to be out and about, mingling, joining the rest of the World in a joint commitment of Living.

AUGUST 28, 2011
6:09 AM

SITTING IN A TRAVEL plaza off the I90 W interstate in New York. Four hundred miles in and four hundred miles which has to be the longest drive to Dunkin' Donuts ever. But here I sit, silently and independently, sipping a DD brew coffee and watching updates on Hurricane Irene. I have been driving since 8:00 last night. I should arrive in Chicago Monday morning, given that I sleep for longer than an hour stretch at a time. I did take a little power nap back in MA. It has been difficult thus far to even see twenty feet in front of me as I drive. The rain whiplashes the windshield and the darkness spreads like an underground cavern. It has been dark, dark, dark. I am much surprised I didn't go off the road during the night it's been so dark. As it is, the morning sun is set to rise and it will be heralded in my rearview mirror. There is something so endearing about watching the sun rise in my rearview mirror. Perhaps that has to do with the fact the east is behind me as I head west. There is always something quite sentimental about hitting the road heading West. I already miss certain people. Hurricane Irene: I don't expect the wind to rain ratio is going to put the state of Maine underwater. I would have liked to get online here but there is a connectivity problem that I can't seem to remedy so my updates will have to wait and my family will have to continue to guess where I am in this little world of mine. I cannot wait to get to my destination; Chicago, Indianapolis, and finally, home sweet home, Fairmount, IN.

<u>7:46 AM</u>

At yet another travel station, waiting out the sleepiness, staving off the desire to fall asleep for ten hours straight. I suppose I really should try to get some sleep but it seems a useless endeavor as I appear to be wired at the moment. You go for so long without sleep and you begin to wonder if you really need to. I haven't much to write about yet. Nothing has happened so far which is both a blessing and a curse because I am bored, bored, bored. My anxiety hasn't piqued at all since I've been on the road. I contribute this to the fact that it is in my car where I am most comfortable. I also contribute this to the fact my anxiety hasn't reached its peak in a few weeks now. Where has this anxiety gone? I am glad to be rid of it. It always had a tendency to get in the way of things before. My depression, still, is a no show. I am glad to be rid of that as well. I have my moments when I feel the darkness begin to seep into my thoughts once again but I shove those thoughts away and remind myself of how far I've come and what I've to look forward to. I have much in this life to look forward to. The least of which is this trip that will find me back 'home' after a two year absence. I cannot really fathom that it has been so long since I've been to Fairmount but there it is. The truth can never be denied. One may try and try, but the truth is steadfast and any other emotion is merely a lie. I'm done lying to myself. I'm done trying to be someone I am not. It takes far too much energy to repeat that cycle again and again. The rain is falling down still. In five hundred miles there has not been a dry sky anywhere. Attribute this to Irene if you will.

AUGUST 29, 2011
12:09 PM CHICAGO TIME

HERE I SIT, IN a lonely little Starbucks café in the Woodfield Mall in Chicago, IL. I am trying to make this font as small as possible in order to ward away potential onlookers who wish to read whatever it is that I am writing. Little do they know that I am writing nothing of importance as it is. I'm just rambling on and on. Where this situation would have caused massive anxiety on my part just a few months ago, I feel nothing but a calmness within that is at once enjoyable and perplexing. I say it is perplexing because I still am not used to this little feeling of tranquility. I am glad it is finally here, after all these years, but it is still surprising, the marked difference in how I feel.

I am stuck here at the mall until around three o'clock when Jerri gets out of work and we can then coordinate a plan in order to meet up. I do hope he comes to the mall because I'm not sure I'll be able to find my way out of here. I was here this morning for a bit before losing my car and frantically searching for about an hour for it. I found it.

I'm enjoying my staple white chocolate mocha as I sit

and people watch. People are fascinating creatures. I notice people looking and when I notice them looking they look away. I suppose I do the same thing but I don't look away as though I was caught doing something I was not supposed to be doing. I don't know if others are ashamed of their prying eyes intrusion or embarrassed by it.

AUGUST 31, 2011
1:54 PM
FAIRMOUNT, IN

MADE IT. I'M HERE at the gallery. My dear friends graciously offered to put me up for however long it is that I'm going to be staying. They are so great. I'm in my little room and ready for a nap. I'm sure I'll be writing again soon, perhaps after the nap. I ended up getting a pretty good nights' sleep last night in my car, thanks in no small part to the fact I took my Remeron. I'm tired, tired, tired still. I do think a nap will serve me well. I guess I'll try to do that.

Just got back from my friend's house, again. We stayed on the porch for a few hours listening to vinyl records. He gave me even more records. He bought some for me today as well. He has been far too generous to me this year but I appreciate it very much. I have the greatest friends on earth, I think. Emily will be coming up here tomorrow. Carole will be here for the Deaner breakfast. I get to see them both and that will be a good day regardless of anything else. I just have to learn how to live in the moment instead of living in the past and hoping for the future. The future is now. The future is here every second of the day and I can't be worried about what may happen in a week's time or what may or may not happen on any given day. Today is now. Live it.

OCTOBER 17, 2011
5:45PM

MY TIME IN INDIANA was well spent. That trip, at the very least, gives me fond memories to look upon during any time of great distress. Such memories make life easier to take in moments of despair or uncertainty. Think of the good times. Change the view, the perspective, and create a positive atmosphere. You do have friends. You do have people that care about you. You are not alone in this world even when you feel you are. Reach out and grab hold of someone who offers their hand.

OCTOBER 18, 2011

I HAD MY SESSION with my therapist today. It was my last session with her as well. I get no real benefits from having these sessions. What needs to happen, I think, is to find the right therapist. A therapist with whom I am comfortable. Try a few out like a car before buying into the pitch.

OCTOBER 20, 2011
11:29 AM

I FEEL RELIEF THAT I will no longer be going to see my former therapist. There is something about the very idea of therapy that does not jibe well with me. It's not that I don't believe in it or the benefits it can bestow on people but for me it just isn't productive. For one thing, I usually lie about things. For another thing, I hate talking about my "feelings" and answering questions that begin with "why" or the dreaded "what's the worst that can happen?" That is what I despise most. I don't know 'why', I just know what I know. Sometimes there are no answers to that query. I don't believe so anyway. Some things you just feel without a definitive answer to 'why'.

NOVEMBER 2011

WHAT HOLDS ME BACK is fear. It's the same old fear which has controlled my life until this point. It's not abated and not disappeared but it seems to intensify ever more so as the days pass. Things have progressed so fast and I feel powerless to the momentum. I am in fear that many things will end. If it does, the blame will more than likely rest with me and my own inability to follow through with things. I'm not going to let go though. I'm not going to give into the hesitations which always before have held me at bay. There is no sense in fear. There is no reason to fear the things that mean the most to us. And yet there is fear because we care so deeply for people, for things, for life that we become fearful of its end. We become fearful of a rejection that at once seems imminent and at other times seems impossible. My friends mean the world to me. The bonds forged throughout a lifetime are lasting. The importance of such bonds cannot be overestimated. It is the bonds of friendship and love which make a person whole. I have finally begun to allow myself to be loved, to feel worthy of love. Worthlessness has always encapsulated me within its all too powerful grasp. The emotion, the feeling of being worthless is a monster which feasts on insecurity. My insecurities are a glaring reminder of past transgressions. My insecurity leaves me with feelings of hopelessness despite the fact I realize their fleeting power. And it is a fleeting power. It ebbs between high and low. On days when my insecurities run rampant I begin to think every situation is hopeless. On days when my insecurities are low, I feel the potential coursing through my veins like blood itself. It is a life-sustaining feeling to diminish those insecurities. Though they are omnipresent, they are not overriding. If I have not given up yet chances are I won't. I have the potential to make this work, I just need to try. As for my pretending everything is alright, I still do. It is a habit of which seems impossible to break. When one goes for so long pretending to be someone they are not, they lose themselves to the actions of false pretense.

NOVEMBER 2011

I'M GOING TO HAVE to pull myself out from underneath the wreckage that is my mind if I'm ever going to be able to make it in the world. It's a struggle. It has always been a struggle, but if not now, when? Now is the time to beat it into submission. I've been submissive to it for the better part of my life and I think it's time the tables are turned.

I finally have the potential for a good life, with friends and family, and I can't let it all slip through my fingers again. I want to hold onto it all, hold onto them all, for all I'm worth because without them I become nothing again. I become an existence and that's all. Existing is not living. Living with fervor, purpose, love, and loyalty is the only way to make it in the world today. I have all of these things at my disposal and I must utilize them and gratefully take them for all they are worth. I love these people in my life. I would do anything for them, within my power. They keep me going.

DECEMBER 4, 2011

MY ANXIETY HAS NOT overpowered me into a stasis as of late. I am still much surprised at my lack of anxiety and my lack of depression.

I don't feel like I'm the same girl I used to be. In fact, I know that I am not. The girl from not so long ago would never have gone out to get a job; would never have gone out alone to a bar to meet people; would never have socialized away from her inner sanctum of people; would never have initiated conversations with strangers; would never have dared ask questions if she didn't know what she was doing; would never have disclosed to anyone she is bipolar; but I have done just that on many occasions. The girl I used to be would never had admitted to being in love. The girl I used to be would never have even allowed herself to love and that, I admit, is something I wish hadn't changed because love can be a painful emotion, especially when not reciprocated.

The girl I am now is honest and quite forthright. The girl I am now isn't afraid of mingling with the rest of common society. On the contrary, I rather crave the attention. The significance with which I feel my life spiraling is optimistic rather than the usual downtrodden outlook I once I had in life. I find great hope in the here and now. Yes, the girl I used to be would never have admitted to having a problem but the girl I am now isn't afraid of saying, "This is me. Take me or leave me. I am not going to change for you any longer". I am not going to bend my life around someone else's perception of me and I am not going to go out of my way to appease all because that is an impossible and arduous task. I am going to be who I am and I am going to take both the good and the bad with a grain of salt in order to temper down the hostile emotions that may bubble up to the surface on occasion. Those feelings are still there, they have not disappeared but they have dissipated. Every now and then a thought crosses my mind that finds me back in that old frame of mind but the thoughts no longer linger indefinitely. They come and they pass. I am not suddenly an infallible human being that no longer feels to the depth of her inner core but I am a fallible human being who feels emotional undercurrents with an especially sensible frame of mind, something of which, in the past, was not something I could do. I used to dwell unnecessarily on the negative without giving a second glance to all the positive that surrounds. But I am able to see both now. The glass is neither half full nor half empty; it is just a glass. There are no emotions of which I feel I cannot handle.

For the first time in my life I feel as though I can breathe. It's a wonderful feeling.

DECEMBER 8, 2011

SOCIAL INTERACTION IS BENEFICIAL to my well-being. My well-being; my rose-colored glasses, on for viewing the world. It can be a desperate little place without those glasses, but the optimism with which I feel I now possess certainly helps the view.

As per my other 'issues', I've not dealt with any real fallout recently. There are always certain circumstances which one would rather not endure, but that's life. Life is not always going to go the way you want it to and disappointment is just one facet of a long line of components that make up this little thing we call Life. There are circumstances now that leave me feeling out in the cold but what can one do but forge ahead and hope for the best? Hope can be tricky; it can leave one helpless at its whims; it can whittle away peace of mind when it goes unrequited but still it lingers, hanging on with a zealousness that cannot be overcome. Hope is the glowing ember which needs only one little breath of wind to set it ablaze. My own glowing ember of hope has come close to being extinguished time and time again recently but then someone comes along and breathes new life into me and I'm rescued; the fire burns brightly for a while before slowly diminishing into that ember once again. It's a cycle that can get wearying in its own right but its Life's cycle for us.

Time is interludes of emotion. Not everything is going to be sunshine and roses but when it is, how sweet life can be.

On the other hand, when it's not, how desperate we become. The neuroses with which I used to dwell on these interludes of emotion, particularly the negative has ebbed away and I'm able to rationalize and move on from them. Before, I would dwell and fixate upon them; my mind becoming nothing more than a haven for negativity and abashment. Self-loathing was at the core of my soul. I always resigned myself to the depressive episodes I deemed deserving. Now I feed off the optimism of the moments marked with this new life. And a new life is what it feels to be.

I am a different person than I was three or four months ago. Where four months ago would have found me desperately forging ahead into that familiar and abysmal mindset of depression and melancholy demeanor, I suffer momentarily and then move on, leaving behind the dejected self that used to linger indefinitely. Not to say I don't have my moments still. I don't think I'd be human if I did not. There are circumstances which surround that are not conducive to my peace of mind but what can one do about something that has no satisfactory answer to an existing predicament? Moving on from anything that one must move on from is difficult in its own right and it is made even more difficult when whatever it is hangs on like a burr to the soul, clutching and clawing its way up the ladder of the soul trying to reach the summit of the forefront of the mind where it burrows so deeply one thinks there is no way to rid themselves of the thought. Yes, I still have my moments but what makes these moments so different from the moments before, is my ability to cope. I think of life as B.M.B. and A.M.B. which refers to "Before Meds Began" and "After Meds Began". The difference is astounding. My coping skills have improved dramatically and I sincerely give due credit to the meds. I feel a different person, a better person, a person worthy of life and love and optimism. It is a new experience, a new endeavor I am embarking upon and it, for the most part, feels wonderful. I still feel intense emotions which often lend themselves to momentary despair for certain circumstances but the intensity, for all its force, doesn't crash into me as violently and jarringly as it once did. The intensity is still there but it feels more controlled than before. But I still feel. I feel emotionally, passionately, and unyieldingly. When one feels emotions this intensely, it's difficult to find absolution. But onward I go, stepping brightly into the future as it unfolds before my eyes. All I have is NOW. Now is all we ever have. Why waste a moment?

DECEMBER 25, 2011
7:51PM

MY POETRY CAN BE dark sometimes. Poetry is supposed to expose the innermost feelings, thoughts, and emotions. It is supposed to reveal the hidden seeds of thought that frolic and leap amidst one's mind. Poetry enables one to release all hidden neuroses through an expression that is at once personal and gratifying and it is left up to the interpretation of others when they read the words. It is the interpretation that makes poetry unique and individual. My poems mean something to me and only I know what they truly represent. To another, my poetry could mean something else entirely. No one knows the thought process of my poetry and no one can truly understand the inner workings of my mind.

There are times when I myself don't understand the inner workings of my mind. There is still a frenzy of thought that overtakes me at the most inopportune of times. It is the voice. It is still there, echoing throughout the chambers of my mind. It ricochets off my skull and reverberates throughout my entire soul. The voice knows no reason and no shame. It consumes the mind as though the mind is wallowing in quicksand, being consumed slowly, steadily, and irrevocably. The voice whispers and sings. But it is a melancholy tune. Sad and depressing, the tune carries despair and desperation. The voice is a self-induced panic which resounds with a dizzying consistency of self-loathing. It is still there, in my mind. It hangs on with razor sharp talons which dig into my psyche like claws into flesh. My mind bleeds with anger at this destructive force and it aches with unassuming submissiveness for its existence for there is no way around it, no way to avoid it. It is a leech, bearing down on my flesh and sucking the life from my soul. I long to be apathetic to its maligning presence yet the persistence of it doesn't allow me the leeway of indifference. It is an omnipresent force to contend with. The potency of its destructive nature is what keeps me awake at night still. The incessant noise of its existence leaves one wary of sound for in every sound there is the chance it will be heard. It is carried by the wind and it washes ashore with the waves. Every sound conveys a manifestation of this voice so it cannot be drowned out. It cannot be relegated to absence. Absentia is not in its realm for its realm is all its own and it has taken residence in my mind with an unrelenting lease in my psyche.

Lost Love.

The voice is still there. Still it flows through my body with a reverberating consistency. To stop the torrent of sound I would wish to be deaf but it is an internal foe that cannot be easily discarded. I have fought with this voice for my entire life and while, lately, I have been able to subdue it to merely a murmur of imperceptible white noise, it still finds moments to scream.

So I come to you to seek the solace I crave from another human being. There is no one to answer my call; my pleas; my one longing and desperate cry. I feel as though a part of my soul has been wrenched away from me by a force so powerful it leaves nothing but disaster in its wake. The disaster, the remnants of my life, scattered on the land that overlooks my desires, dreams, ambitions, and regrets. The regrets fester in the whirlpools of time that accumulate along the river bed. My land of desires, dreams, and ambitions is overcome with weeds and branches which block the view to a better future. The skies are dark grey, fog engulfs the land laying a carpet of grey mist that rises from the soil. Tombstones of memories litter the fields as my skeletons turn over in their graves.

You are my skeleton. You are the one hidden passion found hanging in my closet. You are the skeleton that cannot come to life. You hang limp and bloodless in my memory, refusing to dissemble yourself from my mind, refusing to relinquish your hold on my thoughts, refusing to seek your own safe tomb.

You are my despair. You hang so low in my mind that I am pulled down by the weight of your anchor, chained to all the excuses you threw at me as I waded down into the trenches trying to drown my life from yours; an effort to escape the onslaught of desire that catapults my mind into frenzying thoughts of you and I.

You are my skeleton; your bones enmesh with mine, becoming one, impossible to break, impossible to shatter or separate. Your memories are my memories and my reflections of our time spent together list about in my mind as the monsoon of memories weathers the dizzying ride. You thrash about inside of me with such force it's a wonder I am able to stand upright at all.

You are my skeleton; the one immovable object within my heart and soul; you linger on my tongue, my body, my skin; I am soaked through to my bones, saturated with your body and soul. One night and your skeleton crashed into mine, your body rolled with mine on this sea of desire and became entwined with mine.

You are my skeleton; you wish for me to be gone and yet you hid the key to the mausoleum and I am trapped with your memory. I am trapped in your denial. I am trapped with this skeleton of time that my memories can't erase. Eroded regrets loiter in this mausoleum; they blend with the shadows and darken my room. My mind is the mausoleum; you are the skeleton that will not let me go.

My skeletons are screaming inside the closet of my mind still. My mind runs through and through the memories of you and I can't shake the feeling of hope, the false feeling of hope, which infiltrates my thoughts. I know there is no hope and yet still I hang on. I hang on with one finger on the ledge; one finger separating me from the fall. I have already fallen for you and that is where the problem lies. I fell for you a long time ago and so much time has passed. Yet my mind won't let go of the thoughts of you and I together.

You are the ghost traipsing through the corridors of my mind. Your foot falls heavy in my thoughts provoking me to turn to various means in an effort to dissociate myself from you but you linger, linger, linger. My body is wracked with emotions that fly through my mind; emotions so heavy handed they press on my brain, suffocating me; baring down on my soul with a heaviness so encompassing I am being asphyxiated by its might. My pores absorbed you and you became a part of my body, relinquishing my peace of mind in favor of ravaging my notions of you and me. You gave me hope and you took it away as quickly as you gave it to me. My mind is wrapped around thoughts of you that tighten the grip on my mind; like a vice you squeeze and compress; my head aches and my body is overcome with desire.

If someone could save me someday, save me from you, I would be indebted forever. But I can't forget you. I can't forget your kiss or the way your body felt beneath mine. My hands covered you with a longing so sincere it burns my fingertips with a sense memory. My fingertips are raw by memories; my fingertips tingle with recollections of how your skin felt beneath mine. My body vibrates with recognition. Every time I see you those thoughts rush back at me, toppling me over with remembrance.

I feel half dead because of you. I feel half alive because of you. You have split me in half; longing for you, despising you. But I can't hate you no matter how I try; I can't hate you because I love you. Though your rebuke pains me, your subtle friendship remains a constant reminder of pain. The last time I kissed you, I didn't know it would be the last time. The last time I held you, I didn't know it would be the last time. The last time I saw you, I didn't realize the agony that would entwine my soul with yours.

You bettered me and you destroyed me. I am destroyed.

My mind left in a wreckage of you. Scattered pieces of my mind and soul litter the ground surrounding my every step. You are my shadow that never disconnects from my darkness. You follow me like a refugee. You seek my contentment and turn it over in your hands, relinquishing me to the darkness of your memory.

But still you linger. When thoughts of you disappear, I remember what it's like to be me. When thoughts of you invade, I remember what it's like to be with you. I long to touch you; I long to be with you in any capacity you will allow.

You are intoxicating. You are my drug and I am addicted. Thoughts of you make me high. But the higher I get, the farther I fall. I have fallen for you time and time again when I only want to climb to the summit of mending; to mend my heart; to stitch it back together; to recuperate from your onslaught would be relief. There is no relief from you. You are my skeleton, saturating my bones, overtaking my body with remembrances of you. You are my skeleton that will not let me go because I love you.

DECEMBER 26, 2011
7:46PM

THOUGHTS HAVE A LIFE of their own. They invade peace of mind even when not provoked to do so. Thoughts linger indefinitely and it seems the harder one tries to forget something, the more persistent the thought becomes. Certain thoughts breathe life into a soul while other thoughts infiltrate and destroy. I am not yet sure what the consequences of these thoughts are going to cater to me. Right now I am on the fence and could fall either way; either into an arena of peaceful resignation or into the void of despairing consumption. It is a consumption with no remedy. It consumes the peaceful reserves built through days, weeks, and months of dogged determination; determination to acquiesce to the pressure of the thought on the mind and accept the facts of the circumstances without resentment or remorse. To come to terms with a significant event, whether it reside in relationships or occupation or simply Life itself, is a feat of will. Thoughts carry an indefatigable life force of their own. Without compunction, they fester; they gather momentum and strength as the hours and days ware on. To rid oneself of thought is impossible. Only by occupying the mind with distraction can one overcome the incessant presence of certain thoughts but then, as suddenly as you find yourself remembering that you forgot about a thought, it rears back with more potency than before. To give into the thoughts may be the only way to forget about them. Though they remain, and perhaps always will, their might dwindles and they soon become just an afterthought to reflect upon and easily dismiss. Thoughts cannot be discarded but they can lessen their grip on the mind over the course of time. Time is perhaps the one adversary to thought. Time is an antagonist which slowly dissipates the thought into nothing more than a remembrance of one transitory moment.

DECEMBER 28, 2011
9:49AM

IT WAS A LONG day yesterday, rife with discontent and mild panic. But my panic didn't reveal itself in the way it used to. As I wrote yesterday, rational and level-headed. I must be that way when other people are concerned. I need one definitive escape plan. I need a job so I can put that escape plan into action. Now that the job at LL Bean has ended, I feel adrift. I have streamlined my journals into a comprehensive book. I have gone through and reedited all my poetry and now I am left with no little projects to occupy my time. I cannot write like I used to write, though I feel desperate to do so. My words have become stunted. My thoughts too erratic. What were they before if not erratic, you wonder. I do too. I could at least focus on one objective in my writing before but now I just jump around from thought to thought, oftentimes meaningless in their substance, and try to kill time by the slow hand of tapping fingers. But time, as we know, has an uncanny way of bending and shifting out of its linear form making it feel as though it is slowing down, stopping, speeding up, or staying consistently aloof in its passing. Time measures itself not by seconds or hours but by moments. These moments mark time, making time something tangible, with merit. But shifts of time alter our world and it distinguishes itself in a manner of identifiable interludes. My time feels agonizingly slow. It feels as though I am waiting for a grand awakening, waiting for an event, anticipatory and excited, I wait for this event to take hold and mark my time with significant moments but time lingers on, tiptoeing ever so quietly, making its way into the oblivion of my consciousness. I don't know what this event is that I am anticipating but there must be one. Or maybe it is just an epiphany with which I am eagerly anticipating. Like most epiphanies, I won't know the context of such until it comes to be. Only then will I be able to raise my finger and say, "aha. That is what it's all about." And then I will know. And what will knowing do for me? What is knowledge if it is never put to use? Unused knowledge sits on the shelf of the mind, being dusted over with a fine coating of inactivity, while slowly evaporating to white mist. Misused knowledge festers in the mind and provokes irrational responses to its learned information. Knowledge put to good use intensifies and instigates productivity. What knowledge is it that I am waiting for? Knowledge of my own Self; an effort to determine a greater purpose? What greater purpose is there other than existing for others? Helping others? Understanding others? Where knowledge really becomes purposeful is when it is used in a way to better the world around us and the people who inhabit this little realm of subjective interpretations. We are not all going to see eye to eye, but with knowledge comes understanding. We may all speak different languages, we may all have different beliefs and different customs, but knowledge, true knowledge, indisputable knowledge, connects us all and allows us an understanding of one another that cannot be denied. Knowledge is the source of understanding, both the world around us and each other. And what knowledge have I that constitutes this verifiable form of understanding? What do I know that can better the world or better some of the lives in this world? What do I know? I know what it's like to want to die and to have to fight with myself to live. I know what it's like to destroy myself on the outside while I'm withering away from uncertainty on the inside. I know how anxiety becomes a palpable adversary in any given situation. I know the unprovoked misery that consumes the mind and destroys the desire to actively participate in the world. I know what it feels like to live each day under the glaring microscope of internal examination. Living in the mind rather than living in the world. Caging oneself up so tight the air becomes stale and you wonder why it's still keeping you alive. I know what it's like to give into desirous temptation and then suffer the fallout of such. I know what it's like to wish for disaster to unfold at one's doorstep in an effort to still your mind and voice and body. I know what it's like to care about other people so intensely that it hurts. I know what it's like to want to better the world around me but feeling utterly incapable of doing so. I know disappointment. I know failure and I know success. I know the demons that lurk within my mind, feasting off my sanity and yearning to gain ultimate control. They skulk around the corners of the psyche waiting for the right moment to leap and jump and attack solemnity with a vicious and unrelenting torrent of destructive thought. I know destructive thoughts and how they linger within every shadow of the mind; how they wait for the most inopportune time to lash out with fury. I know what it's like to want to participate in the world, having an insatiable desire to do so but how fighting with the anxiety is often a losing battle. I know I've missed out on a large portion of my life because of these maligning thoughts and suicidal ideations. I've missed opportunity, I've missed time with my friends, and I've missed living for the sole purpose of living. I know what it's like to want to stop the flow of voices that run through my mind with worry and doubt; what it's like to always acquiesce to these dominant thoughts because they are of more strength and power than I. Their omnipresence overtakes and overrides every defense I have built up. I know what it's like to watch those walls of self-preservation crumble and disintegrate into nothingness. I know what it's like to overcome only to fall back once more into the trenches. To pick oneself up, brush off, and try again, time after time after time; I know what it feels like to keep trying and to keep failing, of never reaching the pinnacle of success I desire simply because of the demons who pull me back with their scaly hands time and time again. I know what it's like to kill those demons only to have them resurrect themselves. I know what it's like to persevere but I don't yet know what it's like to triumph. These battles we are forced to fight are exhaustive; the battles that rage in the mind where no one can go. It is only you. It is only me. It is only an individual experience and a solitary fight. I know what it's like to fight, fight, fight; to gain the upper-hand and then be thrown mercilessly to the ground. I know what it's like to want to raise the white flag in surrender but never have I. We fight because it's our natural instinct to do so. The flight or fight syndrome. Where I used to choose the former, I ultimately realized it never ends successfully. So I fight. I have been fighting my entire life and while I've been beaten many times I have not submissively given up. I have not thrown my hands up and surrendered to the laws of contrition which encircle my mind. This remorse I feel has no bearing and no relevance and yet it is there in all its damning glory. I suppose it is remorse for being who I am or perhaps who I am not. I still struggle with the image I create for myself wondering, pondering, is it really me? I know what it's like to wear different personalities for different people in my life. These costumes and masks inhibit me and yet I wear them when I'm in fear of exposing myself to the realities of who and what I am. If I even know. Uncertainty encloses upon me even when I feel self-assured and in control. There still resides a little voice of hesitation within my mind that questions every little thing I do. To second-guess always creates dissention in the mind. I know what it's like to fight with myself, and lose. I haven't lost everything yet though. So still I fight. It may be a battle that never ends but the one thing I don't know how to do, is give up.

Final Thoughts

As I SIT BACK and contemplate the journey that has led me to where I am today, I realize I have but one regret. That being, I did not seek help sooner. For more than a decade, I faced these disorders alone. I was a solitary fighter trying, often in vain, to navigate my way through the painful emotions that held me captive.

It must be known, and said, that there is no shame in having these disorders or asking for help. In fact, asking for help shows strength and initiative by taking the steps to securing a better quality of life. These disorders are not a weakness. They may initially inhibit you from actively participating in the world around you but they are not so powerful as to control you, if you seek treatment.

These disorders are not something you recover fully from. There is no cure, no magical elixir that will evaporate fully the struggles these disorders induce. But they can be managed. One must never forget that. It is a fight, a battle, a struggle to maintain control when seemingly everything is against you. But it is the mindset with which you approach these disorders that can, and will, allow you to manage and cope with them.

The fact is, trying to face these disorders alone does nothing but wear you down more. It is emotionally exhausting and can cause physical ailments as well.

Many people try to pretend nothing is wrong. I tried to pretend nothing was wrong for a very long time. When the fateful night came and I found myself in the ER, I realized I could no longer pretend, I could no longer manage on my own. I did initially rebel against the idea that I had these disorders but once I accepted the fact I learned I could move ahead with my life instead of stagnating in the pool of despair that encircled my life.

I'm not going to lie, these disorders can make one's life hell. So if you, or anyone you know, suffers from these disorders, seek help and urge others to do so as well.

In the past few years, after being on medication, I have become more content, more at peace with myself. My relationships with family and friends has improved. I still have my struggles, but with the support of my family and friends I have been able to maintain a more positive outlook on life.

What it comes down to is this: Life is meant to be lived. Life is not meant to be feared or to face struggles alone. You don't have to face anything alone if only you allow yourself to be helped. Take it from someone who lived a decade in turmoil, it can get better. Life can be enjoyed when you allow yourself to acknowledge the fact you need help.

Remember, there is no shame in having these disorders. There is no shame in seeking help. You are stronger than you realize.

© 2014 Katherine L. Fogg

Printed in the United States
By Bookmasters